WITHDRAWN

jQuery FOR DUMMIES®

by Lynn Beighley

WILEY

Wiley Publishing Inc.

jQuery For Dummies®

Published by
Wiley Publishing, Inc.
111 River Street
Hoboken, NJ 07030-5774
www.wiley.com

Copyright © 2010 by Wiley Publishing, Inc., Indianapolis, Indiana

Published by Wiley Publishing, Inc., Indianapolis, Indiana

Published simultaneously in Canada

For general information on our other products and services, please contact our Customer Care Department within the U.S. at 877-762-2974, outside the U.S. at 317-572-3993, or fax 317-572-4002.

For technical support, please visit www.wiley.com/techsupport.

Wiley also publishes its books in a variety of electronic formats. Some content that appears in print may not be available in electronic books.

Library of Congress Control Number: 2010926840

ISBN: 978-0-470-58445-3

Manufactured in the United States of America

10 9 8 7 6 5 4 3 2 1

About the Author

Lynn Beighley has been a Web developer and computer book author long before jQuery was a glimmer in John Resig's eye. This is her eleventh book. Lynn shares her off-kilter 1920's home with her husband, Drew, and two Bernese Mountain Dogs who are much too big to be the lap dogs they think they are.

Dedication

To Drew.

Author's Acknowledgments

I'd like to thank Kyle Looper for offering me the chance to write a second *Dummies* book on another great topic, and Susan Pink for her amazing dedication. She's a stickler for detail, and this book benefits greatly from it!

Publisher's Acknowledgments

We're proud of this book; please send us your comments at http://dummies.custhelp.com. For other comments, please contact our Customer Care Department within the U.S. at 877-762-2974, outside the U.S. at 317-572-3993, or fax 317-572-4002.

Some of the people who helped bring this book to market include the following:

Acquisitions, Editorial

Project Editor: Susan Pink

Acquisitions Editor: Kyle Looper

Copy Editor: Susan Pink

Technical Editor: Cody Lindley

Editorial Manager: Jodi Jensen

Editorial Assistant: Amanda Graham

Sr. Editorial Assistant: Cherie Case

Cartoons: Rich Tennant
(www.the5thwave.com)

Composition Services

Project Coordinator: Katherine Crocker

Layout and Graphics: Joyce Haughey

Proofreaders: Lindsay Littrell, Toni Settle

Indexer: BIM Indexing & Proofreading Services

Publishing and Editorial for Technology Dummies

> **Richard Swadley,** Vice President and Executive Group Publisher

> **Andy Cummings,** Vice President and Publisher

> **Mary Bednarek,** Executive Acquisitions Director

> **Mary C. Corder,** Editorial Director

Publishing for Consumer Dummies

> **Diane Graves Steele,** Vice President and Publisher

Composition Services

> **Debbie Stailey,** Director of Composition Services

Contents at a Glance

Table of Contents

Introduction

*j*Query is all around you. You see it on hugely popular sites such as Twitter and Facebook. When you visit Yahoo! or Google, there it is. Someone's Aunt Mary has a snazzy Web site with jQuery effects for her pet photography business. But there you are, using animated gifs. Your site looks dated, and you aren't keeping up with your competition. It's time for you to add the power of jQuery to your site.

Welcome to the first edition of *jQuery For Dummies,* the book that was written especially for people who want to include jQuery code and plug-ins on their Web sites but haven't a clue how to start.

Maybe you've already tried to add jQuery to your site, but the documentation you've found is targeted to programmers. You want to know how to add some simple but compelling jQuery effects to your pages or some great pre-built jQuery plug-ins, but you don't have the time to dig through tedious and yawn-inducing technical explanations of how to make it all work.

You need this book.

In *jQuery For Dummies,* I use everyday language to show you how to write jQuery code and use jQuery plug-ins. I don't assume that you know to program. You don't even need to know how to write HTML, although you'll get more out of this book if you do. The goal of this book is to show you, without the technical jargon, how to take advantage of jQuery with only a few lines of code added to your HTML pages.

About This Book

This isn't the kind of book you need to read from start to finish. You can pick up this book, turn to just about any page, and start reading. Each of its 22 chapters covers a specific aspect of jQuery — such as downloading jQuery, building simple jQuery effects, using amazing jQuery plug-ins, or integrating jQuery with popular Content Management Systems such as Drupal, Joomla!, and WordPress.

How to Use This Book

This book works like a reference. Decide on a topic you want to find out about. Look for it in the table of contents or in the index. Then turn to the area of interest and read as much as you need.

You don't have to memorize anything. This is a need-to-know book. Need to know how create an accordion menu? Pick up the book. Need to know how to fade in or fade out something on your Web page? Pick up the book. Want to find an awesome jQuery plug-in to display your photographs in an image gallery? You're all set.

This book rarely directs you elsewhere for information — just about everything that you need to know about jQuery is right here.

Finally, this book contains a lot of code. You can type the code or download it from the companion Web site at www.dummies.com/go/jqueryfd.

Foolish Assumptions

I'm making only one assumption about who you are: You're a nonprogrammer who has heard of jQuery and wants to add it to your own site. Both Macintosh and Windows users can use this book.

How This Book Is Organized

Inside this book, you find chapters arranged in seven parts. Each chapter breaks down into sections that cover various aspects of the chapter's main subject. The chapters are in a logical sequence, so reading them in order makes sense. But the book is modular enough that you can pick it up and start reading at any point.

Here's the lowdown on what's in each of the seven parts.

Part 1: Getting Started with jQuery

The chapters in this part are a layperson's introduction to what jQuery is all about, where to get it, and how to use it in a Web page. This part is a good place to start if you've never looked at jQuery code, aren't clear on what a Web server is, and don't know how to build a basic Web page.

The best thing about Part I is that it starts at the very beginning and doesn't assume that you know how to download, upload, and build Web pages. It also covers the most fundamental parts of using jQuery: connecting the jQuery library to a Web page, selecting elements on your Web page, and making special effects happen when you want them to. When you finish Part I, you'll be able to change the content or appearance of elements on your page when a visitor mouses over a link on your page, clicks an image, and more.

Part II: Affecting Elements with Effects

The goal of the chapters in Part II is to show you how to start changing the appearance of your Web page in response to user actions with jQuery. I take you beyond simply showing and hiding elements on a page to fun actions such as fading in and out and animating.

Part III: Manipulating Your Web Page

Whereas Part II focuses on making elements on your page move, fade in and out, and animate, Part III gets to the heart of the matter. This is where you find out how to change the text and content on your page.

Part IV: Using Plug-ins and Widgets

You take your site to a new level in Part IV, where you discover the plentiful free jQuery plug-ins developed by scores of talented programmers. The plug-ins are just waiting for you to download and integrate into your own site. And did I mention that they're free?

Part V: Building AJAX Applications

In Part V, you gain a broad understanding of AJAX and integrate some robust jQuery AJAX plug-ins into your own site. AJAX is complicated and can involve the integration of several programming languages. It's a topic that could easily fill up an entire book, but this part gives you a simple introduction and points you in the right direction for getting started.

Part VI: Integrating jQuery with Content Management Systems

Content Management Systems (CMS) are wildly popular, and it's no wonder. With a CMS, you can build an entire robust Web site in just a few hours. And three of the most widely used CMS — Drupal, Joomla!, and WordPress — support jQuery. Part VI gives you pointers on including jQuery with all three.

Part VII: The Part of Tens

This wouldn't be a *Dummies* book without a collection of lists of interesting snippets: ten jQuery plug-ins or add-ons for your Web site, ten jQuery design tricks, and ten sites you can visit to find out even more about jQuery. You find all this in Part VII.

Icons Used in This Book

Those nifty little pictures in the margin aren't there to just pretty up the place. They also have practical functions.

Hold it — technical details lurk just around the corner. Read on only if you want to find out a little more about the inner workings of jQuery. But if your eyes glaze over, move on.

Pay special attention to this icon; it lets you know that some particularly useful tidbit is at hand — perhaps a shortcut or a little-used command that pays off big. And sometimes tips point you to important information in other parts of this book.

This icon indicates important, often basic, information that you should try to remember. You will need this information again and again, both in the examples in this book and in your own jQuery explorations.

Danger, Will Robinson! This icon highlights information that may help you avert disaster. And by disaster, I mean your code won't run, your plug-in won't function, and your day will be shot. You'll spend far too long trying to track down the problem. Instead, give this icon special attention.

Where to Go from Here

Yes, you can get there from here. With this book in hand, you're ready to add exciting jQuery effects and functionality to your Web pages. Browse through the table of contents and decide where you want to start. Your Web pages will never be the same!

Part I
Getting Started with jQuery

"We should cast a circle, invoke the elements, and direct the energy. If that doesn't work, we'll read the manual."

In this part . . .

You have to begin somewhere, and here's the place. Before you can use jQuery, you have to get the jQuery library. Then you need to know what to do with it. And just what is jQuery, anyway? These chapters give you all the answers.

After you have the jQuery library squared away, it's time to use it. Simply follow the clear, easy examples to add code to your Web page.

You'll also discover how to pinpoint Web page elements, such as images, divs, and links. And how to call jQuery when specific events occur, such as when an element is clicked or a div is moused over.

If you don't know anything about jQuery, or you don't know how to select elements, or you don't know how to detect events, start here.

Chapter 1

Getting Up and Running
with jQuery

Perhaps you're reading this book because you need to create an image viewer for your Web site. Maybe you want to make something on your page fade in and out. Or maybe you want to give visitors to your site a way to upload files. jQuery can help you add hundreds of impressive interactive effects to your Web page quickly and easily.

In this chapter, you find an overview of how jQuery works, how to use it in your own Web pages, and how to create your first simple Web page with a jQuery effect.

Finding Out What jQuery Can Do for You

jQuery gives Web developers and designers an easy way to create sophisticated effects with almost no coding. Because jQuery is so easy to implement, its popularity is growing. You see examples of jQuery all over the Web. Facebook and Twitter, for example, use a number of jQuery effects.

When you post a new tweet on Twitter, the page doesn't reload. Instead, the code behind the Web page calls a jQuery function to make your new tweet appear and all the other tweets on your page move down. Another jQuery feature on Twitter is the notification you receive when a new tweet arrives, as shown in Figure 1-1.

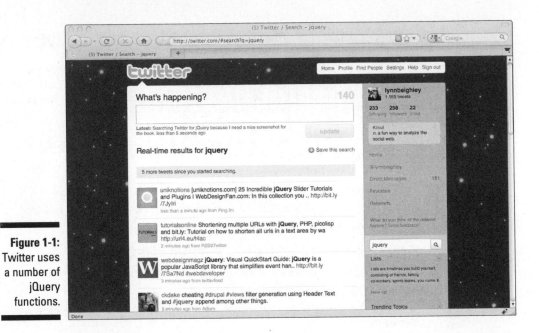

Figure 1-1:
Twitter uses
a number of
jQuery
functions.

If you click the notification, the new tweets appear on your page, and the older tweets slide down. The Web page never reloads; instead, the content on the page changes dynamically.

Defining jQuery

To understand jQuery, it helps to know a little about JavaScript, a programming language that your Web browser understands. JavaScript code can interact with images and text on your Web page — for example, hiding an image, moving text, or changing content after a certain period of time or when a visitor to your page does something, such as roll his mouse cursor over a link. JavaScript code can make an image appear when someone visiting a Web page clicks a button, can make a window pop up 30 seconds after you browse to a Web page, or can check to make sure a visitor to your site filled out a Web form correctly. JavaScript is robust and commonly used to add interactivity and dynamic effects to Web pages. But JavaScript is a complete programming language, and to use it effectively, you have to learn to program.

jQuery is an add-on library for JavaScript. Think of jQuery as JavaScript code that's been written for you. In general, all you have to do is include a line or two of code in your page that calls the jQuery code. jQuery does the hard JavaScript coding work for you.

Understanding jQuery effects and events

jQuery lets you easily change the appearance, location, or behavior of an element on a Web page. In Chapter 2, I discuss HTML elements in depth, but for now think of an *element* as something on a Web page such as an image, a block of text, a hyperlink, a table, or a heading.

jQuery code gives the text and image elements on a Web page various special effects, including the following:

- **hide:** Hides an element on your Web page.
- **show:** Displays an element on your Web page if the element is hidden.
- **slideDown:** Slides down an element on your Web page.
- **slideUp:** Slides up an element on your Web page.
- **fadeIn:** Fades in a hidden element on your Web page, making the element visible.
- **fadeOut:** Fades out an element on your Web page, making the element invisible.
- **animate:** Animates an element on your Web page in a particular direction.

You can use jQuery effects on elements on your page, but jQuery also lets you control when these effects take place. You can make an element on your page fade, slide, animate, and so on when you specify. Here are a few of the events that jQuery can use to trigger an effect:

- **load:** The effect occurs when a Web page has finished loading in the Web browser or when an element in a page has loaded, such as an image.
- **mouseover:** The effect occurs when the mouse cursor moves over a specific location on a Web page.
- **mouseout:** The effect occurs when the mouse cursor moves off a specific location on a Web page.
- **change:** If the value of something (for example, the text in a field on a Web form) changes, an event occurs. This is useful for making sure someone enters the correct information in a text box.

Using plug-ins

The true power of jQuery is in the many hundreds of plug-ins that use it to create amazing effects. *Plug-ins* are JavaScript programs that use and expand jQuery. To see an example of a popular and impressive plug-in, visit the Lightbox plug-in Web site at `http://leandrovieira.com/projects/jquery/lightbox`. This plug-in lets visitors to your page click an image and see a larger version of the imaged overlaid (see Figure 1-2).

Figure 1-2:
A jQuery
Lightbox
plug-in.

Throughout this book, you find out about quite a few jQuery plug-ins, all free and easy to use, that turn a simple Web site into a robust and dynamic destination.

Installing jQuery

Before you can use jQuery, you need to download a copy of it. Then you need to decide where you want it to live. In this section, I discuss the basic steps involved in getting a copy of jQuery and then saving it to the right location depending on whether you're working on your personal computer or on a remote Web server. Later, you see how to include a line of code in your HTML file or Web page to see jQuery effects on your Web page.

Downloading jQuery

To get a copy of jQuery, follow these steps:

1. **Browse to `jquery.com` and click the Download jQuery button, which is on the right (see Figure 1-3).**

   Clicking this button takes you to a page on `http://code.google.com` with a link to the latest version of jQuery. In my case, the filename is `jquery-1.4.min.js`. Your version may be newer and have a different number, but that won't make any difference for the code and examples in this book.

Figure 1-3:
Download
the latest
version of
jQuery from
jquery.
com.

The letters `min` in the filename indicate that the file is minimized. This means that extra spaces and comments that don't do anything are removed, making the overall file size smaller. In general, it's best to download the minimized version of jQuery.

2. Click the link to the jQuery file.

A dialog box appears, asking you whether you want to open or save this file, as shown in Figure 1-4.

Depending on the browser you use to download the jQuery `.js` file, you might not see the dialog box asking you to save the file. You may instead be presented with a page full of JavaScript code. If that happens, choose File➪Save Page As and save the file.

3. Save this file to a directory on your computer that you will remember.

Setting up a testing directory

Now that you have a local copy of the jQuery file, you need to set up a location on your computer where you can create HTML files that use jQuery. To do this, follow these steps:

1. Create a directory or folder on your computer that's easy to browse to and name it webtest.

On a PC, if you create the directory on the `C:/` drive, the directory would be `C:/webtest`. On a Mac, you can create the directory on the desktop.

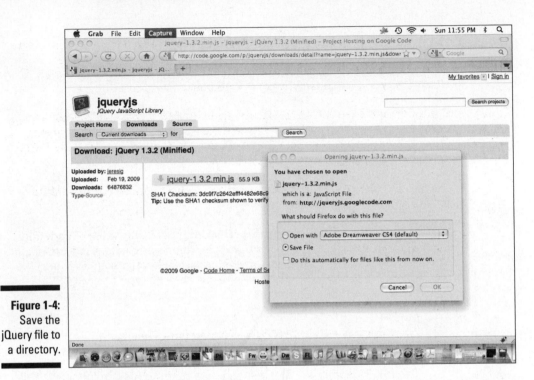

Figure 1-4:
Save the
jQuery file to
a directory.

2. **Inside the webtest directory, create two directories, naming them js and images.**

   Figure 1-5 shows my directory named webtest and the folders in it.

3. **Copy or move the jQuery file (jquery-1.4.min.js in my case) into the js directory.**

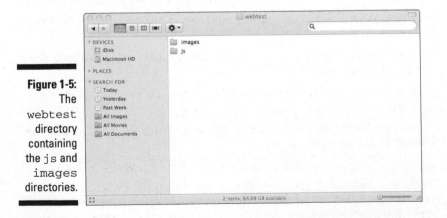

Figure 1-5:
The
webtest
directory
containing
the js and
images
directories.

Calling jQuery from a Web page

After you have your directory set up and the jQuery file saved in the `js` directory, you can create your first Web page.

For much of the rest of this book, you need an HTML editor or at least a text editor. If you're using a PC, you can use the Notepad program by choosing Start⇨All Programs⇨Accessories⇨Notepad. On the Mac, you can use TextEdit by choosing Applications⇨TextEdit.

If you use TextEdit on the Mac, make sure you first choose Format⇨Make Plain Text.

In the following steps, you create an HTML page and add a line of code that connects the page to the jQuery library. This page won't do anything exciting, but correctly inserting the jQuery code in your Web page is vital. jQuery won't work if even a single character is incorrect, so type carefully.

To create your page, do the following:

1. **Open the text editor or HTML editor of your choice.**

2. **Type the following code into the text document:**

```
<!DOCTYPE html PUBLIC "-//W3C//DTD XHTML 1.0 Strict//EN"
          "http://www.w3.org/TR/xhtml1/DTD/xhtml1-strict.dtd">
<html>
<head>
<title>My Test Page</title>
</head>
<body>
<p>This is my test page.</p>
</body>
</html>
```

3. **Save this file as `test.html` in the `webtest` directory you created in the last section.**

   No matter which editor you use, make sure you save your files with the `.html` extension, not `.txt`.

   You still need to add the line of code that connects the jQuery library to this page.

4. **Right after the HTML code `<title>My Test Page</title>`, add the following line of code:**

```
<script type="text/javascript" src="js/jquery-1.4.min.js"></script>
```

   The jQuery filename (`jquery-1.4.min.js` in the preceding line of code) must match the name of the file you downloaded from `jquery.com`. This line of code calls the jQuery code library. Later, when you add simple code to this Web page that uses jQuery, your Web browser will know how to find jQuery.

5. **Save your test.html file again.**

   This time your file is saved with the line of code you just added.

Viewing a Web page on your computer

You've created a simple HTML page, and now you should look at it in your browser. To open your page, follow these steps:

1. **Start the browser of your choice.**

   In this example, I use Firefox.

2. **Choose File⇨Open File.**

   An Open File dialog box appears.

3. **Browse to the webtest directory and select the file you created earlier, test.html.**

4. **Click OK.**

   Your Web page now appears in your browser, as shown in Figure 1-6.

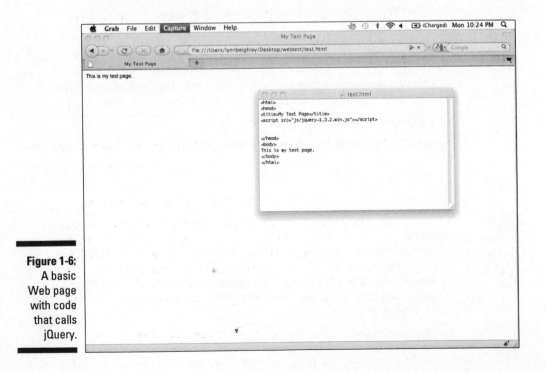

Figure 1-6:
A basic
Web page
with code
that calls
jQuery.

This page displays the title, My Test Page, and a line of text, This is my test page. The jQuery code is accessible by your Web page, but you're not using it for any effects in your page yet.

Creating Your First jQuery Code

Now that you know how to create a simple Web page with a <script> tag that calls, or includes, the jQuery library, you can create your first jQuery effect. In this section, you add an image to your page and add jQuery code that displays information about the image in an alert box. It isn't the most exciting use of jQuery, but it demonstrates the basic techniques you will use throughout this book.

To add an image to your HTML page:

1. **Locate a small .gif image file and save it in the images directory you created earlier inside the webtest directory.**

   Try to find one that's no larger than 300x300 pixels.

   If you don't have a .gif image handy, grab one by browsing to this location:

   ```
   http://media.wiley.com/spa_assets/site/dummies2/include/images/topnav/home.
          gif
   ```

   This file is a small image of a house. Choose File⇨Save File As and save this image to the images directory under webtest.

2. **Open test.html in a text editor.**

3. **Add the following code after the line <p>This is my test page</p>:**

   ```
   <img src= "images/home.gif" height="28" width="28" alt="This is a test
          image.">
   ```

   Make sure to change home.gif to match the file you're using.

   Take a close look at this <img> tag. It contains bits of code known as *attributes*. The attributes are src, height, width, and alt. Each of these contains information about the image. The src attribute contains the filename and location of the image. The height and width attributes contain the dimensions of the image in pixels. The alt attribute is additional text to display when the image is moused over or can't be displayed.

4. **Save your test.html file but leave it open in your text editor.**

If you view your page in a Web browser now, the image appears as shown in Figure 1-7.

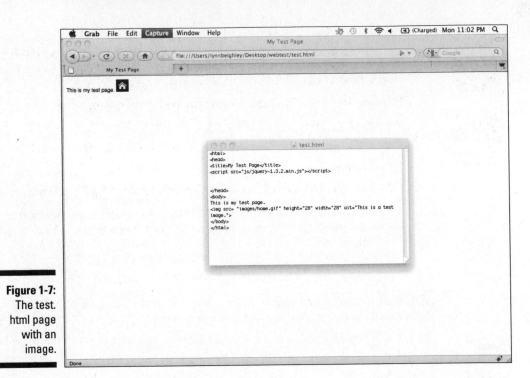

Figure 1-7:
The test.
html page
with an
image.

You're ready to add some jQuery code. In the following steps, you add code that displays information about the image:

1. **If `test.html` is not already open in your text editor, open it.**

2. **Locate the `<script>` line of code that you added that calls jQuery.**

3. **Below that line of code, after the `</script>` tag, add the following code:**

```
<script type="text/javascript">
$(document).ready(function(){


//Do things here


});
</script>
```

You will see this code again and again throughout this book. The `$(document).ready` code is calling a jQuery function that tells the browser that when a certain portion of the page has finished loading, do something. You still need to tell it what to do.

When you see the dollar sign in code, it means the code is interacting with jQuery by calling a jQuery function. The `$` character is a stand-in for the code word `jQuery`.

The `//Do things here` line is a comment. The two forward slash characters tell the Web browser to ignore the text that follows them on the same line. It's often handy to put comments in your code to tell yourself what you still need to do or what you have done.

4. Replace the `//Do things here` line with this code:

```
alert(jQuery('img').attr('alt'));
```

Remember the $ sign? The preceding code line can also be written like this:

```
alert($('img').attr('alt'));
```

5. Save your file but leave it open in your text editor. View it in a browser.

The line of code you added tells the browser to open a JavaScript alert box when the page is ready. Figure 1-8 shows this alert box. The alert displays the text that is in the image tag following the `alt` attribute. Figure 1-8 also displays the entire source code for `test.html`.

Figure 1-8:
An alert box displaying the text from the image's `alt` attribute.

```
<html>
<head>
<title>My Test Page</title>
<script src="js/jquery-1.3.2.min.js"></script>
<script type="text/javascript">
$(document).ready(function(){

alert($("img").attr("alt"));

});
</script>

</head>
<body>
This is my test page.
<img src= "images/home.gif" height="28" width="28" alt="This is a test image.">
</body>
</html>
```

6. Change the `alert` code to display the height of the image by modifying it to

```
alert(jQuery('img').attr('height'));
```

7. Save `test.html` and view it in your Web browser.

You now see the height of the image displayed in the alert box.

How jQuery works with your Web page

At its most basic, a Web page contains a `<script>` tag that includes the jQuery library and a `<script>` block of JavaScript code that contains calls to functions from the jQuery library.

Using JavaScript code to call jQuery functions is a bit confusing at first, but don't worry. The important point is to get a sense of how the code you used in this chapter works and what all the pieces mean. In this section, I take you through `test.html` line by line so it will be clearer:

- ✔ `<!doctype...>`: This long element tells the Web browser which version of HTML is used in the code that follows. You should always include it at the beginning of any HTML pages you create.

- ✔ `<html>`: This element begins the HTML page.

- ✔ `<head>`: This element designates the beginning of the head section. This section usually contains the title and any script element.

- ✔ `<title>My Test Page</title>`: This line displays the title of the page.

- ✔ `<script src="js/jquery-1.4.min.js"></script>`: This line provides the location of the jQuery library.

- ✔ `<script type="text/javascript">`: This script tag tells the browser that everything inside is JavaScript code.

- ✔ `$(document).ready(function(){`: The dollar sign is an alias for the jQuery function. The `ready` function waits for the Web page to load, and then the code contained inside it is executed.

- ✔ `alert(jQuery('img').attr('height'));`: The `alert` function opens a pop-up alert box. The dollar sign that follows is calling the jQuery `attr` function. This function returns the value of whatever attribute is in quotes, in this case, the height. Notice that `img` precedes the `attr` function. In short, this function means, "look for all `img` elements you find in the HTML code, and return the value of the `height` attribute of the first one."

- ✔ `});`: This punctuation is closing the braceand parenthesis started in the `$(document).ready(function(){` line.

- ✔ `</script>`: This tag closes the `<script>` tag and ends the JavaScript code block.

- ✔ `</head>`: This tag closes the head section of the HTML.

- ✔ `<body>`: This tag begins the body section, where the main content consisting of HTML code, text, and images is written.

- ✔ `<p>This is my test page.<p>`: This line is a line of text that appears in the page.

- ✔ `<img src= "images/home.gif" height="28" width="28" alt="This is a test image.">`: This `img` element displays on the Web page an image with several attributes.

- ✔ `</body>`: This tag ends the content section of the page.

- ✔ `</html>`: This tag ends the HTML page.

You can use single or double quotes around elements and text in jQuery functions, but the best practices is to always use single quotes. Double quotes are best used in HTML code. For example, this is a jQuery function with single quotes:

```
alert($('img').attr('width'));
```

and this is HTML code with double quotes:

```
<img src= "images/home.gif" height="28" width="28" alt="This is a test image.">
```

Chapter 2

Accessing HTML Elements

· ·

In This Chapter

▶ Finding out the elements of elements

▶ Getting HTML element attribute values

▶ Changing HTML element attribute values

▶ Displaying attribute values

▶ Changing HTML and text code inside HTML elements

· ·

jQuery is great for manipulating elements on a Web page. But to use it effectively, you need to know what an element is and which jQuery functions can be used on the elements you want to manipulate. In this chapter, I discuss the most common elements and how you can use jQuery to get and set element values. I also show you how to get and set the HTML code inside an HTML element to change the content of your Web page.

Understanding Elements

jQuery allows you to interact with and manipulate elements on your Web pages. *HTML elements* make up HTML pages and are denoted by tags, which are letters or words in angle brackets, < and >. For example, <img> is an image element.

Overview of elements

Consider the HTML code that you created at the end of Chapter 1:

```
<!DOCTYPE html PUBLIC "-//W3C//DTD XHTML 1.0 Strict//EN"
              "http://www.w3.org/TR/xhtml1/DTD/xhtml1-strict.dtd">
<html>
<head>
<title>My Test Page</title>
<script type="text/javascript" src="js/jquery-1.4.min.js"></script>
<script type="text/javascript">
$(document).ready(function(){
```

```
alert(jQuery('img').attr('alt'));
});
</script>
</head>
<body>
<p>This is my test page.</p>
<img src= "images/home.gif" height="28" width="28" alt="This is a test
             image." />

</body>
</html>
```

This code contains eight elements, which I discuss in the next section, Common HTML Elements: `<html></html>`, `<head></head>`, `<title></title>`, `<script></script>` (used twice), `<body></body>`, `<img>`, and `<p></p>`.

When you open this content in a browser (see Figure 2-1), the only visible elements are the title, the text in the `<p>` element, and the alert box from the jQuery function in the second `<script>` element.

With the exception of the `<html>` element that surrounds everything else in the HTML code, elements are always nested inside other elements. For example, the line of text, `This is my test page.` is nested inside `<p>` tags, which are inside `<body>` tags, which are inside `<html>` tags. Think of Russian stacking dolls.

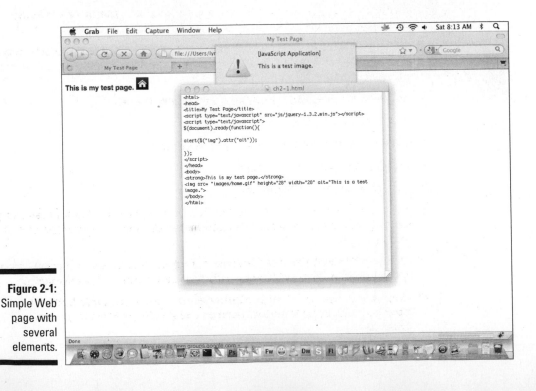

Figure 2-1:
Simple Web
page with
several
elements.

When you think about elements, keep these rules of order in mind:

- ✔ **An element inside another element is the child of the outer element.**
- ✔ **The outer element is the parent of the inner element.**
- ✔ **An individual element can, and often is, simultaneously both a parent and a child.**

Common HTML elements

You may already be familiar with HTML. If not, here's a closer look at a few of most common HTML elements you should know:

- ✔ **<html></html>:** Tells the Web browser that everything inside the tags should be considered a Web page.

- ✔ **<head></head>:** Contains information that controls how the page is displayed. Elements responsible for JavaScript and CSS code and calls to other files are generally placed between these tags.

- ✔ **<title></title>:** Contains the title of the Web page, displayed on the title bar at the top of the browser.

- ✔ **<body></body>:** Holds all the content of the page.

- ✔ **<style></style>:** Controls the appearance and behavior of elements on your Web page.

- ✔ **<script></script>:** Makes JavaScript and other specified code available, either by calling a file or code placed between these tags. jQuery is included on the page with this tag.

- ✔ **<strong></strong>:** Boldfaces any text within the tag.

- ✔ **<h1></h1>:** Creates header text.

- ✔ **<div></div>:** Creates a container of content.

- ✔ **<p></p>:** Creates a paragraph.

- ✔ **<a></a>:** Creates a hyperlink.

- ✔ **<img />:** Displays an image. Note that this tag doesn't have a matching end tag, so a slash character is used inside the tag to denote the end of the tag.

- ✔ **<form></form>:** Creates a Web form that can send user-submitted information to another Web page or code that can process this information.

- ✔ **<input></input>:** Creates a form element, such as a radio button, text input box, or a Submit button. Used as a child element inside <form> </form>.

> ✔ **
**: Inserts a line break. No matching end tag is needed.
>
> ✔ **<table></table>**: Creates a table, along with child tags <tr></tr> and <td></td>.

TIP

A more complete list of HTML elements is located at www.w3.org/TR/REC-html40/index/elements.html.

Getting and Setting Element Values

jQuery allows you to get and set values associated with your elements. In this section, I describe element attribute values and show you how to get them and how to change the elements by setting values for them with jQuery.

Understanding element attribute values

One feature of jQuery that makes it so powerful is that it allows you to manipulate the attribute values of elements. An *attribute* is an HTML code word that controls an aspect of the element. For example, consider this <img> element:

```
<img src= "images/home.gif" height="28" width="28" alt="Little house" />
```

This line of code has the following four attributes:

> ✔ **src:** The URL or location of the image file to display
>
> ✔ **height:** The image height in pixels
>
> ✔ **width:** The image width in pixels
>
> ✔ **alt:** The text that appears in lieu of an image or, in some browsers, when the image is moused-over for a few seconds

These are a few of the many possible attribute values that an <img> element can have. Other elements have different attributes.

The *value* of an attribute is the text that follows the equal sign after the attribute name. This value is typically surrounded in double quotes. For example, in the <img> element just shown, the height attribute has a value of 28.

Getting element attribute values

If you want the value of an attribute, you can use the jQuery attr() function. The attr() function takes the name of an attribute on your page, such as attr('src'), and gives you the value of that attribute, that is, the information on the right side of the equal sign.

Consider this line of code:

```
var imageSource = $('img').attr('src');
```

To use the `attr()` method, you call a function method in the jQuery library. You have to include a call to the name of the jQuery function in your code. The `$` function tells the browser to use the jQuery function and specifies which element you are interested in.

The `$` is a shorthand way of calling jQuery. The following line of code works the same way as the preceding code:

```
imageSource = jQuery('img').attr('src');
```

This code stores the value of the `src` attribute from an `<img>` element into the `imageSource` variable.

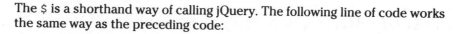

A *variable* is a place to store values. Think of a variable as a box containing whatever is on the other side of the = sign. In the preceding example, I created a variable named `imageSource` and stored in it whatever was in the `src` attribute of the `<img>` tag.

In the following steps, you get the value of the `src` attribute. Then you save it in a variable and display it in an alert box:

1. **Create a Web page containing the following code:**

```
<!DOCTYPE html PUBLIC "-//W3C//DTD XHTML 1.0 Strict//EN"
          "http://www.w3.org/TR/xhtml1/DTD/xhtml1-strict.dtd">
<html>
<head>
<title>My Test Page</title>
<script type="text/javascript" src="js/jquery-1.4.min.js"></script>
<script type="text/javascript">
$(document).ready(function(){

// Your code goes here.

});
</script>
</head>
<body>
<strong>This is my test page.</strong>
<img src= "images/home.gif" height="28" width="28" alt="This is a test
          image." />
</body>
</html>
```

You can browse to `www.dummies.com/go/jquery` and copy this code and paste it into your text editor or Web editor. Look at Chapter 1 for instructions on creating Web pages using Notepad (Windows) or TextEdit (Mac) and viewing them in your Web browser.

Make sure you name your file with .html at the end of the name.

2. **Replace** `// Your code goes here.` **with the following two lines of code:**

```
var imageFile = $('img').attr('src');
alert (imageFile);
```

The first line says, "Get the value of the `src` attribute for the `<img>` element and save it in the `imageFile` variable. The second line says, "Display in an alert box the value stored in the `imageFile` variable."

You can name your variables anything you want, as long as the name contains no spaces and no special characters. Stick to letters, and avoid numbers. It's best to give your variables meaningful names, so you remember the purpose of each variable.

3. **Save this file and then open it in your browser.**

You see an alert box displaying the source directory and filename of the image on the page, as shown in Figure 2-2.

Displaying an attribute value in an alert box is not a particularly useful trick. But the point here is to understand how to get those values and store them in variables.

There are specific rules for naming variables:

✔ JavaScript variable names start with a letter, $, or an underscore.

✔ Names can contain only letters, numbers, $, and underscores; no spaces or other special characters are allowed.

✔ You can't use reserved words (which have special meanings) as variable names.

Getting element content

Some HTML elements have text elements between their opening and closing tags that you can manipulate using jQuery. Consider this code:

```
<p>This is some text.</p>
```

With jQuery, I can get the text between the opening and closing `<p>` tag. To get an element's content with jQuery, do the following:

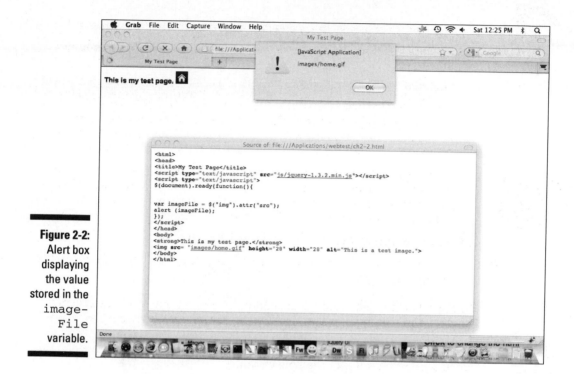

Figure 2-2:
Alert box
displaying
the value
stored in the
`image–`
`File`
variable.

1. **Create a Web page containing the following code:**

```
<!DOCTYPE html PUBLIC "-//W3C//DTD XHTML 1.0 Strict//EN"
        "http://www.w3.org/TR/xhtml1/DTD/xhtml1-strict.dtd">
<html>
<head>
<title>My Test Page</title>
<script type="text/javascript" src="js/jquery-1.4.min.js"></script>
<script type="text/javascript">
$(document).ready(function(){

// Your code goes here.

});
</script>
</head>
<body>
<strong>This is my test page.</strong>
<p>This is some text.</p>
</body>
</html>
```

You can browse to www.dummies.com/go/jquery and copy this code
and paste it into your text or Web editor.

2. **Replace** `// Your code goes here.` **with the following two lines of code:**

```
var pContent = $('p').text();
alert (pContent);
```

The first line says, "Get the HTML content of the <p> element and save it in the pContent variable. The second line says, "Display in an alert box the value stored in the pContent variable."

3. **Save this file, and then open it in your browser.**

You see an alert box displaying the content of the <p> element, as shown in Figure 2-3.

Setting element attribute values

Suppose that you want to change an image displayed on a page. Because the displayed image is based on what is stored in the <img> src attribute, changing the src value will change which image is displayed on the page.

For the next example, you need two image files of the same height and width. You can download cover1.jpg and cover2.jpg from www.dummies.com/go/jquery. Save these files to your webtest directory in the images directory.

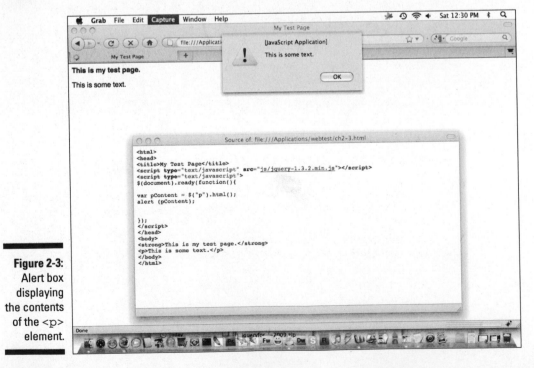

Figure 2-3:
Alert box displaying the contents of the <p> element.

To change the attribute value of an HTML element, follow these steps:

1. **Create a Web page containing the following code:**

```
<!DOCTYPE html PUBLIC "-//W3C//DTD XHTML 1.0 Strict//EN"
          "http://www.w3.org/TR/xhtml1/DTD/xhtml1-strict.dtd">
<html>
<head>
<title>My Test Page</title>
<script type="text/javascript" src="js/jquery-1.4.min.js"></script>
<script type="text/javascript">
$(document).ready(function(){

// Your code goes here.

});
</script>
</head>
<body>
<strong>This is my test page.</strong>
<img src="images/cover1.jpg" alt="cover1" />
</body>
</html>
```

2. **Save this file, and then view it in your browser.**

   Note that the image that appears is `cover1.jpg`.

3. **Replace `// Your code goes here.` with the following code:**

```
$('img').attr({src: 'images/cover2.jpg', alt: 'cover2'});
```

   This code says, "Find the `<img>` element, and change the `src` attribute to `images/cover2.jpg` and the `alt` attribute to `cover2`."

4. **Save this file, and then open it in your browser.**

   This time, the image that appears is `cover2.jpg`, as shown in Figure 2-4.

Removing element attribute values

Removing an attribute value is easy; you just use the `removeAttr()` function. For example, the following code removes the `height` attribute from an `<img>` tag:

```
$('img').removeAttr('height');
```

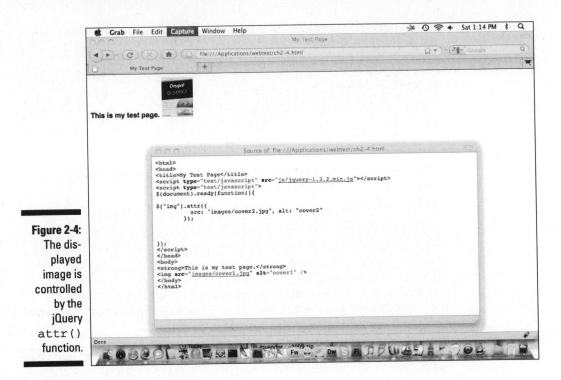

Figure 2-4:
The displayed image is controlled by the jQuery `attr()` function.

Changing HTML Content

Earlier in the chapter, you copied the HTML content from an element and displayed it in an alert box. After you copy HTML content, you can place it inside any other HTML element on the page.

To copy HTML content from one element and place it in another, follow these steps:

1. **Create a Web page containing the following code:**

```
<!DOCTYPE html PUBLIC "-//W3C//DTD XHTML 1.0 Strict//EN"
          "http://www.w3.org/TR/xhtml1/DTD/xhtml1-strict.dtd">
<html>
<head>
<title>My Test Page</title>
<script type="text/javascript" src="js/jquery-1.4.min.js"></script>
<script type="text/javascript">
$(document).ready(function(){

// Your code goes here.

});
```

```
</script>
</head>
<body>
<strong>This is the code in the STRONG element.</strong>
<p>This is the code in the P element.
<img src="images/cover1.jpg" alt="cover1" /></p>
</body>
</html>
```

2. **Save the file, and then view it in your browser.**

    Note the text in the `<strong>` and `<p>` elements (see Figure 2-5). They each have HTML `<em>` tags that italicize parts of the text.

3. **Replace `// Your code goes here.` with the following code:**

```
var strongContent = $('strong').html();
var pContent = $('p').html();
```

    The first line gets the HTML content inside the `<strong>` element and stores it in the `strongContent` variable. The second line stores the content of the `<p>` element in the `pContent` variable. Now that you have the content from each element, you need to set it in each element.

4. **Add this code below the two lines you just added:**

```
$('strong').html(pContent);
$('p').html(strongContent);
```

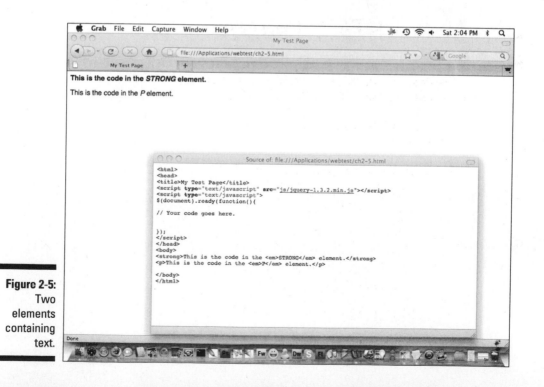

Figure 2-5:
Two elements containing text.

The first line puts the HTML code stored in pContent in the <strong> element. The second puts the HTML code stored in strongContent in the <p> element.

5. **Save this file, and then open it in your browser.**

The code that was originally in the <strong> element is now in the <p> element, and vice versa (see Figure 2-6).

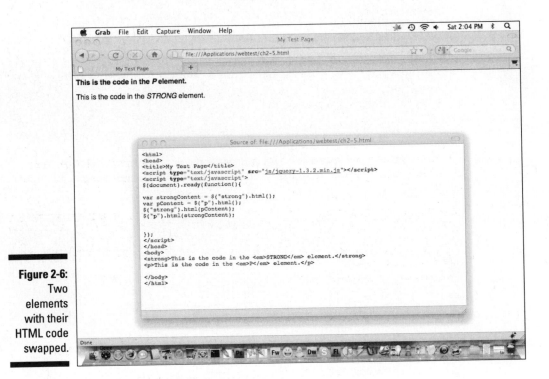

Figure 2-6:
Two
elements
with their
HTML code
swapped.

Changing Text Content

Sometimes you don't want the actual HTML code in an element; you want only the text. To do so, replace the html() function with the text() function. In the preceding example, you swapped the HTML code. If you want to swap only the text and not the HTML code, use this code:

```
<!DOCTYPE html PUBLIC "-//W3C//DTD XHTML 1.0 Strict//EN"
          "http://www.w3.org/TR/xhtml11/DTD/xhtml1-strict.dtd">

<html>
<head>
<title>My Test Page</title>
<script type="text/javascript" src="js/jquery-1.4.min.js"></script>
```

```
<script type="text/javascript">

$(document).ready(function(){

var strongContent = $('strong').text();
var pContent = $('p').text();

$('strong').text(pContent);
$('p').text(strongContent);

});
</script>
</head>
<body>
<strong>This is the text in the <em>STRONG</em> element.</strong>
<p>This is the text in the <em>P</em> element.</p>
</body>
</html>
```

Note that the <em> tags are no longer present, so nothing is italicized (see Figure 2-7). Using the text() method strips out HTML elements.

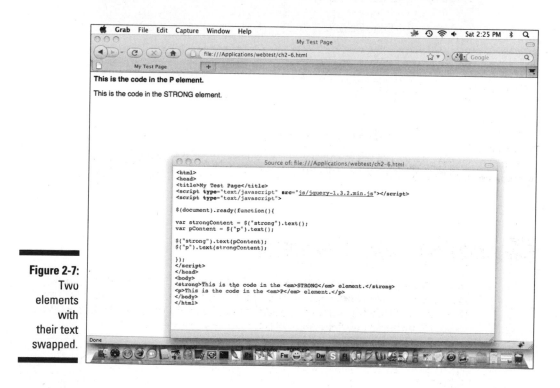

Figure 2-7:
Two
elements
with
their text
swapped.

Chapter 3

Selecting HTML Elements, Attributes, and Positions

....

....

In Chapter 2, you find out how to get and set an element's attributes and HTML inside elements. All the examples in that chapter focus on getting and setting values in a single element type on a page. But when you have multiple elements of the same type, sometimes you need to filter a particular element or elements and leave other ones alone. This is where jQuery selectors come in handy.

You can use a selector to choose a particular type of element and also to select an element based on its attributes, id, CSS class, and order on the page (for example, the third <img> or the fifth <p>). You can even choose elements based on their parents or children.

After you select the element or elements you want, you can use other jQuery functions to manipulate them. This chapter is all about selecting elements with jQuery selectors.

Using jQuery Selectors

In this section, you select all the elements of a single type. You also find out how to filter elements based on id values, CSS classes, and their order on the page.

Selecting specific element types

You may not realize it, but you use a selector in Chapter 2. Take a look at the following code, which changes the `src` and `alt` attributes for `<img>` elements:

```
<!DOCTYPE html PUBLIC "-//W3C//DTD XHTML 1.0 Strict//EN"
            "http://www.w3.org/TR/xhtml1/DTD/xhtml1-strict.dtd">
<html>
<head>
<title>My Test Page</title>
<script type="text/javascript" src="js/jquery-1.4.min.js"></script>
<script type="text/javascript">
$(document).ready(function(){

$('img').attr({src: 'images/cover2.jpg', alt: 'cover2'});

});
</script>
</head>
<body>
<strong>This is my test page.</strong>
<img src="images/cover1.jpg" alt="cover1" />
</body>
</html>
```

This code changes the `src` and `alt` attributes for an `<img>` element. The code `$('img')` is selecting the `<img>` element.

You use the same selector with the jQuery `html()` and `text()` functions to change the HTML code or text in all matching elements on a page. To see this in action, follow these steps to change the text in all the `<strong>` elements on a page:

1. **Create a Web page containing the following code:**

```
<!DOCTYPE html PUBLIC "-//W3C//DTD XHTML 1.0 Strict//EN"
            "http://www.w3.org/TR/xhtml1/DTD/xhtml1-strict.dtd">
<html>
<head>
<title>My Test Page</title>
<script type="text/javascript" src="js/jquery-1.4.min.js"></script>
<script type="text/javascript">
$(document).ready(function(){

// Your code goes here.

});
</script>
</head>
<body>
<strong>some name</strong>
```

```
<p>Some text<p>
<strong>another name</strong>
<p>More text<p>
<strong>another name</strong>
<p>Even more text<p>
<strong>your name</strong>
<p>Last bit of text<p>
</body>
</html>
```

You can download this code from www.dummies.com/go/jquery. If you instead type the code yourself, the text inside the <strong> and <p> elements doesn't matter, so use whatever you want. The important point is to have several <strong> elements.

2. Save the file, and then view it in your browser.

Note the bold text in the <strong> elements (see Figure 3-1).

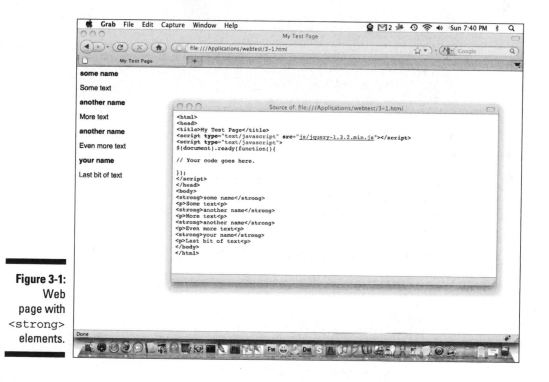

Figure 3-1:
Web
page with
<strong>
elements.

3. Replace `// Your code goes here.` with the following code:

```
var strongContent = 'jQuery for Dummies';
```

The `strongContent` variable stores the text *jQuery for Dummies*. Now that you have the content you want in the `<strong>` elements, you need to use a selector to select all the `<strong>` elements and change the text in them with the `text()` function.

4. **Add this code below the line you just added:**

```
$('strong').text(strongContent);
```

This code puts the text stored in `strongContent` in all the `<strong>` elements on the page.

5. **Save this file, and then open it in your browser.**

The text that was originally in the `<strong>` elements has been replaced, as shown in Figure 3-2.

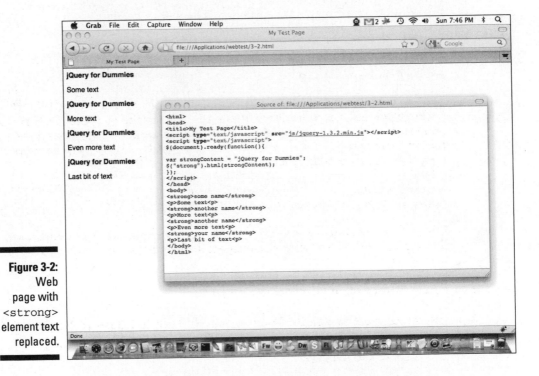

Figure 3-2:
Web page with `<strong>` element text replaced.

Selecting all elements

You can select every element on a page by using the `*` character. For example, if I wanted to add an `id` attribute to every element in the preceding code, I could use this line of code:

```
$('*').attr({id: 'myNewID'});
```

You shouldn't use the * character with some jQuery functions. Consider this line of code:

```
$('*')text('Not a good idea.');
```

When this line of code executes, it first replaces the outermost element's text. Because the outermost parent element of any HTML page is the <html> element, you end up with this HTML code on your page:

```
<html>Not a good idea.</html>
```

In general, it's practical to use the * selector when you want to assign a CSS style or an attribute to every element on a page or can narrow the results further in some other way.

Selecting an id

In Chapter 2, you see src, alt, height, and width attributes used for <img> elements. There are other attributes, such as the id attribute, that you can assign to all elements. The id attribute contains a unique identifier that you can use with a selector to pinpoint a specific element. For example, here is code that assigns ids to two <p> elements:

```
<p id='someTxt'>Some text<p>
<p id='moreTxt'>More text<p>
```

The first <p> element has the someTxt id. The second has the moreTxt id. If I want to select the second <p> element, I can use the id name moreTxt in a selector.

Several rules govern id attributes. An id

- **An id must be unique.** You can use an id only once per HTML page.
- **An id can contain only letters, numbers, hyphens, underscores, colons, and periods.**
- **An id must begin with a letter.**
- **An id is case-sensitive.** The id you use in the HTML tag must match the one you use in your selector.
- **An id is used in jQuery with a pound sign (#) in front of the id name.** In my HTML code, for example, I use id = 'myidname'. But when I use the id with a selector in the jQuery code, I place a pound sign in front of the id name, that is, '#myidname'.

Pay attention to how the pound sign is used in the following example. You see the pound sign used only in the code in the `<script>` section, not in the HTML `<p>` tag.

To display an attribute from an element using an `id` selector, follow these steps:

1. **Create a Web page containing the following code:**

```
<!DOCTYPE html PUBLIC "-//W3C//DTD XHTML 1.0 Strict//EN"
           "http://www.w3.org/TR/xhtml1/DTD/xhtml1-strict.dtd">
<html>
<head>
<title>My Test Page</title>
<script type="text/javascript" src="js/jquery-1.4.min.js"></script>
<script type="text/javascript">
$(document).ready(function(){

// Your code goes here.

});
</script>
</head>
<body>
<p id='someTxt'>Some text<p>
<p id='moreTxt'>More text<p>
</body>
</html>
```

2. **Locate this line in the code: `// Your code goes here`. Replace that line with the following code:**

```
alert ($('#moreTxt').text());
```

This code opens an alert box containing the text stored in the selector named with the `id` attribute `moreTxt`.

3. **Save this file, and then open it in your browser.**

The text in the `<p>` element with the `moreTxt` attribute displays in an alert box, as shown in Figure 3-3.

Selecting classes

Using `id`s to select specific elements gives you a lot of control over the elements on your page. But because `id`s are unique, you have to select each element by `id`. If you want to select four elements on your page, for example, you have to use all four `id`s in your code. For example, to set the `src` attribute for four `<img>` elements on a page, you would use the following code:

```
$('#anid').attr('src') = 'images/newImage.gif';
$('#anotherid').attr('src') = 'images/newImage.gif';
```

```
$('#myid').attr('src') = 'images/newImage.gif';
$('#hereisanid').attr('src') = 'images/newImage.gif';
```

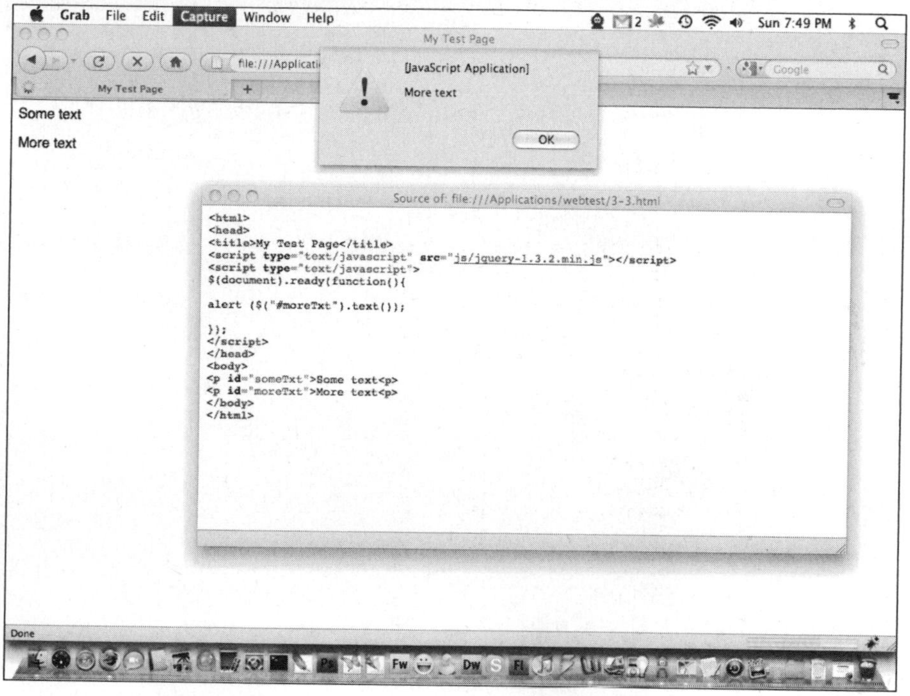

Figure 3-3:
Web page
with alert
box display-
ing the text
from the
element
with
moreTxt
id.

To select elements by `id`, the code in the HTML contains `id` attributes for each element without a pound sign.

Each of these lines sets the `src` attribute of a particular `<img>` element. If you use a special attribute known as a `class`, you can select all elements with that attribute with a single line of code, such as:

```
$('.someClass').attr('src') = 'images/newImage.gif';
```

Several rules govern `class` attributes.

✔ **A class may be used by more than one element.** You can use an `id` only once per HTML page.

✔ **An element may contain more than one class.** If you want to give an element multiple class attributes, use a space between class names. For example, here are three class attributes assigned to a single `<p>` element:

```
<p attribute="firstclass anotherclass dogclass catclass">
```

✔ **A class attribute is used in jQuery with a period (.) in front of the class name.** In HTML code, for example, I use `class = "myclass"`. But when I use the `class` with a selector in the jQuery code, I place a period in front of the `class` name, that is, `'.myclass'`.

To change the text in `<p>` and `<strong>` elements with the same class, do the following:

1. **Create a Web page containing the following code:**

```
<!DOCTYPE html PUBLIC "-//W3C//DTD XHTML 1.0 Strict//EN"
          "http://www.w3.org/TR/xhtml1/DTD/xhtml1-strict.dtd">
<html>
<head>
<title>My Test Page</title>
<script type="text/javascript" src="js/jquery-1.4.min.js"></script>
<script type="text/javascript">
$(document).ready(function(){

// Your code goes here.


});
</script>
</head>
<body>
<strong class="changemytext">some name</strong>
<p class="changemytext">Some text<p>
<strong>another name</strong>
<p>More text<p>
<strong>another name</strong>
<p>Even more text<p>
<strong class="changemytext">your name</strong>
<p class="changemytext">Last bit of text<p>
</body>
</html>
```

Four elements have the same class attribute, `changemytext`. Note that a class can be used as often as you want, and different types of elements can share a class. If you save and open this file in a browser, you see the same page shown previously in this chapter in Figure 3-1.

2. **Replace `// Your code goes here.` with the following code:**

```
$('.changemytext').text('This is new text.');
```

This code changes the text in all the `<strong>` and `<p>` elements with the `changemytext` class attribute to the new text.

3. **Save this file, and then open it in your browser.**

The text originally in the `<strong>` and `<p>` elements with the class attribute `changemytext` has been replaced, as shown in Figure 3-4.

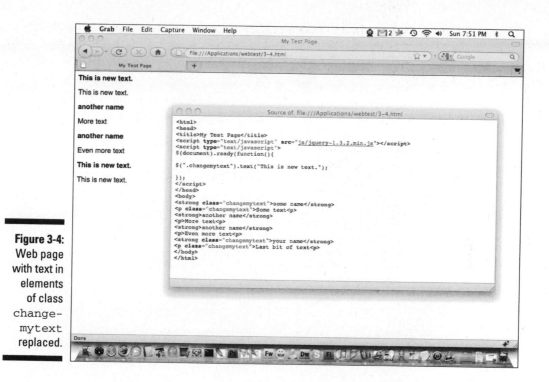

Figure 3-4:
Web page with text in elements of class change-mytext replaced.

Selecting by order

When you have several of the same type of elements on a page, you may want to select by order. For example, you might want to select the third <p> element on the page. jQuery has a set of functions that lets you select based on an element's position on the page.

When using lists of things in the jQuery library, the first item in the list is always considered number 0, not number 1. Code examples in this section that choose an element based on its position in a list count from the beginning of the list starting with 0.

Consider this code with several different elements, <p>, <strong>, and <img>. There are eleven total elements, four <p> tags, four <strong> tags, and two <img> tags:

```
<!DOCTYPE html PUBLIC "-//W3C//DTD XHTML 1.0 Strict//EN"
                "http://www.w3.org/TR/xhtml1/DTD/xhtml1-strict.dtd">
<html>
<head>
<title>My Test Page</title>
<script type="text/javascript" src="js/jquery-1.4.min.js"></script>
<script type="text/javascript">
```

```
$(document).ready(function(){

// Your code goes here.

});
</script>
</head>
<body>
<strong>Element, first strong tag</strong>
<p>Element, first p tag<p>
<strong>Element, second strong tag</strong>
<p>Element, second p tag<p>
<strong>Element, third strong tag</strong>
<p>Element, third p tag<p>
<img src="images/cover1.jpg" alt="Element"/>
<strong>Element, fourth strong tag</strong>
<img src="images/cover1.jpg" alt="Element" />
<p>Element, fourth p tag<p>
<img src="images/cover2.jpg" alt="Element" />
</body>
</html>
```

Following are some order selectors and examples of their use with elements in the preceding code:

Try the code in the following examples by replacing the `//Your code goes here` line in the preceding code.

✔ **:first:** Selects the first matching element. This code returns the value of the src attribute of the first `<img>`, which is `images/cover1.jpg`.

```
$('img:first').attr('src');
```

✔ **:last:** Selects the last matching element. This code returns the value of the `src` attribute of the last `<img>`, which is `images/cover2.jpg`.

```
$('img:last').attr('src');
```

✔ **:even:** Matches even elements, starting with 0. This code changes the text of the first and third `<strong>` elements (see Figure 3-5).

```
$('strong:even').text('Changed this text.');
```

✔ **:odd:** Matches odd elements, starting with 1. This code changes the text of the second and fourth `<strong>` elements.

```
$('strong:odd').text('Changed this text.');
```

REMEMBER

Lists of things used with jQuery begin numbering at 0, not 1. To select the first element, use an index of 0. The second element has an index of 1, the third an index of 2, and so on.

✔ **:eq(index):** Matches a specific element by counting from the first element to the index value. Suppose that you want to choose the third `<strong>` element on the page. Because the count starts with 0, to select the third `<strong>` element, do the following:

```
$('strong:eq(2)').text('Changed this text.');
```

✔ **:gt(index):** Selects all elements with an index value greater than the index. Selected elements are elements below the selected element on the page.

✔ **:lt(index):** Selects all elements with an index value less than the index. Selected elements are above the selected element on the page.

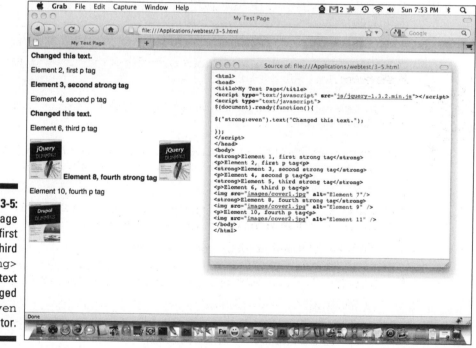

Figure 3-5: Web page with first and third `<strong>` element text changed by even selector.

Selecting from Forms

jQuery has a special set of filters just for selecting elements in HTML forms. The examples in this section work with the following code to select form elements:

```
<!DOCTYPE html PUBLIC "-//W3C//DTD XHTML 1.0 Strict//EN"
            "http://www.w3.org/TR/xhtml1/DTD/xhtml1-strict.dtd">
<html>
<head>
<title>My Test Page</title>
<script type="text/javascript" src="js/jquery-1.4.min.js"></script>
<script type="text/javascript">
$(document).ready(function(){

// Your code goes here.

});
</script>
</head>
<body>
<form action="" method="post">
Your name<input type="text" />
<input type="checkbox" />
<input type = "radio" />
<select><option>First Choice</option></select>
<input type="submit" />

</form>
</body>
</html>
```

The following are some of the form element selectors and examples of their use on elements in the preceding code:

✔ **:input:** Selects all form elements including `<input />`, `<select>`, `<textarea>`, and `<button>`. This code shows the number of input elements in my form in an alert box:

```
alert( $(':input').length);
```

When a selector selects more than one element, the result is a list of values known as an *array*. When I select all the inputs on my page, I get back an array of all the elements. The `length` keyword tells me how many elements are in my array.

✔ **:text:** Selects all elements with the type attribute set to `text`. The following code returns the value 1 in an alert box:

```
alert( $(':text').length);
```

✔ **:radio:** Selects all elements with the type attribute set to radio. The following code returns the value 1 in an alert box:

```
alert( $(':radio').length);
```

✔ **:checkbox:** Selects all elements with type attribute set to radio. The following code sets the checked attribute to true for all check boxes (see Figure 3-6):

```
$(':checkbox').attr({checked:'true'});
```

✔ **:checked:** Selects all check boxes and radio buttons that are checked.

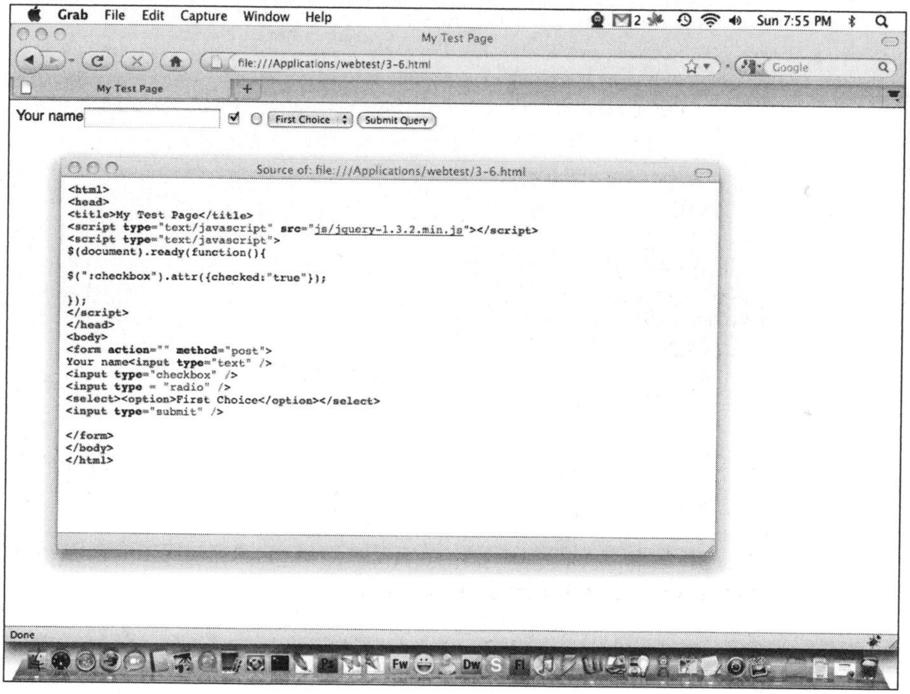

Figure 3-6:
Selected check boxes checked using the check-box selector.

Selecting Attributes

Elements can be selected by using their attributes and attribute values. Here are some attribute filters:

✔ **[attribute]:** Selects all elements with a specific attribute. The following code displays the number of `<img>` elements with a `height` attribute:

```
alert( $('img[height]').length);
```

You can leave off the name of the element to select all the elements with a particular attribute. For example, the following code returns all elements with a `height` attribute, whether or not they are `<img>` elements:

```
alert( $('[height]').length);
```

✔ **[attribute=value]:** Selects all elements with a particular attribute set to a specific value. The following code displays the number of elements with a `class` attribute set to `myclass`:

```
alert( $('[class=myclass]').length);
```

✔ **[attribute!=value]:** Selects all elements with a particular attribute not set to a specific value. The following code displays the number of elements with a `class` attribute that isn't `myclass`. Elements with no `class` attribute are ignored:

```
alert( $('[class!=myclass]').length);
```

Selecting Visibility

Being able to hide and show elements are some of the fun things you can easily do with jQuery. In Chapter 5, you find out how to hide elements. The following selectors will come in handy then:

✔ **:hidden:** Selects all hidden elements

✔ **:visible:** Selects all visible elements

Selecting Parents and Children

Often the elements you need to select are nested inside other elements. The following code shows two `<div>` elements, each with the same content inside:

```
<!DOCTYPE html PUBLIC "-//W3C//DTD XHTML 1.0 Strict//EN"
          "http://www.w3.org/TR/xhtml1/DTD/xhtml1-strict.dtd">

<html>
<head>
<title>My Test Page</title>
<script type="text/javascript" src="js/jquery-1.4.min.js"></script>
<script type="text/javascript">
```

```
$(document).ready(function(){

// Your code goes here.

});
</script>
</head>
<body>
<div id="myfirstdiv">
<strong class="changemytext">some name</strong>
<p class="changemytext">Some text<p>
<strong>another name</strong>
<p>More text<p>
</div>
<div id="myseconddiv">
<strong class="changemytext">some name</strong>
<p class="changemytext">Some text<p>
<strong>another name</strong>
<p>More text<p>
</div>
</body>
</html>
```

The outer element is considered the parent, and inner elements are the children.

To select elements based on their parents or children, try these selectors:

- ✔ **:first-child:** Selects the first child element. The following code selects the first child of the first `<div>` and changes the text of the selected element:

  ```
  $('div:first-child').text('Change me.');
  ```

- ✔ **:last-child:** Selects the last child element. The following code selects the last child of the second `<div>` and changes the text of the selected element:

  ```
  $('div:last-child').text('Change me.');
  ```

- ✔ **parent > child:** Selects the child element of the parent element. This code changes the text of every `<strong>` element that is a child of a `<div>` element (see Figure 3-7).

  ```
  $('div > strong').text('Change me.');
  ```

Keep in mind that the selectors in this chapter are not all the available jQuery selectors. Fortunately, knowing how to use these will make it easy to use any that aren't discussed here. You can find the complete list of selectors at http://api.jquery.com/category/selectors/.

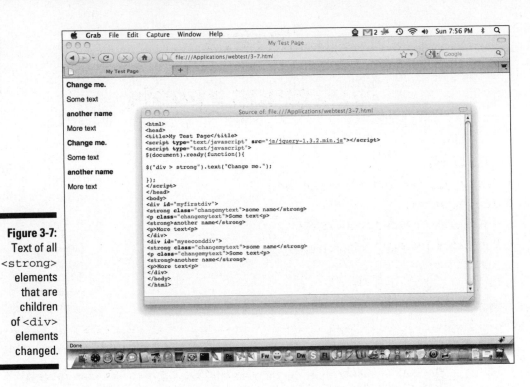

Figure 3-7:
Text of all
`<strong>`
elements
that are
children
of `<div>`
elements
changed.

Chapter 4

Managing Events

· ·

In This Chapter

▶ Calling jQuery when a Web page loads

▶ Handling an event

▶ Reacting to clicks and double-clicks

▶ Detecting when an element gets focus

▶ Noticing keyboard events

▶ Catching mouse movements

▶ Simplifying your code with interaction helpers

· ·

C hapter 2 shows you how to change the values of HTML elements and attributes. Chapter 3 reveals how to select precisely the element or set of elements you want to manipulate. In those chapters, every change you make to a selected element happens when the Web page loads.

But what if you want to change something on your page when someone clicks a link? In jQuery, clicking a link is an *event*. Other events are buttons being clicked, the mouse cursor moving a location on the page, and the page being closed. This chapter tells you how to manipulate HTML elements with jQuery in response to events.

Using jQuery When the Page Loads

To make something happen when a Web page loads in a browser, you use the `ready()` function. This function tells the Web browser to carry out any commands inside the parentheses following the `ready` command.

The following code calls the jQuery `ready()` function. Any code inside that function is executed:

```
<!DOCTYPE html PUBLIC "-//W3C//DTD XHTML 1.0 Strict//EN"
          "http://www.w3.org/TR/xhtml1/DTD/xhtml1-strict.dtd">
<html>
<head>
<script src="js/jquery-1.4.min.js"></script>
<script>
$(document).ready(function(){
var myImage= $('img').attr('src');
$('div').text(myImage);
});
</script>
</head>
<body>
<img src= "images/home.gif" height="28" width="28" alt="Little house">
<div></div>
</body>
</html>
```

You use jQuery functions to grab the `src` attribute from an `<img>` element and display that attribute as text in a `<div>` element. More specifically, the `ready()` function contains commands to first locate the `<img>` element and save the `src` attribute value in the `myImage` variable. The next line uses a selector to locate the `<div>` tag and sets the text inside the `<div>` element to the value stored in the `myImage` variable. All this code takes place when the HTML code in the page is loaded. Images and other media may still be loading, but as soon as the HTML code has loaded, the `ready()` event will fire.

In the examples in this chapter, the event code is placed inside the `ready()` function. You can leave out the `ready()` function and include only the code inside it, but it's a good practice to make sure the HTML code is loaded before you allow any other code to execute. Putting your event code inside the `ready()` function ensures that all the HTML code is present.

Handling Events

Being able to tell when visitors to your page do something, such as moving their mouse over a link or double-clicking an image, is how your Web page becomes *dynamic*. The elements on your page respond to what visitors do.

Before jQuery, you detected events with JavaScript code. However, you had to write a lot of code, and each browser type required different code. For example, the code to detect mouse actions in the current version of Internet Explorer differs from the code for the current version of Safari. Fortunately, jQuery takes care of browser differences for you. With jQuery, the same code works no matter which browser your visitor uses. And you need just a line or two of code rather than many lines.

In this section, you take a look at some specific events and how to use them to make your Web page respond to your visitor's actions.

Clicking and double-clicking

One of the most common events you want to detect is when an element on your Web page is clicked. The following example shows you how you make an alert box open when someone clicks text on your page:

1. **Create a Web page containing the following code:**

```
<!DOCTYPE html PUBLIC "-//W3C//DTD XHTML 1.0 Strict//EN"
          "http://www.w3.org/TR/xhtml1/DTD/xhtml1-strict.dtd">
<html>
<head>
<title>My Test Page</title>
<script type="text/javascript" src="js/jquery-1.4.min.js"></script>
<script type="text/javascript">
$(document).ready(function(){

//Your code goes here.

});
</script>
</head>
<body>
<div class="clickme">Do something</div>
</body>
</html>
```

You can download this code from www.dummies.com/go/jquery. If you do create this file yourself, make sure you include a <div> element with the class="clickme" attribute and text between the open and close <div> tags.

2. **Save the file, and then view it in your browser.**

3. **Click the text in the <div> element (see Figure 4-1). Nothing happens.**

4. **Replace // Your code goes here. with the following code:**

```
$('.clickme').click(function() {
alert('You clicked on something.');
});
```

A selector attaches the click event to the clickme class. You can name your class whatever you want.

Chapter 3 shows you how to use a selector to find all elements on a page with a specific class attribute. Keep in mind that you can use any of the selectors in Chapter 3 with the events discussed in this chapter.

5. **Save this file, and then open it in your browser.**

6. **Click the text.**

An alert box pops up in response to the click event, as shown in Figure 4-2.

The problem with using a `click` event with something such as text on a Web page is that visitors to your page won't know that it's something they can click. In general, the `click` event should be used with things that look like they are clickable, such as buttons or images that act like buttons.

In the following example, we use a small image as a button. This example uses the `dblclick` event, which means the element has to be double-clicked to execute the event code:

1. **Create a Web page containing the following code:**

```
<!DOCTYPE html PUBLIC "-//W3C//DTD XHTML 1.0 Strict//EN"
        "http://www.w3.org/TR/xhtml1/DTD/xhtml1-strict.dtd">
<html>
<head>
<title>My Test Page</title>
<script type="text/javascript" src="js/jquery-1.4.min.js"></script>
<script type="text/javascript">
$(document).ready(function(){

//Your code goes here.

});
</script>
</head>
<body>
<div class="clickme"><img src="images/home.gif"></div>
</body>
</html>
```

This code uses the `home.gif` image in the `images` directory inside my Web directory. See Chapter 1 for more information on how the files in this book's examples are organized.

2. **Save the file, and then view it in your browser.**

3. **Click the text in the `<div>` element (refer to Figure 4-3); nothing happens.**

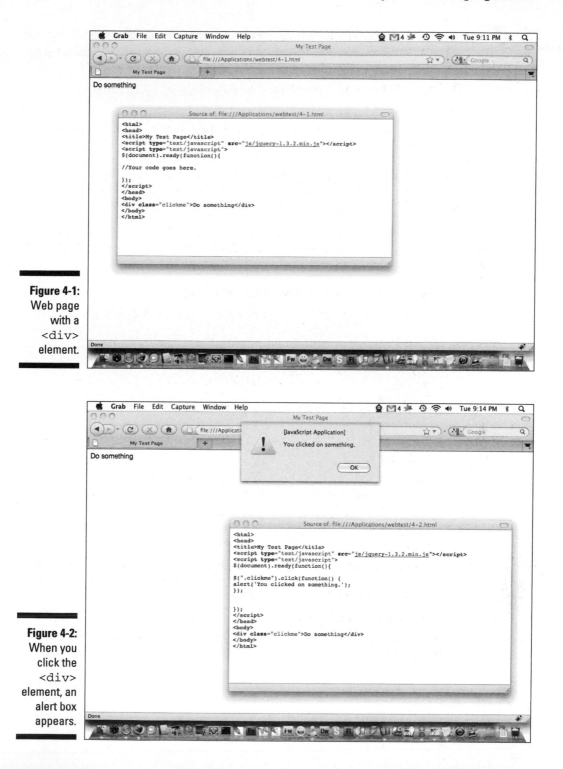

Figure 4-1:
Web page with a `<div>` element.

Figure 4-2:
When you click the `<div>` element, an alert box appears.

Figure 4-3:
Web page
with an
image inside
a <div>
element.

4. Replace // Your code goes here. with the following code:

```
$('.clickme').dblclick(function() {
alert('You double-clicked on something.');
});
```

A selector attaches the dblclick event to elements that have a class value of clickme. The <div> element has a clickme class and contains an img element.

5. Save this file, and then open it in your browser. Double-click the image.

An alert box pops up in response to the double-click event, as shown in Figure 4-4.

The <div> element with the clickme class is now clickable. Double-clicking the <div> element, which includes everything inside it, will open an alert box.

You aren't limited to using alert boxes in response to events. In later chapters, you find out how to make elements appear, disappear, fade out, animate, and do other effects. Any effect you can use in jQuery can be used in response to an event.

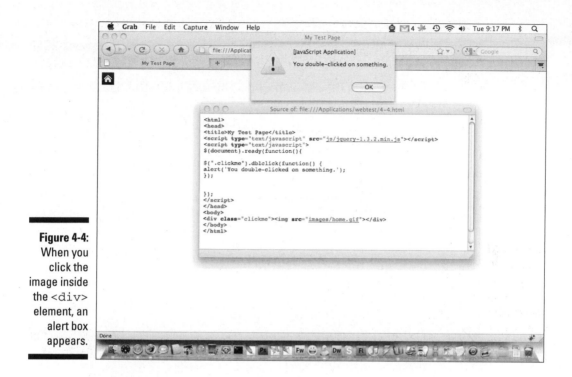

Figure 4-4:
When you click the image inside the `<div>` element, an alert box appears.

Giving an element focus

An element on a Web page gains focus when you click it with the mouse or press the tab key. To see how this works, follow these steps:

1. **Create a Web page containing the following code:**

```
<!DOCTYPE html PUBLIC "-//W3C//DTD XHTML 1.0 Strict//EN"
        "http://www.w3.org/TR/xhtml1/DTD/xhtml1-strict.dtd">
<html>
<head>
<title>My Test Page</title>
<script type="text/javascript" src="js/jquery-1.4.min.js"></script>
<script type="text/javascript">
$(document).ready(function(){

//Your code goes here.

});
</script>
</head>
<body>
First Name: <input type="text" id="textbox1" />
```

```
<br />
Last Name: <input type="text" id="textbox2" />
</body>
</html>
```

2. **Save the file, and then view it in your browser. Use the mouse cursor to click in each of the two text boxes.**

   As you click each text box, note the small cursor. When you click in a text box, it becomes the current focus.

3. **Press the tab key on your keyboard several times to see the focus change.**

4. **Replace // Your code goes here. with the following code:**

```
$('#textbox2').focus(function() {
alert('textbox2 has focus');
});
```

5. **Save this file, and then reload the page in your browser. Click inside the bottom text box.**

   An alert box pops up in response to the focus event, as shown in Figure 4-5. You can also use the tab key to give this text box focus.

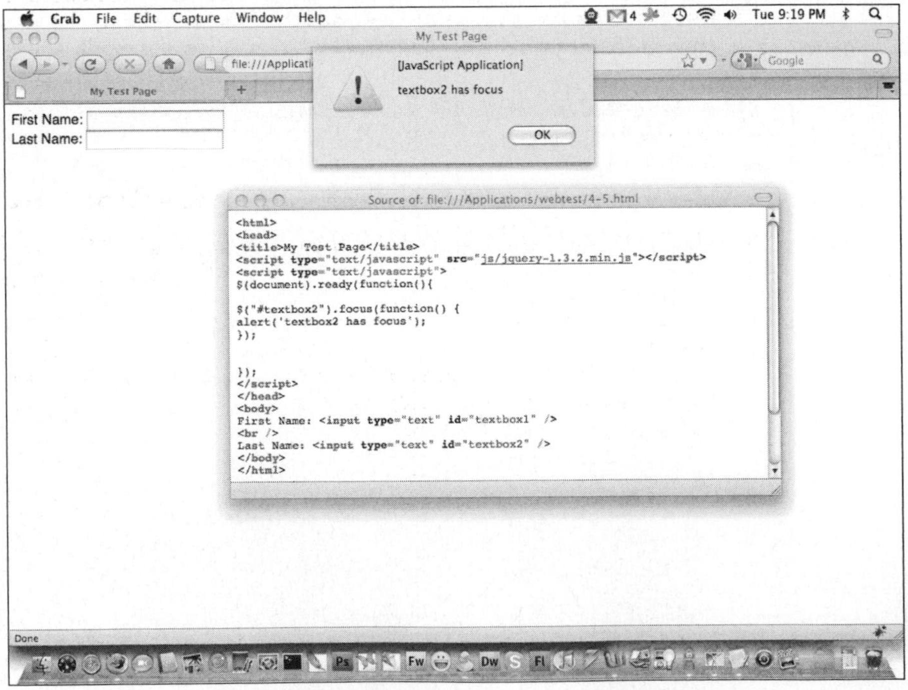

Figure 4-5:
When `textbox2` gains focus, an alert box appears.

This example uses an `id` attribute as the selector rather than a class selector. You can use many other selectors as well. Refer to Chapter 3 for more information about using selectors.

Detecting a keyboard event

It can be useful to detect when a key on the keyboard is pressed by someone visiting your site. The following events are associated with the keyboard, and you can attach events to any of them:

✔ **keydown:** A key is pressed.

✔ **keyup:** A pressed key is released.

✔ **keypress:** A key is pressed and released.

The `keydown` event takes place before the `keyup` event. If someone holds down a key and doesn't release it, the `keydown` event takes place. If someone presses a key and releases it, a `keypress` takes place.

Every key on the keyboard is associated with a numeric value. For example, A equals 65, B equals 66, and Z equals 90. These numbers are called ASCII values. You can see a chart of these values at `www.ascii.cl`. Now that we know these values, we can detect when a particular letter key is pressed.

To detect when someone presses and releases a specific key (the `keypress` event), do the following:

1. Create a Web page containing the following code and save it:

```
<!DOCTYPE html PUBLIC "-//W3C//DTD XHTML 1.0 Strict//EN"
          "http://www.w3.org/TR/xhtml1/DTD/xhtml1-strict.dtd">
<html>
<head>
<title>My Test Page</title>
<script type="text/javascript" src="js/jquery-1.4.min.js"></script>
<script type="text/javascript">
$(document).ready(function(){

//Your code goes here.

});
</script>
</head>
<body>
Type the letter Z: <input type="text" id="textbox1" />
</body>
</html>
```

2. Replace `// Your code goes here.` **with the following code:**

```
$('input').keypress(function (e) {
    if (e.which == 90) alert ('Z was typed.')
});
```

This code contains an `if` statement. The ASCII value from the keyboard is saved as `e.which`, and the `if` statement says, "If the ASCII value is equal to 90, open an alert box." The `e` argument contains the information about which key was pressed.

The secret to this code is all in the `e` argument. Each event has the event object passed into the function, which is how you know which event occurred. To find out more about key and button events, visit `http://api.jquery.com/event.which/`.

3. Save this file, and then open it in your browser. Type some letters, including a capital *Z*, in the input box.

An alert box pops up in response to the capital Z being typed, as shown in Figure 4-6.

Figure 4-6:
When a capital *Z* is typed in the text box, an alert box appears.

Detecting a mouse event

Arguably more useful than detecting keyboard presses are the events that let you detect mouse movements. An earlier example in this chapter shows you how to detect mouse clicks and double-clicks. But you can also detect many other mouse events, including

- ✔ **mousedown:** The mouse button is pressed over an element.

- ✔ **mouseenter:** The mouse cursor enters the selected element but the element is not a child element.

- ✔ **mouseleave:** The mouse cursor leaves the selected element.

- ✔ **mousemove:** The mouse is moved.

- ✔ **mouseout:** The mouse cursor leaves the selected element.

- ✔ **mouseover:** The mouse cursor enters the selected element or any of its child elements.

- ✔ **mouseup:** The mouse button is released.

The following example shows you how to detect when the mouse moves over and leaves an element on the page:

1. Create a Web page containing the following code and save it:

```
<!DOCTYPE html PUBLIC "-//W3C//DTD XHTML 1.0 Strict//EN"
        "http://www.w3.org/TR/xhtml1/DTD/xhtml1-strict.dtd">
<html>
<head>
<title>My Test Page</title>
<script type="text/javascript" src="js/jquery-1.4.min.js"></script>
<script type="text/javascript">
$(document).ready(function(){

//Your code goes here.

});
</script>
</head>
<body>
<img src="images/home.gif" id="mouseoverme">
<div id="outputdiv">This text will change.</div>
</body>
</html>
```

This puts an image on the page with an `id` attribute of `mouseoverme`. The page also has a `<div>` element with the `outputdiv` id attribute. The `<div>` element is used to display text when your mouse moves over the image.

2. **Replace // Your code goes here. with the following code:**

```
$('#mouseoverme').mouseover(function() {
$('#outputdiv').text('You moused over the image.'); });
```

A selector attaches the mouseover event to the <img> element with the mouseoverme id. The second line of code changes the text in the <div> element with the outputdiv id when the <img> element is moused over.

3. **Save this file, and then open it in your browser.**

4. **Move your mouse over the image and notice how the text changes, as shown in Figure 4-7.**

5. **Add the following code below the code you added in Step 2:**

```
$('#mouseoverme').mouseout(function() {
$('#outputdiv').text('You moused out of the image.'); });
```

This block of code is nearly identical to the one you added in Step 2. But instead of using the mouseover event, this code uses the mouseout event and the text that appears in the <div> element changes to indicate that you are mousing out of the <img> element.

6. **Save this file, and then open it in your browser.**

7. **Move your mouse over the image and out of the image and notice how the text changes, as shown in Figure 4-8.**

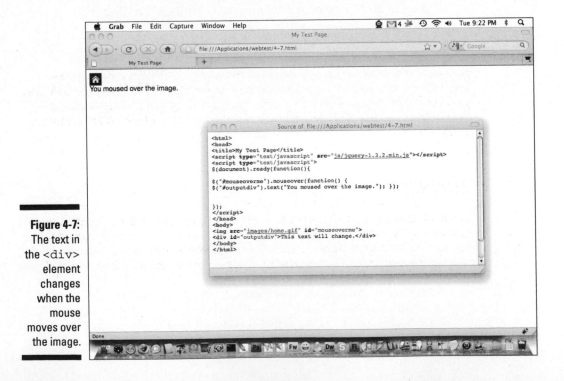

Figure 4-7:
The text in the <div> element changes when the mouse moves over the image.

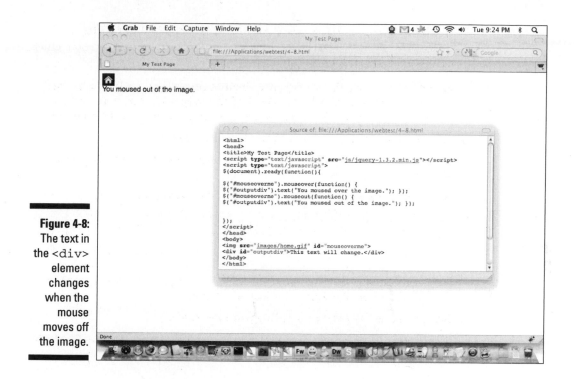

Figure 4-8:
The text in the `<div>` element changes when the mouse moves off the image.

Working with Interaction Helpers

Suppose you want to use `mouseover` and `mouseout` events together frequently, or you want to detect more than one click on an element. jQuery has two event functions to simplify both activities. They are known as interaction helpers. Think of an *interaction helper* as multiple events bundled into a single function to simplify your code.

Hovering

In the preceding example, you used two mouse events together to change the text in a `<div>` element: `mouseover` and `mouseout`. To make things simpler, jQuery has an event known as `hover`, which combines the `mouseenter` and `mouseleave` events. To use the single `hover` event, follow these steps:

1. **Create a Web page containing the following code and save it:**

```
<!DOCTYPE html PUBLIC "-//W3C//DTD XHTML 1.0 Strict//EN"
          "http://www.w3.org/TR/xhtml1/DTD/xhtml1-strict.dtd">
<html>
<head>
<title>My Test Page</title>
<script type="text/javascript" src="js/jquery-1.4.min.js"></script>
<script type="text/javascript">
$(document).ready(function(){

//Your code goes here.

});
</script>
</head>
<body>
<img src="images/home.gif" id="mouseoverme">
<div id="outputdiv">This text will change.</div>
</body>
</html>
```

2. **Replace `// Your code goes here.` with the following code:**

```
$('#mouseoverme').hover(
function() {
$('#outputdiv').text('You moused over the image.');
},
function(){
$('#outputdiv').text('You moused out of the image.');
});
```

A selector attaches the hover event to the <img> element with the mouseoverme id. The first function inside the hover event changes the text in the <div> element with the outputdiv id when the <img> element is moused over. The second function changes the text in the <div> element to indicate that the mouse has moved off the image.

The syntax of the hover event is hover(over, out). The function you put in first happens when the mouseover event takes place. The function you put second, after the comma, happens when the mouseout event takes place.

Be careful with those parentheses, curly braces, semicolons, and the comma in the hover event helper.

3. **Save this file, and then view it in your browser.**

4. **Move your mouse over and off the image and notice how the text changes, as shown in Figure 4-9.**

Figure 4-9:
The text in
the `<div>`
changes
when you
move the
mouse over
the image.

Toggling functions

The `toggle` event allows you to execute different code each time an element is clicked. The following example lets you customize the text in a `<div>` element each time a user clicks an element:

1. Create a Web page containing the following code and save it:

```
<!DOCTYPE html PUBLIC "-//W3C//DTD XHTML 1.0 Strict//EN"
        "http://www.w3.org/TR/xhtml1/DTD/xhtml1-strict.dtd">
<html>
<head>
<title>My Test Page</title>
<script type="text/javascript" src="js/jquery-1.4.min.js"></script>
<script type="text/javascript">
$(document).ready(function(){

//Your code goes here.

});
</script>
</head>
<body>
```

```
<img src="images/home.gif" id="toggleme">
<div id="outputdiv">This text will change.</div>
</body>
</html>
```

2. **Replace // Your code goes here. with the following code:**

```
$('#toggleme').toggle(
function() {
$('#outputdiv').text('You clicked the image once.');
},
function(){
$('#outputdiv').text('You clicked the image twice.');
},
function(){
$('#outputdiv').text('You clicked the image three times.');
});
```

A selector attaches the `toggle` event to the `<img>` element with the `toggleme` id. The first function inside the `toggle` event changes the text in the `<div>` element containing the `outputdiv` id value when you click the `<img>` element the first time. The second function changes the text in the `<div>` element the second time you click the image, and the third function changes the text in the `<div>` element when you click the element a third time.

The syntax of the `hover` event is `toggle(function1, function2, function3, function4, ...)`. The function you put in first happens when the `click` event first takes place. The function you put in second, after the comma, happens when the `click` event takes place again, and so on.

3. **Save this file, and then open it in your browser.**

4. **Click the image repeatedly and notice how the text changes, as shown in Figure 4-10.**

When you reach the end of the list of functions, the first `toggle` function executes again.

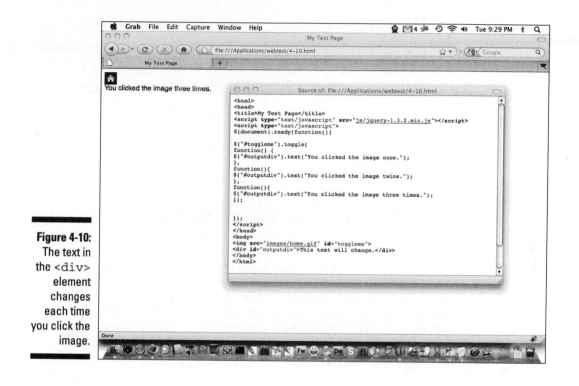

Figure 4-10:
The text in
the <div>
element
changes
each time
you click the
image.

Part II
Affecting Elements with Effects

The 5th Wave   By Rich Tennant

"Why don't you try blurring the brimstone and then putting a nice glow effect around the hellfire."

In this part . . .

Here's where you get to make elements in your pages do magic tricks. Hide them, show them, fade them in and out, and even make them move across the page. It's your turn to pull the rabbit out of your hat.

Chapter 5

Playing Hide-and-Seek with Web Page Elements

*T*wo common, impressive effects often used on Web pages are hiding visible page elements and showing hidden page elements. In this chapter, you find out how to use jQuery to make Web page elements disappear, appear, and toggle between being visible and invisible.

To trigger the hiding or showing of an element, you'll probably want to use an event, such as a button press or an image being moused over. This chapter uses simple events such as the ones discussed in Chapter 4.

Hiding Elements with jQuery

You can hide elements on a page as a result of an event. The examples in this section show you how to hide an element using a variety of selectors and events.

Hiding an element by type with a button

The following example shows you how you make everything inside `<div>` elements disappear when a user clicks a button on your page:

1. **Create a Web page containing the following code:**

```
<!DOCTYPE html PUBLIC "-//W3C//DTD XHTML 1.0 Strict//EN"
         "http://www.w3.org/TR/xhtml1/DTD/xhtml1-strict.dtd">
```

```
<html>
<head>
<title>My Test Page</title>
<script type="text/javascript" src="js/jquery-1.4.min.js"></script>
<script type="text/javascript">
$(document).ready(function(){

//Your code goes here.

});
</script>
</head>
<body>
<div>This will be hidden.</div>
<div>This will be hidden.</div>
<input value="Hide" type="submit">
</body>
</html>
```

This code contains two `<div>` elements and a button.

2. **Save the file, and then view it in your browser.**

3. **Note the text in the `<div>` elements, shown in Figure 5-1. Click the button; nothing happens.**

4. **Replace `// Your code goes here.` with the following code:**

```
$(':submit').click(function () {
    $('div').hide();
});
```

Quite a few things are going on here. The code says, "When the button is clicked, hide everything in the `<div>` elements." This code uses the `:submit` selector and the `click` event to set up the action. The `hide` function, used with the `<div>` selector, hides both `<div>` elements.

Chapter 3 shows you how to use selectors, and Chapter 4 shows you how to use an event, such as the `click` event.

5. **Save this file, and then view it in your browser.**

6. **Click the button.**

Everything in both `<div>` elements is now hidden, as shown in Figure 5-2.

When you clicked the button in this example, you hid all the elements that contained the `<div>` selector in the page. In general, it makes sense instead to pinpoint a specific element to hide as the result of an event.

You can assign an `id` to any HTML element you want. You can also use a class selector if you want to select several elements on a page. Check out Chapter 3 for more information on selectors.

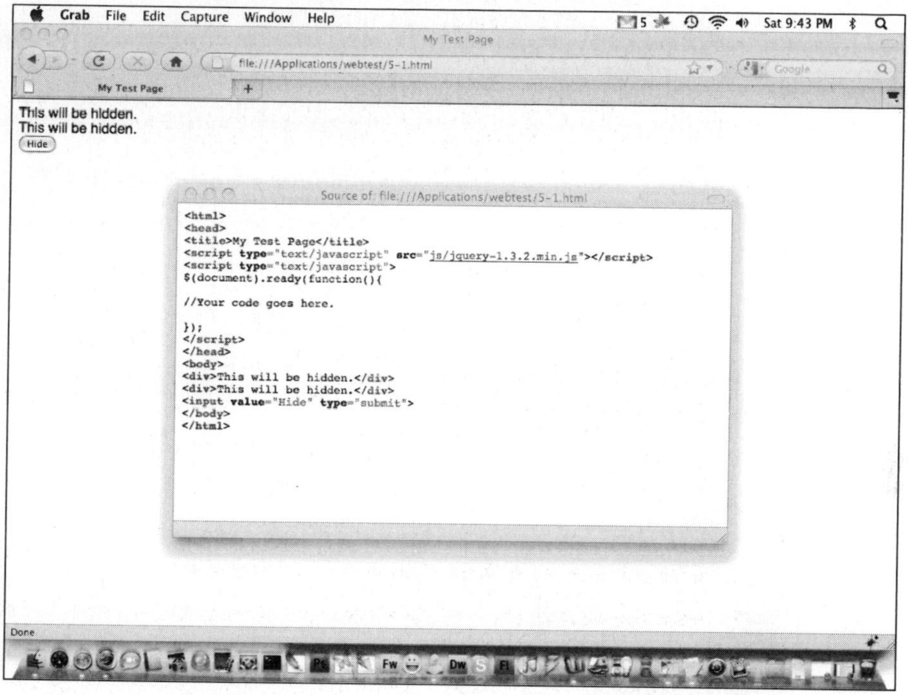

Figure 5-1:
Web page with `<div>` elements and a button.

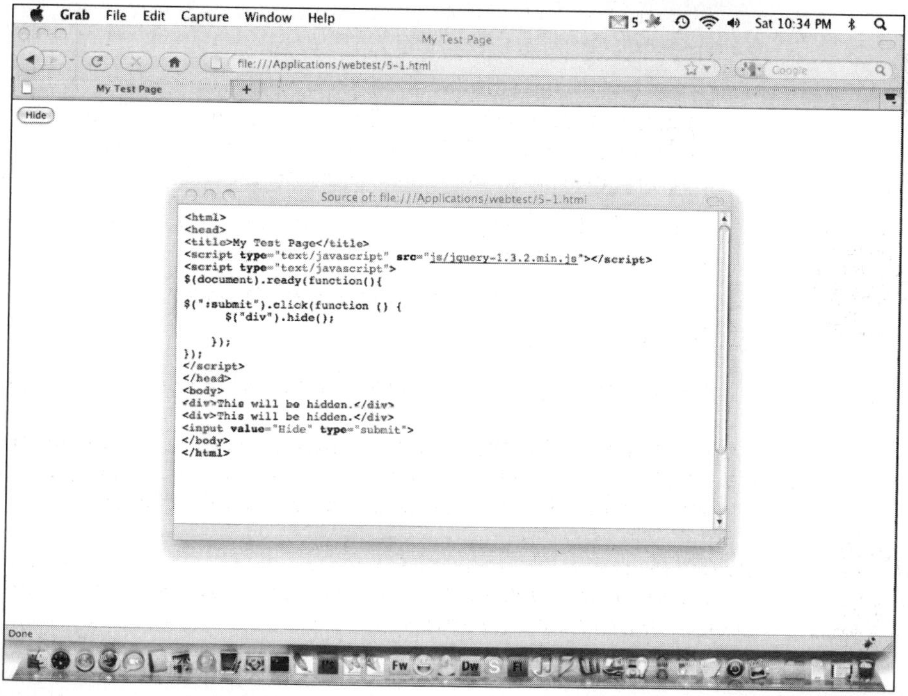

Figure 5-2:
When you click the button, the `<div>` elements disappear.

Hiding an element by id when clicked

The next example shows you how you make everything inside a `<div>` element with an `id` disappear when someone clicks that `<div>` element:

1. **Create a Web page containing the following code:**

```
<!DOCTYPE html PUBLIC "-//W3C//DTD XHTML 1.0 Strict//EN"
          "http://www.w3.org/TR/xhtml1/DTD/xhtml1-strict.dtd">
<html>
<head>
<title>My Test Page</title>
<script type="text/javascript" src="js/jquery-1.4.min.js"></script>
<script type="text/javascript">
$(document).ready(function(){

//Your code goes here.

});
</script>
</head>
<body>
<div id="hideme">This will be hidden.</div>
<div>This will not be hidden.</div>
</body>
</html>
```

   This code contains a `<div>` element with an `id` attribute named `hideme`. Unlike the preceding example, there is no button.

2. **Save the file, and then view it in your browser.**

   Note the text in the `<div>` elements, as shown in Figure 5-3.

3. **Replace `// Your code goes here.` with the following code:**

```
$('#hideme').click(function () {
     $('#hideme').hide();
});
```

   The code says, "When the button is clicked, hide the element with the `hideme` id." The code uses the `:submit` selector and the `click` event to set up the action. The `hide` function, used with an `id` selector, hides the element with the `hideme` id.

4. **Save this file, and then view it in your browser.**

5. **Click the first line of text, "This will be hidden."**

   Everything in both `<div>` elements is now hidden, as shown in Figure 5-4.

Note that the second `<div>` element moves up on the page. When you hide an element, it is not only invisible but also behaves as though it were removed from the page. All the page elements below it move up.

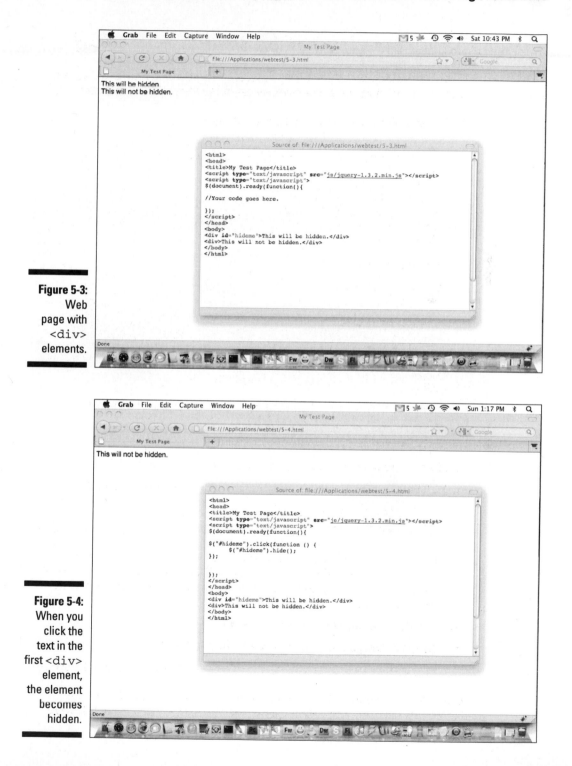

Figure 5-3:
Web
page with
`<div>`
elements.

Figure 5-4:
When you
click the
text in the
first `<div>`
element,
the element
becomes
hidden.

Hiding an element by using the `this` keyword

Take another look at the code you used in the preceding example:

```
$('#hideme').click(function () {
    $('#hideme').hide();
});
```

The outer `click` event is selecting the `hideme` id. The inner `hide` function is also selecting the same `hideme` id. The following code uses the special `this` keyword with the `hide` function and works the same way as the preceding code:

```
$('#hideme').click(function () {
    $(this).hide();
});
```

After you select the `class id`, or use any other selector, functions inside the code block can use the `this` keyword to refer to the selected elements. To test this, repeat the example in the preceding section, but replace `'#hideme'` with `this` in the code in Step 3. Note that you don't use quotes when you use `this`.

Hiding an element with animation

By default, when you hide an element, it disappears instantly. The `hide` function allows you to animate the effect, making it appear as though the element is fading out. To add fade out animations when an element hides, follow these steps:

1. **Create a Web page containing the following code:**

```
<!DOCTYPE html PUBLIC "-//W3C//DTD XHTML 1.0 Strict//EN"
          "http://www.w3.org/TR/xhtml1/DTD/xhtml1-strict.dtd">
<html>
<head>
<title>My Test Page</title>
<script type="text/javascript" src="js/jquery-1.4.min.js"></script>
<script type="text/javascript">
$(document).ready(function(){

//Your code goes here.
```

```
});
</script>
</head>
<body>
<div id="slowhide">This will be hidden slowly.</div>
<div id="fasthide">This will be hidden quickly.</div>
<div>This will not be hidden.</div>

<input value="Hide" type="submit">
</body>
</html>
```

This code contains a button and three `<div>` elements, two with `ids`.

2. **Save the file, and then view it in your browser.**

3. **Note the text in the `<div>` elements, as shown in Figure 5-5. Click the button; nothing happens.**

4. **Replace `// Your code goes here.` with the following code:**

```
$(':submit').click(function () {
   $('#slowhide').hide('slow');
         $('#fasthide').hide('fast');
   });
```

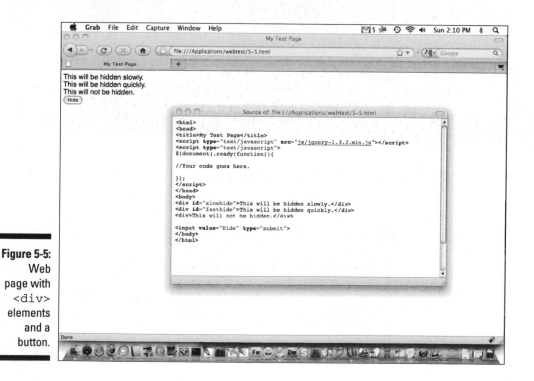

Figure 5-5:
Web
page with
`<div>`
elements
and a
button.

The code says, "When the button is clicked, use a slow speed to hide the element with the slowhide id. Hide the element with the fasthide id quickly." This code uses the :submit selector and the click event to set up the action.

jQuery has two predefined speeds — slow and fast. You can also use a number that representing the number of milliseconds during which you want the animation to occur. For example, if I want a very slow animation, I can replace the line

```
$('#slowhide').hide('slow');
```

with

```
$('#slowhide').hide(1000);
```

Note that you don't use quotes when you use a number. Also, the number 1000 is very slow. Just for fun, try the example using 10000. The fade out is really, really slow. If you don't provide a speed, the default is 400.

5. **Save the file, and then view it in your browser.**

6. **Click the button.**

The <div> elements hide at different rates of speed and the button and remaining <div> element move up, as shown in Figure 5-6.

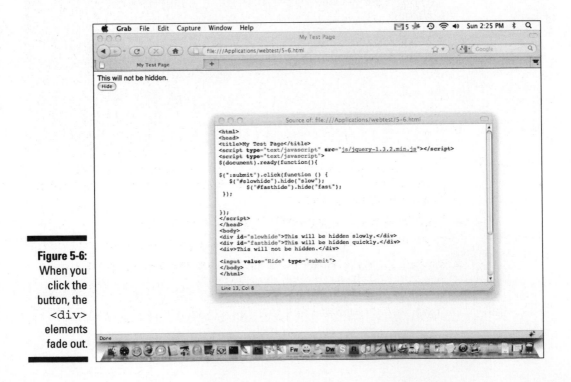

Figure 5-6:
When you click the button, the <div> elements fade out.

Showing Elements with jQuery

Showing hidden page elements is similar to hiding page elements, except you have to have something to display, that is, you must have elements hidden before you can show them. In this section, the example code contains hidden elements that appear in response to events.

Showing an element by id

The following example demonstrates how you make a hidden `<div>` element with an `id` appear when someone clicks a button on your page:

1. **Create a Web page containing the following code:**

```
<!DOCTYPE html PUBLIC "-//W3C//DTD XHTML 1.0 Strict//EN"
          "http://www.w3.org/TR/xhtml1/DTD/xhtml1-strict.dtd">
<html>
<head>
<title>My Test Page</title>
<script type="text/javascript" src="js/jquery-1.4.min.js"></script>
<script type="text/javascript">
$(document).ready(function(){

//Your code goes here.

});
</script>
</head>
<body>
<div id="showme"  style="display:none">This will appear.</div>
<input value="Show" type="submit"></body>
</html>
```

   This code contains a `<div>` element with an `id` attribute named `showme`. This `<div>` element is set as hidden using the CSS `style` attribute set to `display:none`.

2. **Save the file, and then view it in your browser.**

   The `<div>` element does not appear on the page, as shown in Figure 5-7.

3. **Replace `// Your code goes here.` with the following code:**

```
$(':submit').click(function () {
  $('#showme').show();
});
```

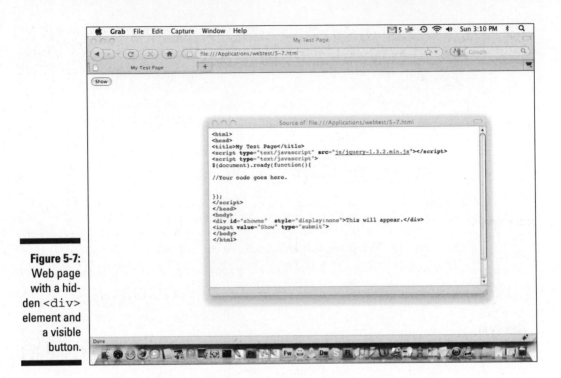

Figure 5-7:
Web page with a hidden `<div>` element and a visible button.

The code says, "When the button is clicked, show the element with the showme id." This code uses the `:submit` selector and the `click` event to set up the action. The `show` function, with an `id` selector, displays the element with the showme id.

4. **Save this file, and then view it in your browser.**

5. **Click the button.**

The hidden `<div>` element is now visible, as shown in Figure 5-8.

Note how the now-visible `<div>` element shifted the button lower. When a hidden element becomes visible, it behaves as though it were added to the page. All the page elements below it move down. This action is called a *browser repaint*.

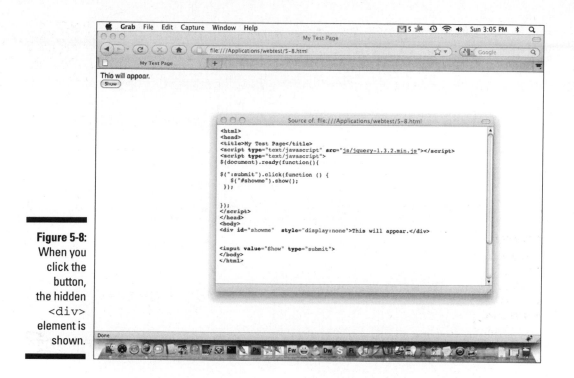

Figure 5-8:
When you
click the
button,
the hidden
`<div>`
element is
shown.

Showing an element with animation

When you show a hidden element, it disappears instantly. As with the `hide` function, the `show` function allows you to make it appear as though the element is fading in. To add fade in animations when elements are displayed, follow these steps:

1. **Create a Web page containing the following code:**

```
<!DOCTYPE html PUBLIC "-//W3C//DTD XHTML 1.0 Strict//EN"
        "http://www.w3.org/TR/xhtml1/DTD/xhtml1-strict.dtd">
<html>
<head>
<title>My Test Page</title>
<script type="text/javascript" src="js/jquery-1.4.min.js"></script>
<script type="text/javascript">
$(document).ready(function(){

//Your code goes here.
```

```
   });
   </script>
   </head>
   <body>
   <div id="slowshow" style="display:none">This will be shown slowly.</div>
   <div id="fastshow" style="display:none">This will be shown quickly.</div>
   <input value="Show" type="submit">
   </body>
   </html>
```

This code contains two `<div>` elements and a button.

2. Save the file, and then view it in your browser.

Note that the text in the `<div>` elements is not visible, as shown in Figure 5-9.

3. Replace `// Your code goes here.` with the following code:

```
$(':submit').click(function () {
   $('#slowshow').show(2000);
        $('#fastshow').show(500);
   });
```

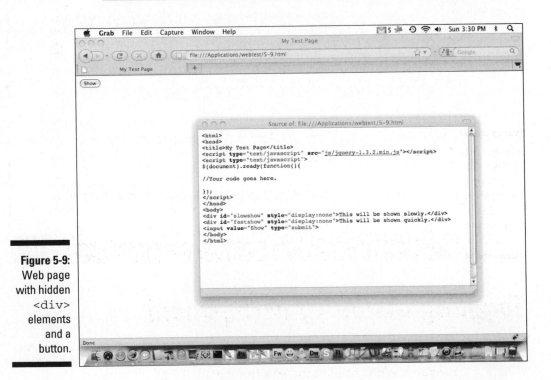

Figure 5-9:
Web page with hidden `<div>` elements and a button.

The code says, "When the button is clicked, show the element with the `slowshow` id at a speed of 2000 milliseconds. Show the element with the `fastshow` id at a speed of 500 milliseconds." This code uses the `:submit` selector and the `click` event to set up the action.

You can use the three predefined speeds — slow, medium, and fast — or a number representing the number of milliseconds during which you want the animation to occur.

4. **Save this file, and then view it in your browser.**

5. **Click the button.**

   The `<div>` elements appear at different rates of speed and the button moves down, as shown in Figure 5-10.

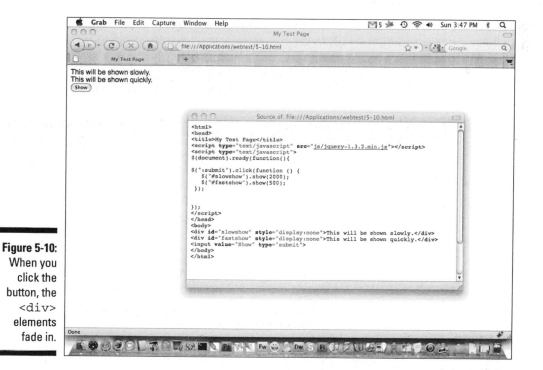

Figure 5-10: When you click the button, the `<div>` elements fade in.

Toggling Visibility with jQuery

Being able to show and hide elements is handy, but what happens when you want to swap back and forth between hiding and showing an element? The `toggle` function handles these tasks for you.

Using a toggle

The following example shows you how to make everything inside `<div>` elements toggle between hidden and shown when someone repeatedly clicks a button on your page:

1. **Create a Web page containing the following code:**

```
<!DOCTYPE html PUBLIC "-//W3C//DTD XHTML 1.0 Strict//EN"
          "http://www.w3.org/TR/xhtml1/DTD/xhtml1-strict.dtd">
<html>
<head>
<title>My Test Page</title>
<script type="text/javascript" src="js/jquery-1.4.min.js"></script>
<script type="text/javascript">
$(document).ready(function(){

//Your code goes here.

});
</script>
</head>
<body>
<div>This will be hidden.</div>
<div>This will be hidden.</div>
<input value="Toggle" type="submit">
</body>
</html>
```

   This code contains two `<div>` elements and a button.

2. **Replace // Your code goes here. with the following code:**

```
$(':submit').click(function () {
      $('div').toggle();
  });
```

   The code says, "When the button is clicked, hide all `<div>` elements if they are shown, and show them if they are hidden." This code uses the `:submit` selector and the `click` event to set up the action. The `toggle` function, used with the `<div>` selector, toggles both `<div>` elements.

3. **Save this file, and then view it in your browser.**

4. **Click the button.**

   Everything in both `<div>` elements is now hidden the first time you click, as shown in Figure 5-11.

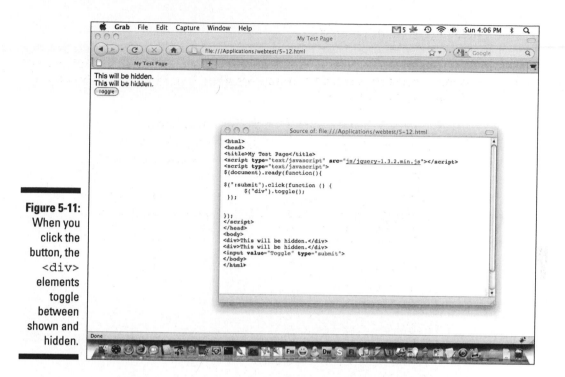

Figure 5-11:
When you
click the
button, the
`<div>`
elements
toggle
between
shown and
hidden.

5. **Click the button again to make everything in the `<div>` elements reappear.**

6. **Locate the second `<div>` in the `<body>` section of the code and replace it with this line:**

```
<div style="display:none">This is initially hidden.</div>
```

This hides the second `<div>` element when the page loads.

7. **Save this file, and then view it in your browser.**

8. **Click the button.**

You now see only the first `<div>` element when you load the page. Clicking the button makes the first `<div>` element disappear and the second one appear, as shown in Figure 5-12.

9. **Click the button again to toggle the two `<div>` elements.**

Figure 5-12:
The `<div>`
elements
toggle
between
shown and
hidden
depending
on their
state.

Toggling with animation

You can toggle with animation by adding a speed setting to the `toggle` function, just as you can with the `hide` and `show` functions. To animate the toggle function, follow these steps:

1. Create a Web page containing the following code:

```
<!DOCTYPE html PUBLIC "-//W3C//DTD XHTML 1.0 Strict//EN"
        "http://www.w3.org/TR/xhtml1/DTD/xhtml1-strict.dtd">
<html>
<head>
<title>My Test Page</title>
<script type="text/javascript" src="js/jquery-1.4.min.js"></script>
<script type="text/javascript">
$(document).ready(function(){

//Your code goes here.
```

```
});
</script>
</head>
<body>
<div>This will be an animated toggle.</div>
<input value="Toggle" type="submit">
</body>
</html>
```

2. Replace // Your code goes here. with the following code:

```
$(':submit').click(function () {
     $('div').toggle('slow');
 });
```

The toggle function in this code is set to a slow speed.

3. Save this file, and then view it in your browser.

4. Click the button.

The <div> element now fades out or fades in slowly each time you click the button, as shown in Figure 5-13.

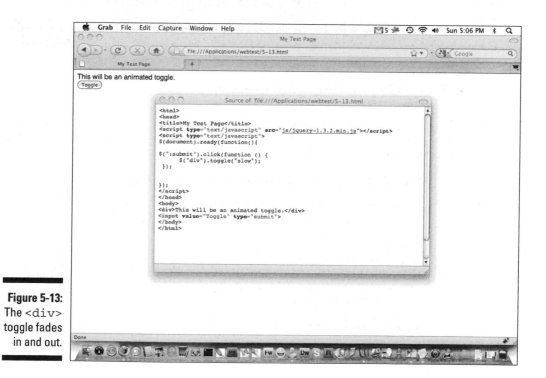

Figure 5-13: The <div> toggle fades in and out.

Using a callback function

All three effects in this chapter — hide, show, and toggle — allow you to add a callback function. A *callback function* is code that executes after the effect is finished. Here's an example of code using a callback function that opens an alert box after you toggle an element:

1. Create a Web page containing the following code:

```
<!DOCTYPE html PUBLIC "-//W3C//DTD XHTML 1.0 Strict//EN"
         "http://www.w3.org/TR/xhtml1/DTD/xhtml1-strict.dtd">
<html>
<head>
<title>My Test Page</title>
<script type="text/javascript" src="js/jquery-1.4.min.js"></script>
<script type="text/javascript">
$(document).ready(function(){

//Your code goes here.

});
</script>
</head>
<body>
<div>This will be an animated toggle.</div>
<input value="Toggle" type="submit">
</body>
</html>
```

2. Replace // Your code goes here. with the following code:

```
$(':submit').click(function () {
    $('div').toggle('slow',
function callback() {
  alert('The toggle is finished')
});
});
```

This code executes an animated toggle on any `<div>` elements. When the toggle animation is finished, an alert box appears.

Take a close look at the syntax of the callback function. The `toggle` function uses the following syntax:

```
toggle(speed, function callback(){};)
```

If you don't want to animate your toggle, you can delete the `speed` setting and use this code:

```
toggle(function callback(){};)
```

3. **Save this file, and then view it in your browser.**

4. **Click the button.**

   The <div> element now fades out or fades in slowly each time you click the button. Then the callback function opens the alert box, indicating that the effect has finished, as shown in Figure 5-14.

You can use callback functions with the show and hide functions as well as the toggle function.

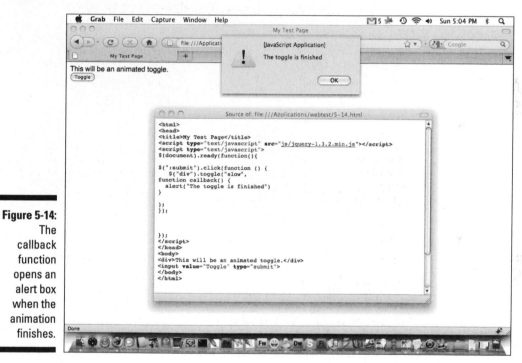

Figure 5-14:
The callback function opens an alert box when the animation finishes.

Chapter 6

Sliding and Fading Web Page Elements

*T*wo impressive effects that jQuery make easy to accomplish are fading and sliding. When an element fades, it goes from fully opaque to semi-transparent or completely transparent. When an element slides, it slowly appears on the page, starting from the top down or the bottom up.

In this chapter, you find out how to slide and fade elements, and also how to control the speed at which these effects happen. You also see how to use a callback function, which is code that executes after the effect is finished.

Sliding Elements with jQuery

The *sliding* effect means an element becomes visible from either the top down or the bottom up. Nothing moves on the page except the element as it becomes visible.

Both the sliding down and sliding up effects are more impressive when you use them with images or blocks with a background color, so the examples in this chapter use `<div>` blocks with background colors and images to demonstrate the effects.

Sliding down

To make a page element appear to slide down, you first need to hide the element. To hidean element, you set its style attribute to display=none.

 Most of the examples in this chapter use images and are more impressive when the image is large. If you don't have a large image file saved to your test images directory, you can grab one from the following:

```
http://media.wiley.com/spa_assets/site/dummies2/include/images/bg/hp-header-bg.
    gif
```

Browse to this location and choose File➪Save As. Save the image to the images directory you are using to test your code, as created in Chapter 1. Name the image big.gif.

To make an element appear on a page using the sliding down effect, follow these steps:

1. **Create a Web page containing the following code:**

```
<!DOCTYPE html PUBLIC "-//W3C//DTD XHTML 1.0 Strict//EN"
        "http://www.w3.org/TR/xhtml1/DTD/xhtml1-strict.dtd">
<html>
<head>
<title>My Test Page</title>
<script type="text/javascript" src="js/jquery-1.4.min.js"></script>
<script type="text/javascript">
$(document).ready(function(){

//Your code goes here.

});
</script>
</head>
<body>
<div style="display:none"><img src="images/big.gif" /> </div>
<input value="Slide Down" type="submit">
</body>
</html>
```

This code contains a hidden <div> element with an image and a button.

2. **Save the file, and then view it in your browser.**

3. **Note that the image doesn't appear (see Figure 6-1). Click the button; nothing happens.**

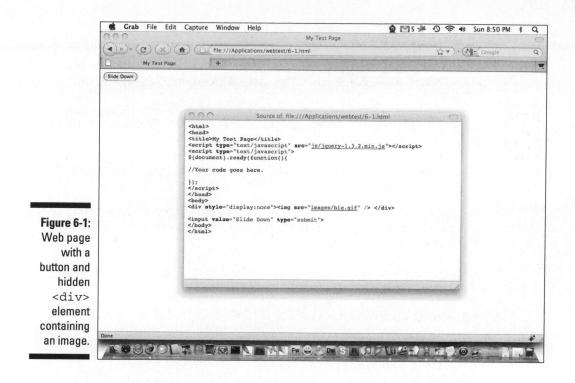

Figure 6-1:
Web page
with a
button and
hidden
`<div>`
element
containing
an image.

4. **Replace // Your code goes here. with the following code:**

```
$(':submit').click(function () {
    $('div').slideDown();
});
```

The code says, "When the button is clicked, make everything in the
`<div>` element appear using the slideDown effect." This code uses the
:submit selector and the click event to set up the action.

Chapter 3 shows you how to use selectors, and Chapter 4 shows you
how to use an event, such as the click event.

5. **Save this file, and then view it in your browser.**

6. **Click the button.**

The slideDown effect makes the image in the hidden `<div>` element
appear from the top down, as shown in Figure 6-2.

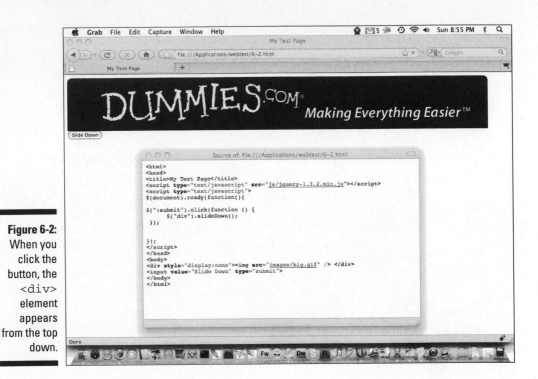

Figure 6-2:
When you
click the
button, the
`<div>`
element
appears
from the top
down.

Sliding up

The slide up effect hides an element by making it slide up.

To make an element disappear on a page by using the slide up effect, follow these steps:

1. **Create a Web page containing the following code:**

```
<!DOCTYPE html PUBLIC "-//W3C//DTD XHTML 1.0 Strict//EN"
        "http://www.w3.org/TR/xhtml1/DTD/xhtml1-strict.dtd">
<html>
<head>
<title>My Test Page</title>
<script type="text/javascript" src="js/jquery-1.4.min.js"></script>
<script type="text/javascript">
$(document).ready(function(){

//Your code goes here.

});
</script>
</head>
```

```
<body>
<div><img src="images/big.gif" /> </div>
<input value="Slide Up" type="submit"></body>
</html>
```

This code contains a `<div>` element with an image and a button.

2. Save the file, and then view it in your browser.

Note that the image appears, as shown in Figure 6-3.

3. Replace `// Your code goes here.` with the following code:

```
$(':submit').click(function () {
    $('div').slideUp();
 });
```

The code says, "When the button is clicked, make everything in the `<div>` disappear using the `slideUp` effect." This code uses the `:submit` selector and the `click` event.

4. Save this file, and then view it in your browser.

5. Click the button.

The `slideUp` effect makes the image in the `<div>` element slide up and then disappear from view, as shown in Figure 6-4.

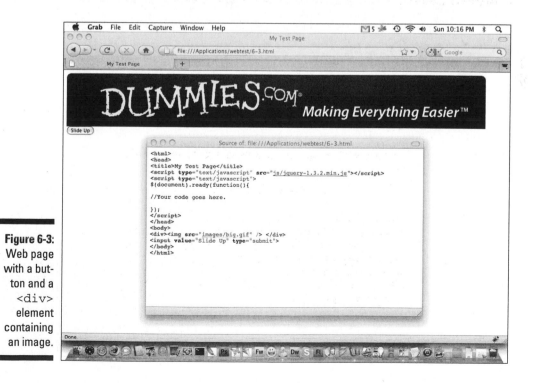

Figure 6-3:
Web page with a button and a `<div>` element containing an image.

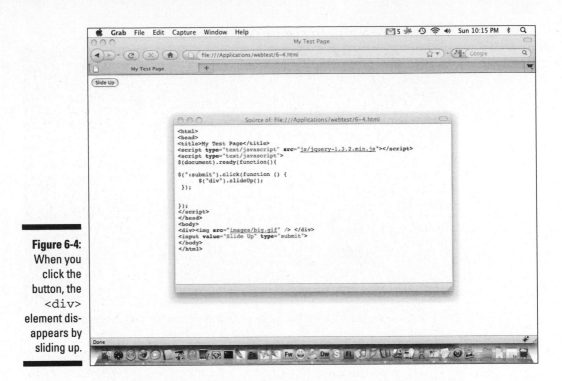

Changing the slide speed

You can control the speed of the slide up or slide down effect with the speed setting. jQuery has three predefined speeds: slow, medium, and fast. You can also use a number that represents the number of milliseconds during which you want the animation to occur. For example, if I want a very slow slide up, I can use the line

```
$('div').slideUp('slow');
```

or

```
$('div').slideUp(1000);
```

Note that you don't use quotes when you use a number. Also, the number 1000 is very slow. The slide down effect operates the same way.

Sliding with a toggle effect

The slide up and slide down effects work together to hide and show elements. You can use the slide toggle effect to allow a visitor to toggle between an event sliding up and sliding down. To use the slide toggle effect, follow these steps:

1. **Create a Web page containing the following code:**

```
<!DOCTYPE html PUBLIC "-//W3C//DTD XHTML 1.0 Strict//EN"
          "http://www.w3.org/TR/xhtml1/DTD/xhtml1-strict.dtd">
<html>
<head>
<title>My Test Page</title>
<script type="text/javascript" src="js/jquery-1.4.min.js"></script>
<script type="text/javascript">
$(document).ready(function(){

//Your code goes here.

});
</script>
</head>
<body>
<div><img src="images/big.gif" /></div>
<input value="Slide Toggle" type="submit">
</body>
</html>
```

This code contains a button and a visible `<div>` element containing an image.

2. **Replace `// Your code goes here.` with the following code:**

```
$(':submit').click(function () {
     $('div').slideToggle();
});
```

The code says, "When the button is clicked, toggle all `<div>` elements to slide up if they are shown and slide down if they are hidden." This code uses the `:submit` selector and the `click` event to set up the action. The `toggle` function toggles the `<div>` elements.

3. **Save this file, and then view it in your browser.**

4. **Click the button.**

Everything in the `<div>` element slides up the first time you click, as shown in Figure 6-5.

5. **Click the button again to make everything in the `<div>` element slide down.**

Sliding with a callback function

The slide up, slide down, and slide toggle effects allow you to use a *callback* function, which is code that executes after the effect is finished. Here's an example of code using a callback function that opens an alert box after an element is toggled:

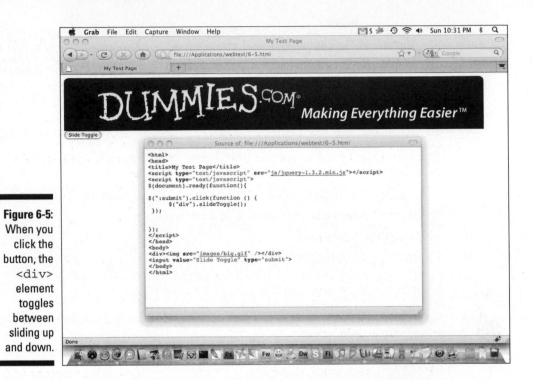

Figure 6-5:
When you
click the
button, the
`<div>`
element
toggles
between
sliding up
and down.

1. **Create a Web page containing the following code:**

```
<!DOCTYPE html PUBLIC "-//W3C//DTD XHTML 1.0 Strict//EN"
          "http://www.w3.org/TR/xhtml1/DTD/xhtml1-strict.dtd">
<html>
<head>
<title>My Test Page</title>
<script type="text/javascript" src="js/jquery-1.4.min.js"></script>
<script type="text/javascript">
$(document).ready(function(){

//Your code goes here.
});
</script>
</head>
<body>
<div><img src="images/big.gif" /></div>
<input value="Slide Toggle" type="submit">
</body>
</html>
```

2. **Replace // Your code goes here. with the following code:**

```
$(':submit').click(function () {
   $('div').slideToggle(
function callback() {
```

```
        alert('The slide effect is finished')
    });
});
```

This code executes a slide toggle on any `<div>` elements. When the slide animation is finished, an alert box appears. The slide toggle function uses the following syntax:

```
slideToggle(speed, function callback(){};)
```

If you don't want to animate your toggle, you can delete the speed setting and use the following code:

```
slideToggle(function callback(){};)
```

3. Save this file, and then view it in your browser.

4. Click the button.

The `<div>` element now slides up or down each time you click the button. Then the callback function opens the alert box, indicating that the effect has finished, as shown in Figure 6-6.

You can use callback functions with the slide up and slide down effects as well as the slide toggle function.

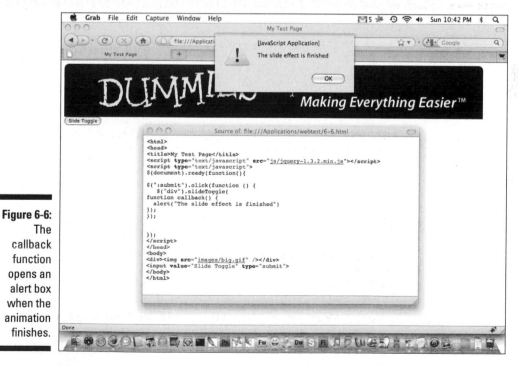

Figure 6-6:
The callback function opens an alert box when the animation finishes.

Fading Elements with jQuery

The *fade effect* is when an element fades out by becoming increasingly transparent over time until it disappears or fades in by becoming less transparent. jQuery has fade out and fade in effects and also allows you to partially fade an element, making it semitransparent.

Fading in

To make a page element fade in, it needs to first be hidden. You do this by setting the style attribute of the element to `display=none`.

To follow along with these exercises, you need an image in the `images` directory that you are using to test your code. Name this image `big.gif`.

To make an element appear to fade in, follow these steps:

1. Create a Web page containing the following code:

```
<!DOCTYPE html PUBLIC "-//W3C//DTD XHTML 1.0 Strict//EN"
        "http://www.w3.org/TR/xhtml1/DTD/xhtml1-strict.dtd">
<html>
<head>
<title>My Test Page</title>
<script type="text/javascript" src="js/jquery-1.4.min.js"></script>
<script type="text/javascript">
$(document).ready(function(){

//Your code goes here.

});
</script>
</head>
<body>
<div style="display:none"><img src="images/big.gif" /> </div>
<input value="Fade In" type="submit">
</body>
</html>
```

This code contains a button and a hidden `<div>` element with an image.

2. Save the file, and then view it in your browser.

The image doesn't appear (see Figure 6-7).

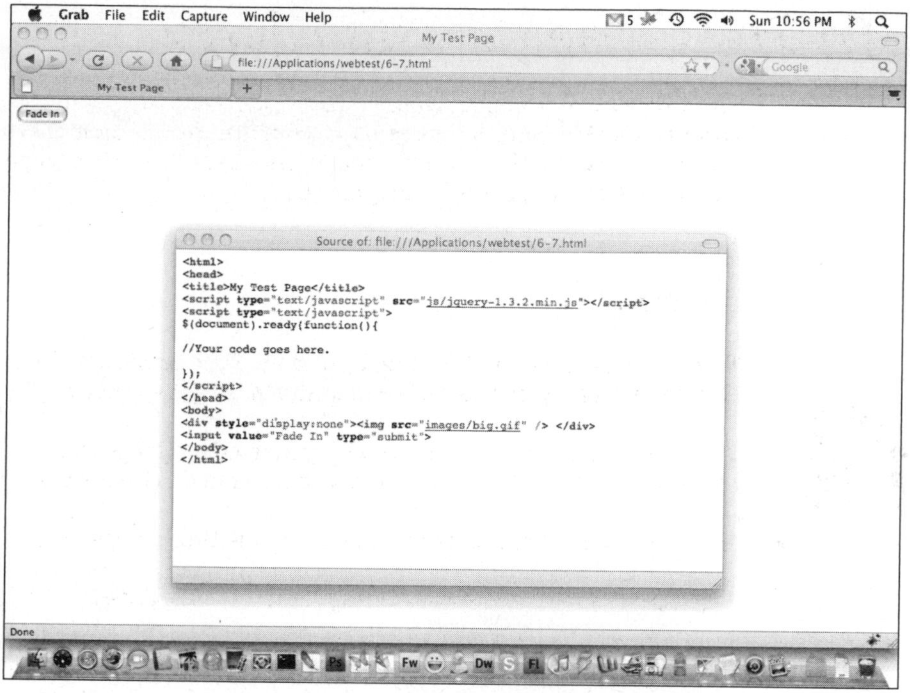

Figure 6-7:
Web page
with a but-
ton and
a hidden
`<div>`
element
containing
an image.

3. **Replace `// Your code goes here.` with the following code:**

```
$(':submit').click(function () {
    $('div').fadeIn();
});
```

The code says, "When the button is clicked, make everything in the
`<div>` fade in." This code uses the `:submit` selector and the `click`
event.

4. **Save this file, and then view it in your browser.**

5. **Click the button.**

The image in the hidden `<div>` element appears to fade in, as shown in
Figure 6-8.

6. **Replace `$('div').fadeIn();` with the following code:**

```
$('div').fadeIn('fast');
```

Now when you save and reload this file in your browser and click the
button, the fade in effect occurs more quickly.

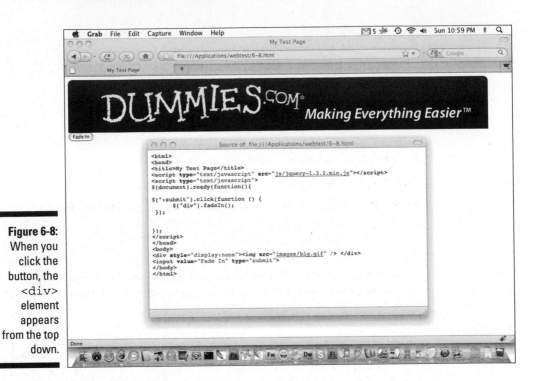

Figure 6-8:
When you click the button, the `<div>` element appears from the top down.

Fading out

The fade out effect takes a visible element and hides it by making it appear to fade out.

To make an element disappear on a page using the fade out effect, follow these steps:

1. **Create a Web page containing the following code:**

```
<!DOCTYPE html PUBLIC "-//W3C//DTD XHTML 1.0 Strict//EN"
          "http://www.w3.org/TR/xhtml1/DTD/xhtml1-strict.dtd">
<html>
<head>
<title>My Test Page</title>
<script type="text/javascript" src="js/jquery-1.4.min.js"></script>
<script type="text/javascript">
$(document).ready(function(){

//Your code goes here.
```

```
});
</script>
</head>
<body>
<div><img src-"images/big.gif" /> </div>
<input value="Fade Out" type="submit"></body>
</html>
```

This code contains a button and a `<div>` element with an image.

2. Save the file, and then view it in your browser.

The image is visible, as shown in Figure 6-9.

3. Replace `// Your code goes here.` with the following code:

```
$(':submit').click(function () {
    $('div').fadeOut();
});
```

The code says, "When the button is clicked, make everything in the `<div>` element disappear using the `slideUp` effect." This code uses the `:submit` selector and the `click` event.

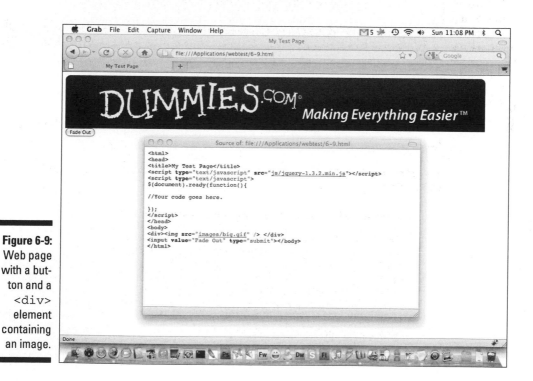

Figure 6-9:
Web page with a button and a `<div>` element containing an image.

4. Save this file, and then reload it in your browser.

5. Click the button.

The image in the `<div>` element fades out and disappears from view (see Figure 6-10).

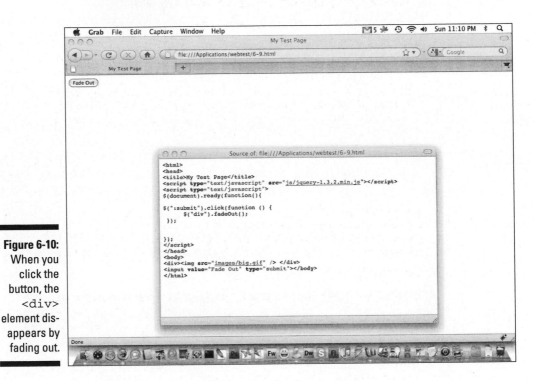

Figure 6-10:
When you click the button, the `<div>` element disappears by fading out.

Partial fading

jQuery has a fade effect that allows an element to fade a certain amount and become transparent. The function syntax is

```
fadeTo(speed, percent, [callback]);
```

The `percent` is expressed as a decimal and is used to control how much to fade out the element. For example, if you want to make something fade out halfway, you use .5 for the `percent` value.

The `callback` function is optional, but you must specify a `speed` and a `percent`. Unlike other effects, the duration must be specified.

To make an element partially fade out, follow these steps:

1. **Create a Web page containing the following code:**

```
<!DOCTYPE html PUBLIC "-//W3C//DTD XHTML 1.0 Strict//EN"
        "http://www.w3.org/TR/xhtml1/DTD/xhtml1-strict.dtd">
<html>
<head>
<title>My Test Page</title>
<script type="text/javascript" src="js/jquery-1.4.min.js"></script>
<script type="text/javascript">
$(document).ready(function(){

//Your code goes here.

});
</script>
</head>
<body>
<div><img src="images/big.gif" /> </div>
<input value="Partial Fade" type="submit"></body>
</html>
```

2. **Save the file.**

3. **Replace // `Your code goes here.` with the following code:**

```
$(':submit').click(function () {
      $('div').fadeTo('slow', .55);
 });
```

The code says, "When the button is clicked, make everything in the `<div>` element fade out at 50 percent."

4. **Save this file, and then view it in your browser.**

5. **Click the button.**

The image in the `<div>` element appears to partially fade out, as shown in Figure 6-11.

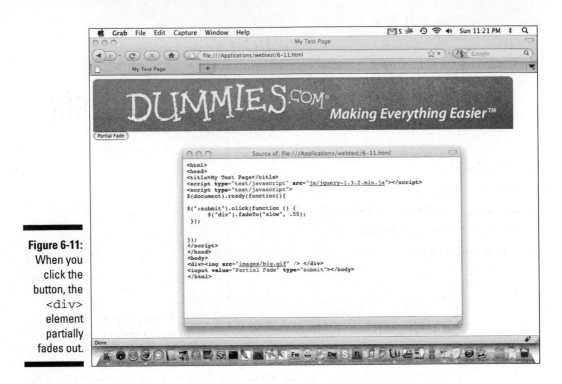

Figure 6-11:
When you
click the
button, the
`<div>`
element
partially
fades out.

Chapter 7

Animating Web Page Elements

* *

In This Chapter

▶ Animating height and width

▶ Animating font size and word spacing

▶ Stopping animations dynamically

▶ Controlling animation speed

* *

Chapter 5 shows you how to animate the hiding and showing of Web page elements. Chapter 6 discusses more animation effects: sliding and fading. In addition to those preprogrammed effects, jQuery allows you to easily animate many CSS style settings of elements. These style settings include the font size, height, and width of an image or the <div> element. In fact, any CSS value that is numeric can be animated. With jQuery animation, you can make page elements grow larger or smaller over time or move across the page.

In this chapter, you discover how to animate elements and element attributes, such as height and width. You also see how to control the speed of animations and how to stop and start them in response to events.

Understanding How jQuery Animation Works

jQuery allows you to animate a number of CSS style settings associated with HTML elements. Consider the following code:

```
<div style="width:200px; height:200px; background-color: gray; border:10px;
            border-color:red; border-style:dotted ">My div</div>
```

This code creates a gray box with a thick, dotted red border, as shown in Figure 7-1.

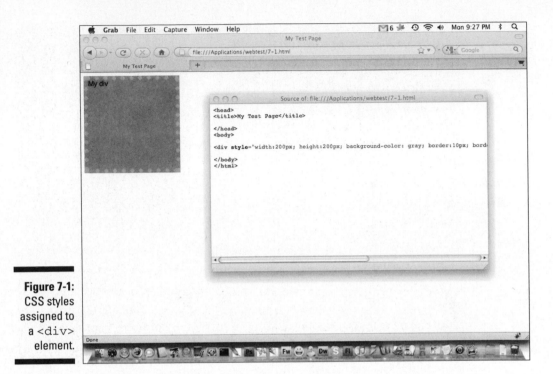

Figure 7-1:
CSS styles
assigned to
a `<div>`
element.

The `<div>` element in this code is associated with the following styles:

- **width:** The width of the `<div>` in pixels
- **height:** The height of the `<div>` in pixels
- **border:** The thickness of the border around the `<div>` in pixels
- **background-color:** The color of the `<div>`
- **border-color:** The color of the border
- **border-style:** The appearance of the border

jQuery can animate the `width`, `height`, and `border`. These are all numeric values, so they can grow or shrink.

Limitations exist about what can be animated. jQuery can't change a style set-ting from one color to another in an animation. Nor can it change the style of a border. However, you can use a plug-in to animate colors. For more informa-tion, go to `http://plugins.jquery.com/project/color`.

Here's an example of code that animates the height and width of a `<div>` ele-ment. Give it a try to get your feet wet. An explanation of what it does follows:

```
<head>
<title>My Test Page</title>
<script type="text/javascript" src="js/jquery-1.4.min.js"></script>
<script type="text/javascript">
$(document).ready(function(){

  $(':submit').click(function(){
    $('div').animate({
            width:'280px',
            height: '140px'

    } );
  });
});
</script>
</head>
<body>



<div style="width:200px; height:200px; background-color: gray; border:10px">My
            div</div>
<br />
<input value="Animate" type="submit">
</body>
</html>
```

This code animates the `<div>` element, changing the width from 200px to 280px and the height from 200px to 140px, as shown in Figure 7-2.

The heart of this code is the `animate` function. A simple form of the jQuery `animate` function syntax is

```
animate(params, duration, callback)
```

The three parts of the function are

- ✔ **params:** A comma-delimited list of style rules to animate. For example:
  ```
  width: '100px', right: '600px'
  ```
- ✔ **duration:** An optional argument controlling the speed of the animation. Acceptable values are slow, medium, fast, or a numeric value representing the speed in milliseconds.
- ✔ **callback:** An optional code that executes after the animation has completed.

  An optional easing argument specifies whether the animation gets faster near the end or begins faster and then slows down. Easing requires an additional plug-in. Read more about it at `jquery.com`.

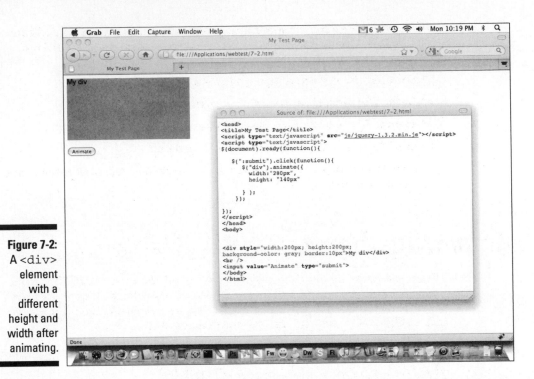

Figure 7-2:
A `<div>`
element
with a
different
height and
width after
animating.

When you're looking at jQuery code samples, you might notice that jQuery style elements are sometimes named slightly differently than CSS style elements. Whereas a CSS style uses a hyphen (for example, `border-width`), the jQuery version omits the hyphen, runs the words together, and capitalizes the second word (for example, `borderWidth`). jQuery can use either version.

The practice of capitalizing the second word of two words run together, such as `borderWidth`, is known as *camel case* because the capital letter makes the expression look like it has a hump in the middle, like a camel. I didn't make this up!

Here are a few more common styles that can be animated with jQuery. The camel case and hyphenated versions both work with jQuery.

- ✔ **borderWidth (border-width):** The width of the four borders. You can also set each border width individually with `border-bottom-width`, `border-left-width`, `border-right-width`, and `border-top-width`.

- ✔ **height:** The height of an element.

- ✔ **width:** The width of an element.

- ✔ **fontSize (font-size):** The font size of text.

- ✔ **margin:** The margin of an element. You can also set each margin individually with `margin-bottom`, `margin-left`, `margin-right`, and `margin-top`.

✔ **padding:** Padding, or space around an element. You can also pad each side individually with `padding-bottom`, `padding-left`, `padding-right`, and `padding-top`.

✔ **bottom:** The bottom margin edge for a positioned box.

✔ **left:** The left margin edge for a positioned box.

✔ **right:** The right margin edge for a positioned box.

✔ **top:** The top margin edge for a positioned box.

✔ **wordSpacing (word-spacing):** An increase or a decrease in the space between words.

Animating Elements with jQuery

This section contains examples of different types of elements and CSS styles that jQuery can animate. Keep in mind that you can mix and match many of the styles with different elements. For example, you can use the `width` style with both a `<div>` element and an `<img>` element.

Animating height and width

To animate an element's height and width, do the following:

1. **Create a Web page containing the following code:**

```
<!DOCTYPE html PUBLIC "-//W3C//DTD XHTML 1.0 Strict//EN"
        "http://www.w3.org/TR/xhtml1/DTD/xhtml1-strict.dtd">
<html>
<head>
<title>My Test Page</title>
<script type="text/javascript" src="js/jquery-1.4.min.js"></script>
<script type="text/javascript">
$(document).ready(function(){

//Your code goes here.

});
</script>
</head>
<body>
<div style="width:200px; height:200px;
background-color: gray; border:10px">My div</div>
<br />
<input value="Animate" type="submit"></body>
</html>
```

This code contains a `<div>` element and a button.

2. **Replace `// Your code goes here.` with the following code:**

```
$(':submit').click(function(){
    $('div').animate({
            width:'280px', height: '500px'
            });
});
```

The code says, "When the button is clicked, make the `<div>` element animate to 280px wide and 500px high." This code uses the `:submit` selector and the `click` event to set up the action.

Chapter 3 shows you how to use selectors, and Chapter 4 shows you how to use an event, such as the `click` event.

3. **Save this file, and then view it in your browser.**

4. **Click the button.**

The `<div>` element animates and grows from 200px by 200px to 280px by 600px, as shown in Figure 7-3.

5. **Replace `width:'280px', height: '500px'` with**

```
width:'20px', height: '50px'
```

This makes the original `<div>` element shrink instead of grow.

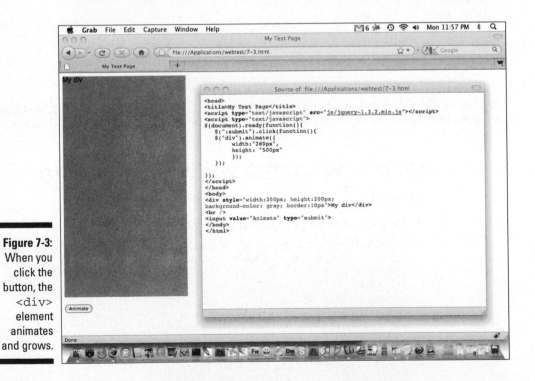

Figure 7-3: When you click the button, the `<div>` element animates and grows.

6. **Save this file, and then view it in your browser.**

7. **Click the button.**

The `<div>` element animates and shrinks from 200px by 200px to 20px by 50px, as shown in Figure 7-4. Note that the text inside the `<div>` element wraps to fit inside the smaller space.

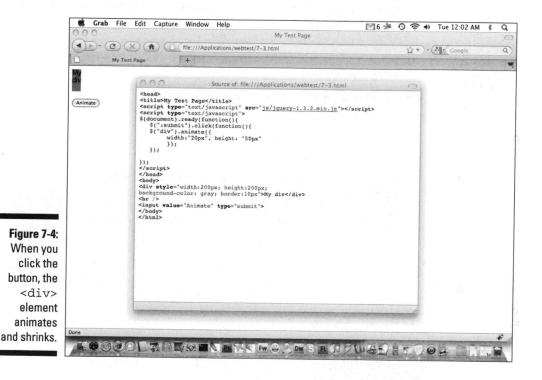

Figure 7-4: When you click the button, the `<div>` element animates and shrinks.

Animating margin width and padding

To animate an element's margin and padding, follow these steps:

1. **Create a Web page containing the following code:**

```
<!DOCTYPE html PUBLIC "-//W3C//DTD XHTML 1.0 Strict//EN"
        "http://www.w3.org/TR/xhtml1/DTD/xhtml1-strict.dtd">
<html>
<head>
<title>My Test Page</title>
<script type="text/javascript" src="js/jquery-1.4.min.js"></script>
<script type="text/javascript">
$(document).ready(function(){

//Your code goes here.

});
```

```
</script>
</head>
<body>
<div style="width:200px; height:200px;
background-color: gray; border:10px">My div</div>
<br />
<input value="Animate" type="submit"></body>
</html>
```

This code contains a `<div>` element and a button.

2. **Replace `// Your code goes here.` with the following code:**

```
$(':submit').click(function(){
    $('div').animate({
           margin:'50px'
           });
  });
```

The code says, "When the button is clicked, animate the `<div>` element's margin to 50px in width."

3. **Save this file, and then view it in your browser.**

4. **Click the button.**

The `<div>` element's margin animates and grows from 0 to 50px, as shown in Figure 7-5.

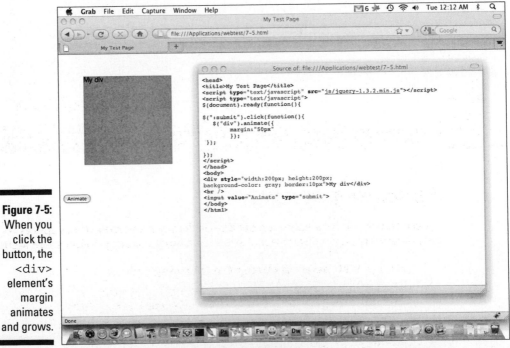

Figure 7-5:
When you click the button, the `<div>` element's margin animates and grows.

5. **Replace** `margin:'50px'` **with**

```
padding:'50px'
```

This code makes the padding — the space inside the `<div>` — grow.

6. **Save this file, and then view it in your browser.**

7. **Click the button.**

The padding inside the `<div>` element animates and grows from 0 to 50px, as shown in Figure 7-6. Note that the text inside the `<div>` element is no longer flush with the upper-left corner.

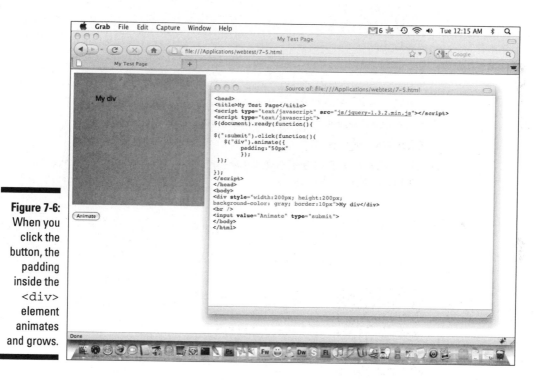

Figure 7-6: When you click the button, the padding inside the `<div>` element animates and grows.

Animating opacity

jQuery allows you to animate the opacity of elements and make them appear to fade to and from a semitransparent state. To animate opacity, follow these steps:

1. **Create a Web page containing the following code:**

```
<!DOCTYPE html PUBLIC "-//W3C//DTD XHTML 1.0 Strict//EN"
        "http://www.w3.org/TR/xhtml1/DTD/xhtml1-strict.dtd">
<html>
<head>
<title>My Test Page</title>
```

```
<script type="text/javascript" src="js/jquery-1.4.min.js"></script>
<script type="text/javascript">
$(document).ready(function(){

//Your code goes here.

});
</script>
</head>
<body>
<div class="fadethis" style="width:200px; height:200px;
background-color: red; border:10px">My div</div>
<br />
<img class="fadethis" src = "images/home.gif" />
<br />
<input value="Animate" type="submit"></body>
</html>
```

This code contains a `<div>` element and an image, both with the same class, `fademe`.

You can name classes anything you want. Classes give you the ability to easily select multiple elements with the same selector.

2. **Replace `// Your code goes here.` with the following code:**

```
$(':submit').click(function(){
   $('.fadethis').animate({
       opacity: 0.25
     });
  });
```

The code says, "When the button is clicked, animate all elements of the `fademe` class to .25 opacity (25 percent)."

3. **Save this file, and then view it in your browser.**

4. **Click the button.**

Both the `<div>` element and the `<img>` element animate and fade to 25 percent opacity, as shown in Figure 7-7.

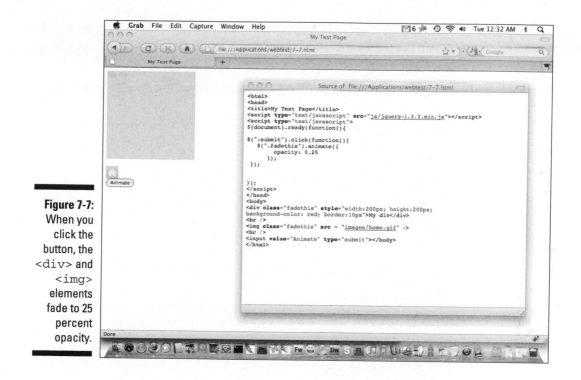

Figure 7-7:
When you
click the
button, the
<div> and
<img>
elements
fade to 25
percent
opacity.

Animating font size and word spacing

To animate shrinking or growing text and change the spacing between words, follow these steps:

1. Create a Web page containing the following code:

```
<!DOCTYPE html PUBLIC "-//W3C//DTD XHTML 1.0 Strict//EN"
          "http://www.w3.org/TR/xhtml1/DTD/xhtml1-strict.dtd">
<html>
<head>
<title>My Test Page</title>
<script type="text/javascript" src="js/jquery-1.4.min.js"></script>
<script type="text/javascript">
$(document).ready(function(){

//Your code goes here.

});
</script>
</head>
```

```
<body>
<div>I'd like to say a few short words.</div>
<br />
<input value="Animate" type="submit"></body>
</html>
```

This code contains a `<div>` element with some text.

2. Replace `// Your code goes here.` with the following code:

```
$(':submit').click(function(){
    $('div').animate({
        fontSize: '100px'
        });
  });
```

Although you're changing the CSS style known as font-size, make sure you use fontSize when you use the animate function.

The code says, "When the button is clicked, animate the text in the `<div>` element, increasing it to a font size of 100px."

3. Save this file, and then view it in your browser.

4. Click the button.

The text in the `<div>` element animates and grows to 100px, as shown in Figure 7-8.

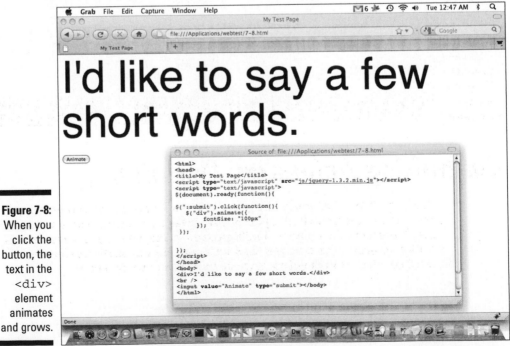

Figure 7-8:
When you click the button, the text in the `<div>` element animates and grows.

5. **Replace** `fontSize: '100px'` **with**

```
wordSpacing:'50px'
```

6. **Save this file, and then view it in your browser.**

7. **Click the button.**

The space between each word in the `<div>` element animates and increases, as shown in Figure 7-9.

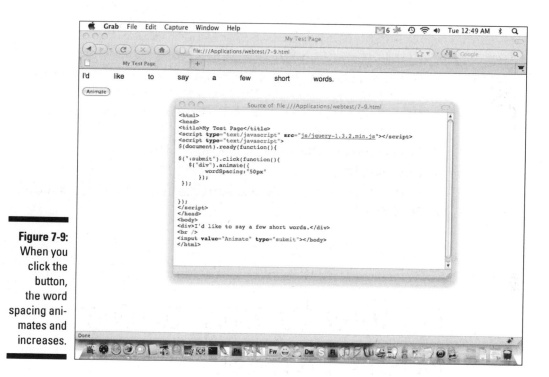

Figure 7-9:
When you click the button, the word spacing animates and increases.

Controlling Animation Duration

You can control the length of any animation with the `duration` parameter. You can use the predefined speeds slow or fast. Or you can use a number that represents the number of milliseconds during which you want the animation to occur. For example, if I want a very slow animation of a change in word spacing, as in the preceding example, I can use the code

```
$('div').animate({
        fontSize: '100px'
    }, 'slow');
```

or

```
$('div').animate({
        fontSize: '100px'
    }, 1000);
```

Note that you don't use quotes when you use a number, and that you need a comma before the duration setting and after the curly brace in both instances.

Animating with Show, Hide, and Toggle

In Chapter 5, you discover how to use the show, hide, and toggle effects. They can be used also inside the animate function in place of a numeric value for a style. For example, the following code uses the toggle effect to hide and then show a <div> element:

```
<head>
<title>My Test Page</title>
<script type="text/javascript" src="js/jquery-1.4.min.js"></script>
<script type="text/javascript">
$(document).ready(function(){

    $(':submit').click(function(){
        $('div').animate({
                width:'toggle',
        } );
    });
});
</script>
</head>
<body>



<div style="width:200px; height:200px; background-color: gray; border:10px">My
            div</div>
<br />
<input value="Animate" type="submit">
</body>
```

The first time you click the Animate button, the width shrinks until the <div> element vanishes. Clicking the button again makes the element expand and reappear.

Disabling All jQuery Animation

It's sometimes useful to provide a way to stop animations. The stop function lets you stop an animation. The following code calls a stop function whenever you click the Stop button:

```
<!DOCTYPE html PUBLIC "-//W3C//DTD XHTML 1.0 Strict//EN"
               "http://www.w3.org/TR/xhtml1/DTD/xhtml1-strict.dtd">
<html>
<head>
<title>My Test Page</title>
<script type="text/javascript" src="js/jquery-1.4.min.js"></script>
<script type="text/javascript">
$(document).ready(function(){

$('#gobtn').click(function(){
   $('div').animate({
       fontSize: '100px'
     },3000);
 });
$('#stopbtn').click(function(){
   $('div').stop();
 });

});
</script>
</head>
<body>
<div>I'd like to say a few short words.</div>
<br />
<input id="gobtn" value="Animate" type="submit"><br />
<input id="stopbtn" value="Stop" type="submit"></body>
</html>
```

This code contains a `<div>` element with text and two buttons. The first button, with the gobtn id attribute, triggers the animate function and makes the text size increase at a slow rate (3000 milliseconds) with the following code:

```
$('#gobtn').click(function(){
  $('div').animate({
      fontSize: '100px'
    },3000);
});
```

The second button, with the stopbtn id attribute, triggers the stop function when you click the button.

If you click the Go button after clicking the Stop button, the animation resumes where it left off.

Part III
Manipulating Your Web Page

The 5th Wave   By Rich Tennant

"Mary-Jo, come here quick! Look at this special effect I learned with jQuery."

In this part . . .

What you say on your Web page matters. And jQuery lets you change what you say dynamically in response to user events such as clicking or mousing over things. You can even grab what your visitor types in forms. This section is all about getting content from your Web page and dynamically adding, editing, and deleting content on your Web page.

And if that wasn't enough, you find out how to replace, remove, and copy any HTML element or group of elements on your page. jQuery gives you total power over the content of your Web pages.

Chapter 8

Making Web Page Content Dynamic

- -

In This Chapter

▶ Controlling text on your page

▶ Changing HTML content dynamically

▶ Putting an element inside another elements

▶ Placing content outside elements

▶ Wrapping elements around elements

▶ Getting values from form elements

▶ Changing the order of elements

- -

Previous chapters discuss adding animation to your pages and hiding content. But jQuery goes far beyond special effects when it comes to making your pages dynamic. With jQuery, you can easily change the content on a Web page without reloading the page. Text and image content can be changed in response to an event, such as an animation completing, a link being clicked, or a cursor moving over an element.

Getting and Setting Text Content

You can retrieve text content from any element on your page that contains text by using a selector and the `text()` function.

The `text()` function will not work with values typed into text boxes. To get values typed into form elements, use `val()` function, discussed later in this chapter in "Getting and Setting Form Values."

To get the text from all `<div>` elements when a user clicks a submit button, follow these steps:

   1. Create a Web page containing the following code:

```
<html>
<head>
<title>My Test Page</title>
<script type="text/javascript" src="js/jquery-1.4.min.js"></script>
<script type="text/javascript">
$(document).ready(function(){

//Your code goes here.

});
</script>
</head>
<body>
<div>This is text from a div.</div>
<div>This is text from a another div.</div>
<br />
<input value="Get Text" type="submit">
</body>
</html>
```

This code contains a button and two `<div>` elements, each with text.

2. **Replace `// Your code goes here.` with the following code:**

```
$(':submit').click(function () {
  alert( $('div').text()  );
  });
```

The code says, "When the button is clicked, display the text from all `<div>` elements in an alert box."

Chapter 3 shows you how to use selectors, and Chapter 4 shows you how to use an event, such as the `mouseover` event.

3. **Save this file, and then view it in your browser.**

4. **Click the button.**

The text from both `<div>` elements appears in an alert box, as shown in Figure 8-1.

When you get text, you pull it in from an element of your page into your code. You can also go the other way and change or set the text in response to an event. To change the text in all `<div>` elements when the user clicks a submit button, follow these steps:

1. **Create a Web page containing the same code as in Step 1 of the preceding exercise.**

2. **Change**

```
<input value="Get Text" type="submit">
```

to

```
<input value="Set Text" type="submit">
```

3. Replace `// Your code goes here.` **with the following code:**

```
$(':submit').click(function () {
 $('div').text('This is new text.') ;
 });
```

The code says, "When the button is clicked, set the text of all `<div>` elements to the text in quotes in the `text()` function."

4. Save this file, and then view it in your browser.

5. Click the button.

The text in both `<div>` elements changes, as shown in Figure 8-2.

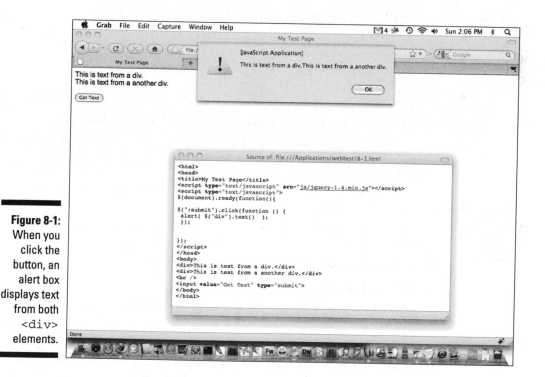

Figure 8-1:
When you click the button, an alert box displays text from both `<div>` elements.

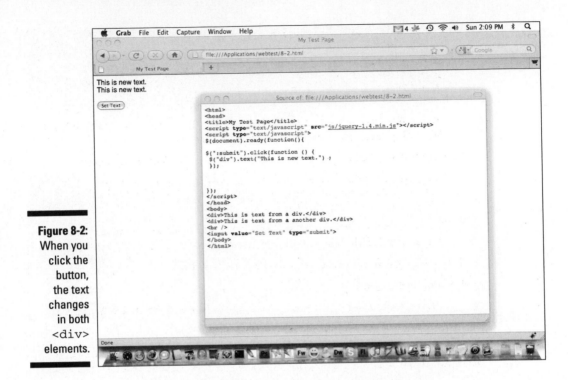

Getting and Setting HTML Content

As with getting and setting text content, you can also get and set any HTML code from any element on your page by using a selector and the `html()` function.

To select the HTML inside a `<div>` element using an `id` attribute when a user clicks a submit button, follow these steps:

1. **Create a Web page containing the following code:**

```
<html>
<head>
<title>My Test Page</title>
<script type="text/javascript" src="js/jquery-1.3.2.min.js"></script>
<script type="text/javascript">
$(document).ready(function(){

//Your code goes here.

});
</script>
</head>
<body>
<div id="outer">
<div>This is text from a div.</div>
<img src = "images/home.gif" />
```

```
<div>This is text from a another div.</div>
</div>
<br />
<input value="Get HTML" type="submit">
</body>
</html>
```

This code contains a button and a parent `<div>` element that contains two `<div>` elements and an `<img>` element.

2. **Replace `// Your code goes here.` with the following code:**

```
$(':submit').click(function () {
 alert( $('#outer').html()  );
 });
```

The code says, "When the button is clicked, open an alert box and display the HTML inside the element with the `outer` id."

3. **Save this file, and then view it in your browser.**

4. **Click the button.**

The HTML from the outer `<div>` element appears in an alert box, as shown in Figure 8-3.

Because the HTML code is displayed in an alert box, it is displayed as just text, not as HTML. But when you set the HTML code on your page, it shows up as HTML, allowing you to control the appearance and add HTML links and images. To set HTML code in your page, do the following:

1. **Create a Web page containing the same code as in Step 1 of the preceding exercise.**

2. **Below the line**

```
<input value="Get HTML" type="submit">
```

add

```
<div id="showcode"></div>
```

This `<div>` element will be used as a place to put the HTML code.

3. **Replace `// Your code goes here.` with the following code:**

```
$(':submit').click(function () {
$('#showcode').html( $('#outer').html());
});
```

The code says, "When the button is clicked, set the HTML inside the element with the `showcode` id to the HTML inside the element with the `outer` id."

4. **Save this file, and then view it in your browser.**

5. **Click the button.**

The HTML in the bottom `<div>` element changes, as shown in Figure 8-4.

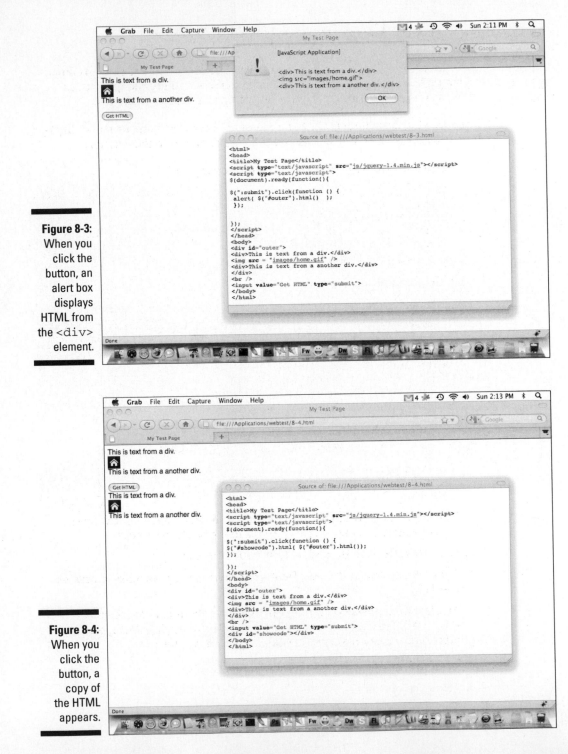

Figure 8-3:
When you
click the
button, an
alert box
displays
HTML from
the <div>
element.

Figure 8-4:
When you
click the
button, a
copy of
the HTML
appears.

Getting and Setting Form Values

The text() and html() functions manipulate text and code that already exists on the page. But if you have a form and want to get the value of an input box, for example, you need to use the val() function instead.

The following example gets the text a user has entered in a text field and displays it on the page as soon as the user removes the cursor from the text field:

1. **Create a Web page containing the following code:**

```
<html>
<head>
<title>My Test Page</title>
<script type="text/javascript" src="js/jquery-1.4.min.js"></script>
<script type="text/javascript">
$(document).ready(function(){

//Your code goes here.

});
</script>
</head>
<body>
<input type = "text" />
<div></div>
</body>
</html>
```

This code contains a text field and a <div> element.

2. **Replace // Your code goes here. with the following code:**

```
$(':text').mouseout(function () {
 alert( $(':text').val()  );
 });
```

The code says, "When the mouse cursor moves out of the text field, open an alert box and display the value inside the text field."

3. **Save this file, and then view it in your browser.**

4. **Type something in the text field, and then move your cursor outside the field.**

An alert box opens containing the text from the text field, as shown in Figure 8-5. This behavior is more than a little annoying. Instead of an alert box, we can display the value in the <div> element.

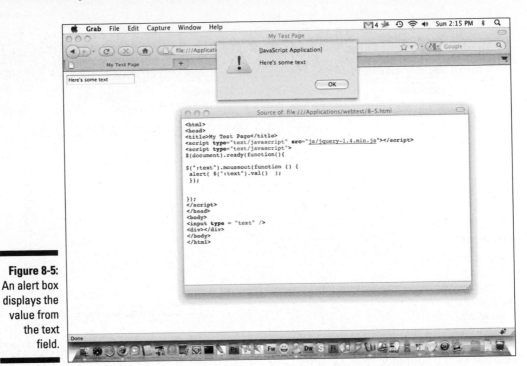

Figure 8-5:
An alert box
displays the
value from
the text
field.

5. **Change**

```
alert( $(':text').val()  );
```

to

```
$('div').text( $(':text').val()  );
```

6. **Save the file, and then view it in your browser.**

7. **Type something in the text field, and then move your cursor outside the field.**

Now the text field text appears in the `<div>` element, as shown in Figure 8-6.

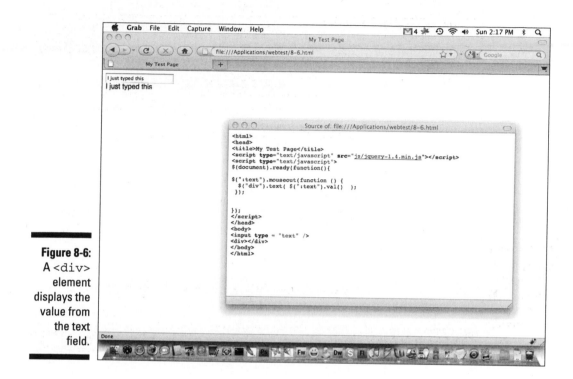

Figure 8-6:
A `<div>` element displays the value from the text field.

To set a value in a form element, follow these steps:

1. **Create a Web page containing the same code as in Step 1 of the preceding exercise.**

2. **Below the line**

```
<input type = "text" />
```

   add this code to create a select box:

```
<select id="colorselect">
<option>Red</option>
<option>Green</option>
<option>Yellow</option>
</select>
```

3. **Replace `// Your code goes here.` with the following code:**

```
$('#colorselect').change(function () {
$(':text').val( ( $(this).val()  ) );
 });
```

   The `change()` function detects when the value in the element with the `colorselect id` has changed. When the select box value has changed, this change event is triggered. The second line assigns the value from the select box to the text field. The outer `val()` function assigns the value in parentheses. The inner `val()` function uses the `this` keyword to get the value from the select box.

The `this` JavaScript keyword means that the code should use the selector that was used in the outer function. In the case of the preceding code, `this` stands in for the `"#colorselect"` code. The `this` keyword doesn't need quotes, but the selector does.

4. **Save this file, and then view it in your browser.**

5. **Select one of the drop-down values.**

   The value in the text field changes to match what you selected, as shown in Figure 8-7.

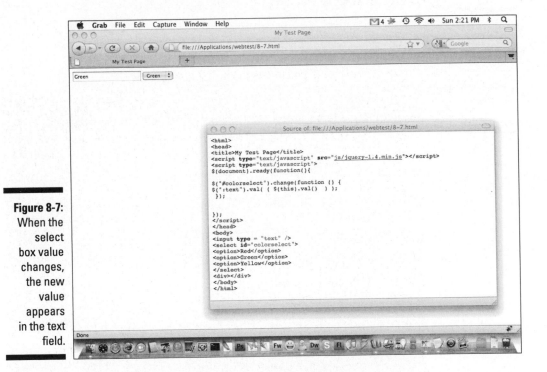

Figure 8-7:
When the select box value changes, the new value appears in the text field.

Inserting Content Inside Elements

Sometimes the `html()` function isn't sufficient. For example, suppose you want to add content to the end of existing content. If all you have to work with is the `html()` function, you could

1. Grab the current content in the element.

2. Save this current content to a variable.

3. Use JavaScript concatenation to combine this content with the new content.

4. Use the `html()` function to put the new combined content back into the original element.

Fortunately, jQuery has functions that combine all four steps into a single easy operation.

Appending content

To append or add content after existing content inside an element, do the following:

1. **Create a Web page containing the following code:**

```
<html>
<head>
<title>My Test Page</title>
<script type="text/javascript" src="js/jquery-1.4.min.js"></script>
<script type="text/javascript">
$(document).ready(function(){

//Your code goes here.

});
</script>
</head>
<body>
<div>My name is</div>
<br />
<input value="Go" type="submit">
</body>
</html>
```

2. **Replace `// Your code goes here.` with the following code:**

```
$(':submit').click(function () {
$('div').append(' Lynn');
});
```

The code says, "When the button is clicked, append this content to the content in the `<div>` element." If the `<div>` element is empty, the content will still be placed in the `<div>` element.

3. **Save this file, and then view it in your browser.**

4. **Click the button.**

The content is appended, as shown in Figure 8-8.

Prepending content

The prepend function allows you to place content in front of a selected element. The following example shows you how to place content in front of an element using the prepend() function:

1. **Create a Web page containing the code from Step 1 of the preceding exercise.**

2. **Replace // Your code goes here. with the following code:**

```
$(':submit').click(function () {
  $('div').append(' Lynn');
  $('div').prepend('<strong>Hi</strong>, ');
});
```

The code says, "When the button is clicked, append this content to the content in any <div> element, then prepend content to the content in any <div> element." Note that you can use regular HTML code as well as text, as long as it's in quotes.

3. **Save this file, and then view it in your browser.**

4. **Click the button.**

The content has now been prepended and appended, as shown in Figure 8-9.

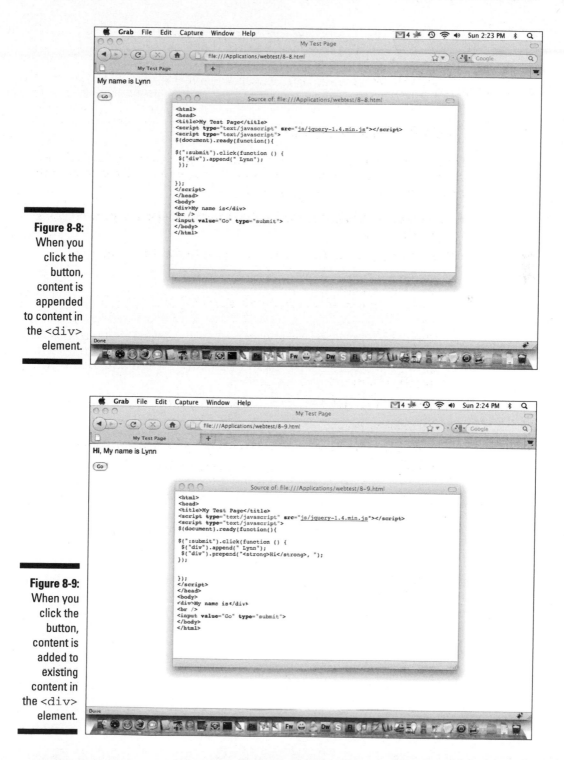

Figure 8-8:
When you click the button, content is appended to content in the `<div>` element.

Figure 8-9:
When you click the button, content is added to existing content in the `<div>` element.

Inserting Content Outside an Element

In addition to appending and prepending content inside elements, jQuery has a simple function that allows you to put content in front of an element or after an element. Prepending and appending functions place content inside selected elements. The before() and after() functions place content outside the selected elements.

To insert content before or after an element, do the following:

1. **Create a Web page containing the following code:**

```
<html>
<head>
<title>My Test Page</title>
<script type="text/javascript" src="js/jquery-1.4.min.js"></script>
<script type="text/javascript">
$(document).ready(function(){

//Your code goes here.


});
</script>
</head>
<body>
<div>Inside <img src = "images/home.gif" /> Inside</div>
<br />
<input value="Go" type="submit">
</body>
</html>
```

2. **Replace // Your code goes here. with the following code:**

```
$(':submit').click(function () {
 $('div').before('Before<br />');
 $('div').after('<br />After');
 });
```

One of the nicest things about jQuery is the sensible way functions are named. It's easy to figure out that the before() function places content before the <div> element and the after() function places content after the <div> element.

3. **Save this file, and then view it in your browser.**

4. **Click the button.**

The content has been placed before and after the <div> element, as shown in Figure 8-10.

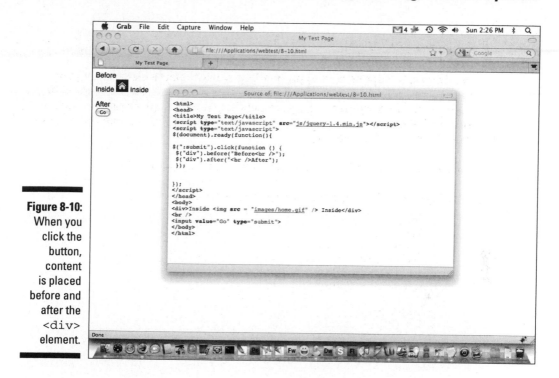

Figure 8-10:
When you click the button, content is placed before and after the `<div>` element.

Moving Elements Around

You can also move elements before or after other elements using the insert-Before() and insertAfter() functions, respectively. For example, suppose your page has an image and a `<div>` element, in that order, but you want the image to follow the `<div>` element after a button is clicked. Do the following:

1. Create a Web page containing the following code:

```
<html>
<head>
<title>My Test Page</title>
<script type="text/javascript" src="js/jquery-1.4.min.js"></script>
<script type="text/javascript">
$(document).ready(function(){

//Your code goes here.

});
</script>
</head>
<body>
<img src="images/home.gif" />
<div>Move the house!</div>
<br />
<input value="Go" type="submit">
```

```
</body>
</html>
```

2. **Replace** `// Your code goes here.` **with the following code:**

```
$(':submit').click(function () {
  $('div').insertBefore('img');
    });
```

The `insertBefore()` function places the `<div>` element before the `<img>` element.

The code is case sensitive. You must use the camel case capitalization with these two functions (`insertBefore()` and `insertAfter()`); otherwise the code will not work.

3. **Save this file, and then view it in your browser.**

4. **Click the button.**

The `<div>` element is placed before the `<img>` element, as shown in Figure 8-11.

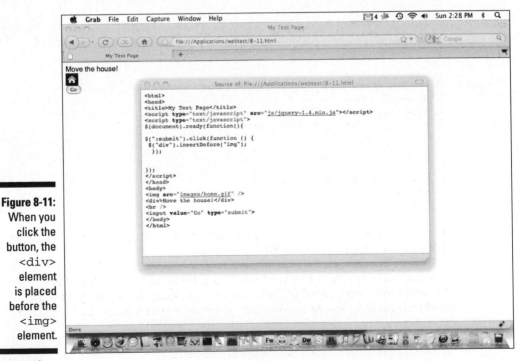

Figure 8-11:
When you click the button, the `<div>` element is placed before the `<img>` element.

We could have used the `insertAfter()` function in the preceding example like so:

```
$(':submit').click(function () {
 $('img').insertAfter('div');
  });
```

This code says to put the `<img>` element after the `<div>` element.

Wrapping Content Around an Element

You can wrap an element around an element on the page with the `wrap()` function. For example, the following code inserts a `<div>` element with a red background color around each `<div>` element on the page when a user clicks a button:

```
<html>
<head>
<title>My Test Page</title>
<script type="text/javascript" src="js/jquery-1.4.min.js"></script>
<script type="text/javascript">
$(document).ready(function(){

$(':submit').click(function () {
$('div').wrap('<div style=background-color:red;></div>');
});
});
</script>
</head>
<body>
<div>Color me red.</div>
<br />
<div>Me too.</div>
<br />
<input value="Go" type="submit">
</body>
</html>
```

This code wraps a red `<div>` element around each `<div>` element when you click the button, as shown in Figure 8-12.

Another function will wrap an element around all matching elements. Suppose that you wanted to make both `<div>` elements in the preceding code wrapped by a single red `<div>` element. Replace the `wrap()` function with the `wrapAll()` function, as shown in Figure 8-13.

The final function in the wrap family is `wrapInner()`. This function wraps all the child elements of the selected element with the specified HTML code.

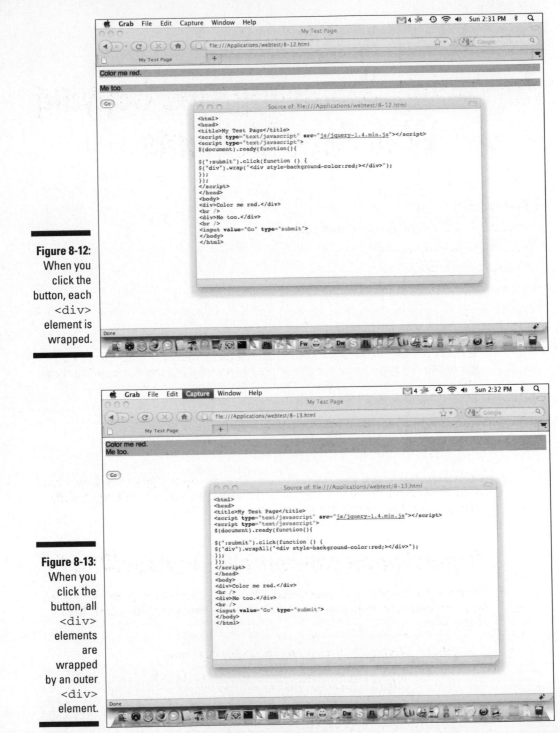

Figure 8-12:
When you click the button, each `<div>` element is wrapped.

Figure 8-13:
When you click the button, all `<div>` elements are wrapped by an outer `<div>` element.

Chapter 9

Replacing, Removing, and Copying Web Page Elements

In This Chapter

▶ Replacing HTML elements with other elements

▶ Deleting elements selectively

▶ Cloning elements and events

▶ Copying elements without events

In Chapter 8, you find out how to change the content on your page. This chapter focuses on locating elements and replacing them, removing them, or copying them elsewhere on the page in response to an event.

Replacing Elements

jQuery has two functions that let you replace elements. These two functions, `replaceWith()` and `replaceAll()`, allow you to select elements, specify what you want to replace them with, and replace them.

Replacing an element with replaceWith()

Suppose you have a `<p>` element that you want to turn into a `<div>` element with formatting in response to a click event. To accomplish this task, follow these steps:

1. **Create a Web page containing the following code:**

```
<!DOCTYPE html PUBLIC "-//W3C//DTD XHTML 1.0 Strict//EN"
        "http://www.w3.org/TR/xhtml1/DTD/xhtml1-strict.dtd">
<html>
<head>
<title>My Test Page</title>
<script type="text/javascript" src="js/jquery-1.4.min.js"></script>
```

```
<script type="text/javascript">
$(document).ready(function(){

//Your code goes here.


});
</script>
</head>
<body>
<p>It will be nice if <strong>this text</strong> and image <image
        src="images/home.gif" /> appear inside a gray div when the
        button is clicked.</p>
<br />
<input value="Replace" type="submit">
</body>
</html>
```

This code contains a button and a <p> element with child elements.

2. **Replace `// Your code goes here.` line with the following code:**

```
$(":submit").click(function () {
  $("p").replaceWith("<div>I am a div</div>") ;
  });
```

The code says, "When the button is clicked, select all <p> elements and replace each with the <div> element."

3. **Save this file, and then open it in your browser.**

4. **Click the button.**

The <p> element is now a <div> element, but all the child elements that were in the <p> element are replaced with the text *I am a div,* as shown in Figure 9-1.

Replacing a parent element while retaining child elements

In the preceding example, the replaceWith() function replaced all selected elements with the content in parentheses. Although this behavior is sometimes useful, it usually makes more sense to keep the current HTML in the element you're replacing so that it appears in the new element.

You can retain the original child elements from the element you're replacing by using the html() function and placing that captured code into the new element. To do this, follow these steps:

1. **Create a Web page containing the same code used in Step 1 of the preceding example.**

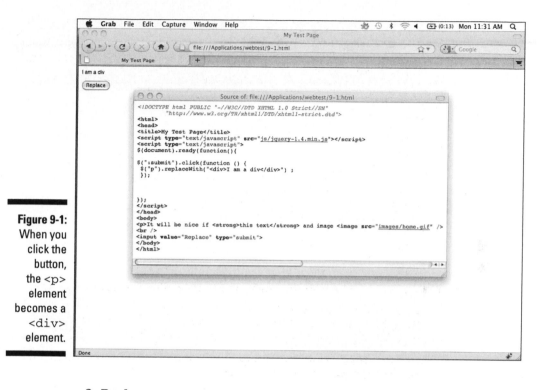

Figure 9-1:
When you click the button, the <p> element becomes a <div> element.

2. **Replace `// Your code goes here.` with the following code:**

```
$(":submit").click(function () {
 $("p").replaceWith() ;
 });
```

3. **Add this line of code inside the parentheses of the `replaceWith()` function:**

```
"<div style=background-color:#aaaaaa>" + $("p").html() + "</div>"
```

Make sure you include the quotes. This code changes the <p> element to a <div> element with the preceding CSS style code. It also says, "Put the HTML that is in the <p> element into the new <div> element."

The `html()` function grabs the content from the <p> element before the `replaceWith()` function changes the <p> element to a <div> element.

4. **Save this file, and then open it in your browser.**

5. **Click the button.**

The <p> element is now a gray <div> element surrounding the HTML that used to be in the <p> element, as shown in Figure 9-2.

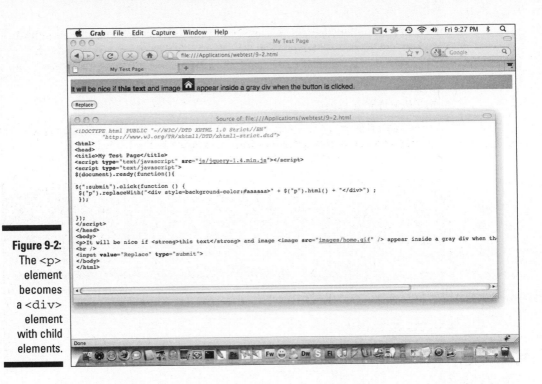

Figure 9-2:
The `<p>`
element
becomes
a `<div>`
element
with child
elements.

Replacing an element with replaceAll()

The `replaceWith()` and `replaceAll()` functions do the same thing, but
their syntax differs. For example, the following code uses `replaceAll()` to
replace a `<p>` element with a formatted `<div>` element:

1. **Create a Web page containing the same code used in Step 1 of the
   preceding example.**

2. **Replace `// Your code goes here.` with the following code:**

```
$(":submit").click(function () {
$().replaceAll("p") ;
});
```

   The code says, "When the button is clicked, call the `replaceAll()`
   function." The code inside the `replaceAll()` function is the selector.
   The function still needs code in the empty parentheses in front of it. The
   code needs to say, "Replace the `<p>` element with a `<div>` element with
   a gray background color."

3. **Add the following line of code inside the empty parentheses in front
   of the `replaceWith` function:**

```
"<div style=background-color:#aaaaaa>" + $("p").html() + "</div>"
```

This code changes the <p> element to a <div> element with attached CSS style code. It also includes the html() function, which puts the HTML that was in the <p> element into the new <div> element.

4. **Save this file, and then open it in your browser.**

5. **Click the button.**

As with the preceding example, the <p> element is now a gray <div> element surrounding the content, as shown in Figure 9-3.

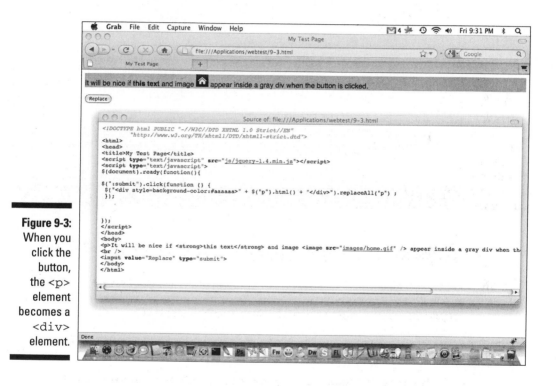

Figure 9-3: When you click the button, the <p> element becomes a <div> element.

Removing Elements

You can use the replaceAll() and replaceWith() functions to remove elements by simply not providing code to replace for each function. In the case of replaceWith(), the following removes all <p> elements and does not replace them with anything:

```
$("p").replaceWith() ;
```

The following code also removes the <p> elements:

```
$("").replaceAll("p") ;
```

But you can also use the `remove()` function to remove elements. And another handy function, `empty()`, removes any child elements from a selected parent element. The next two sections show you examples of these functions.

Removing elements

The following example uses the `remove()` function to remove `<strong>` elements:

1. **Create a Web page containing the following code:**

```
<!DOCTYPE html PUBLIC "-//W3C//DTD XHTML 1.0 Strict//EN"
          "http://www.w3.org/TR/xhtml1/DTD/xhtml1-strict.dtd">
<html>
<head>
<title>My Test Page</title>
<script type="text/javascript" src="js/jquery-1.4.min.js"></script>
<script type="text/javascript">
$(document).ready(function(){


//Your code goes here.



});
</script>
</head>
<body>
<strong>Remove me.</strong>
<br />
<em>Don't remove me.</em>
<br />
Remove the extra word <strong>here</strong> in this sentence.
<input value="Remove" type="submit">
</body>
</html>
```

This code contains two `<strong>` elements.

2. **Replace // Your code goes here. with the following code:**

```
$(":submit").click(function () {
  $("strong").remove() ;
  });
```

The code says, "When the button is clicked, remove all `<strong>` elements and any code inside them."

3. **Save this file, and then open it in your browser.**

4. **Click the button.**

The `<strong>` elements are gone, as shown in Figure 9-4.

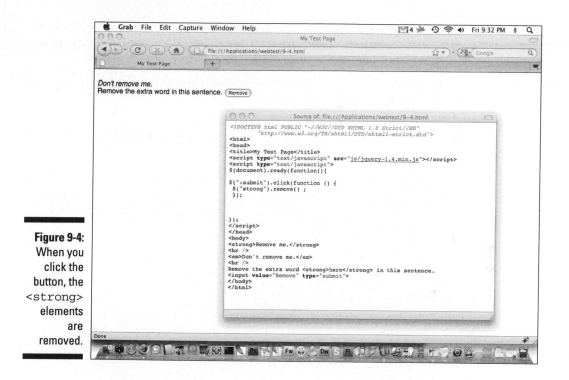

Figure 9-4:
When you click the button, the `<strong>` elements are removed.

Removing content

The `empty()` function removes all content, including elements and text, from a selected parent element. The parent node remains.

The following example uses the `empty()` function to remove everything inside the `<strong>` elements:

1. **Create a Web page containing the following code:**

```
<!DOCTYPE html PUBLIC "-//W3C//DTD XHTML 1.0 Strict//EN"
          "http://www.w3.org/TR/xhtml1/DTD/xhtml1-strict.dtd">
<html>
<head>
<title>My Test Page</title>
<script type="text/javascript" src="js/jquery-1.4.min.js"></script>
<script type="text/javascript">
$(document).ready(function(){

//Your code goes here.


});
</script>
</head>
```

```
<body>
<div> Outside <em> Outside <strong> Inside <p> Inside </p> Inside </strong>
         Outside </em> Outside </div>
<input value="Empty" type="submit">
</body>
</html>
```

This code contains several `<strong>` elements.

2. **Replace `// Your code goes here.` with the following code:**

```
$(":submit").click(function () {
 $("strong").remove();
 });
```

The code says, "When the button is clicked, remove everything inside the `<strong>` element."

3. **Save this file, and then open it in your browser.**

4. **Click the button.**

The content inside the `<strong>` element is gone, as shown in Figure 9-5.

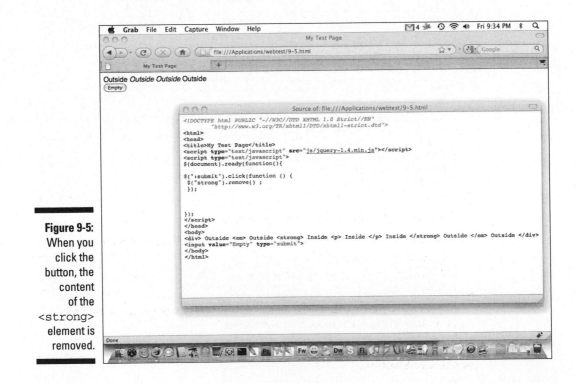

Figure 9-5:
When you click the button, the content of the `<strong>` element is removed.

Cloning Elements

You can use the `clone()` function to copy an element and then duplicate it elsewhere on your page. You can even make the element appear in multiple places.

Cloning elements with events

To clone an `<img>` element multiple times on a page, do the following:

1. **Create a Web page containing the following code:**

```
<!DOCTYPE html PUBLIC "-//W3C//DTD XHTML 1.0 Strict//EN"
         "http://www.w3.org/TR/xhtml1/DTD/xhtml1-strict.dtd">
<html>
<head>
<title>My Test Page</title>
<script type="text/javascript" src="js/jquery-1.4.min.js"></script>
<script type="text/javascript">
$(document).ready(function(){

//Your code goes here.


});
</script>
</head>
<body>
<img src = "images/home.gif" />
<p>Put an image after this line.</p>
<p>Put an image after this line.</p>
<p>Put an image after this line.</p>
<p>Put an image after this line.</p>
<input value="Copy" type="submit">
</body>
</html>
```

This code contains several `<p>` elements.

2. **Replace `// Your code goes here.` with the following code:**

```
$(":submit").click(function () {
  $("img").clone().insertAfter("p");
  });
```

The code says, "When the button is clicked, copy the `<img>` element and place copies after each `<p>` element."

3. **Save this file, and then view it in your browser.**

4. **Click the button.**

The house image now appears after each `<p>` element, as shown in Figure 9-6.

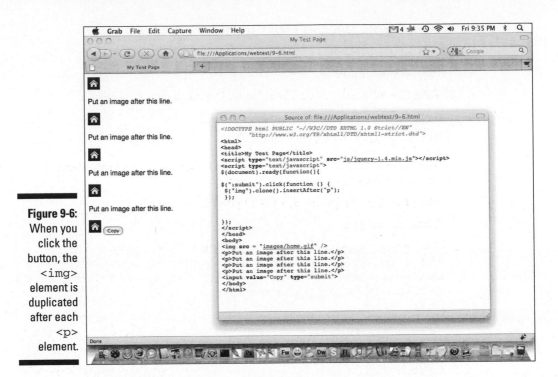

Figure 9-6:
When you click the button, the `<img>` element is duplicated after each `<p>` element.

Copying elements along with their events and data

Suppose you have an image with a mouseover event attached to it. If you want to clone that image as in the preceding example, the new copy of the image wouldn't have the mouseover event attached to it by default. But using the clone() function and the true keyword, you can make a copy of an element and its actions. To see this work, follow these steps:

1. **Create a Web page containing the code from Step 1 of the preceding example.**

2. **Replace // Your code goes here. with the following code:**

```
$('img').mouseover(
function() {alert('mouseover');
 });
```

The code says, "When you mouse over an `<img>` element, open an alert box."

3. **Save this file, and then open it in your browser.**

4. **Mouse over the image.**

   An alert box appears.

5. **Add the following code after the code you inserted in Step 2:**

   ```
   $(':submit').click(function () {
     $('img').clone().insertAfter('p');
   });
   ```

   The code says, "When the button is clicked, copy the <img> element and place copies after each <p> element."

6. **Save this file, and then open it in your browser.**

7. **Click the button.**

   The house image now appears after each <p> element, as shown in Figure 9-7. But only the original <img> element, when moused over, displays an alert box. You need to add the true keyword to the clone function to tell it to copy the image and its events.

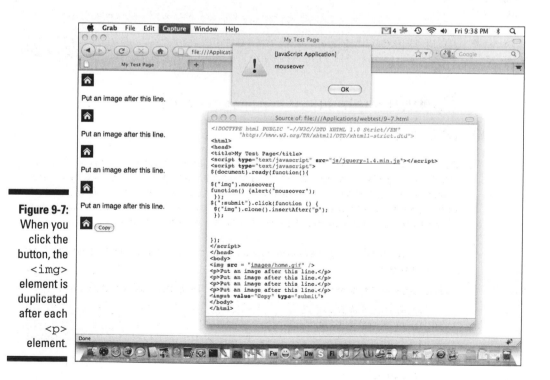

Figure 9-7:
When you click the button, the <img> element is duplicated after each <p> element.

8. Locate the `clone()` function and add the word `true` inside the empty parentheses, like so:

```
$('img').clone(true).insertAfter('p');
```

9. Save this file, and then view it in your browser.

10. Click the button.

Now when you mouse over any image, the alert box opens.

Part IV
Using Plug-ins and Widgets

The 5th Wave

By Rich Tennant

"See? I created a little felon figure that runs around our Web site hiding behind banner ads. On the last page, our logo puts him in a non lethal choke hold and brings him back to the home page."

In this part . . .

Unlike when you were in school, sometimes it's better to use someone else's work. In the next few chapters, you discover a world of jQuery goodness. From plug-ins that let you create gorgeous menus and image galleries to widgets such as calendars complete with a custom color scheme, the next few chapters are full of cool free jQuery stuff.

Chapter 10

Understanding Plug-ins

*P*arts I and II focus on code that uses functions in the jQuery library. Among other things, you find out how to select, animate, and change HTML content in response to events. Putting these techniques together makes your Web page dynamic. But building complicated effects can be a lot of work.

Fortunately, plug-ins do the work for you. *jQuery plug-ins* are free extensions to the jQuery library that create robust JavaScript effects with little effort on your part to install and use them.

This chapter introduces you to jQuery plug-ins, tells you where to get them, and shows you how to install a few small ones.

How jQuery Plug-ins Work

jQuery plug-ins work in much the same way as jQuery. When you find a plug-in you want, you download a .js file and save it to a directory on your Web server. On your Web page, you include the path to that file. For example, the following code contains two lines. The first line connects to the jQuery library, and the second connects to the jquery.columnhover.js JavaScript plug-in file:

```
<script type="text/javascript" src="js/jquery-1.4.min.js"></script>
<script type="text/javascript" src="js/jquery.columnhover.js"></script>
```

After your Web page calls the source code for the plug-in, you have access to it.

Some plug-ins require code in the <script> element, some require CSS code, and most require specific id or class attributes in your HTML elements. Each plug-in has documentation that shows you how to use it.

Getting jQuery Plug-ins

You can find an exhaustive listing of jQuery plug-ins at `plugins.jquery.com`. The plug-ins are divided into categories, as shown in Figure 10-1.

Here are some of the more popular categories of plug-ins:

- **Ajax:** Allow the Web page to pass and receive data from your Web server or database
- **Animation and Effects:** Create interesting animations and special effects
- **Browser Tweaks:** Manage the way specific browsers behave
- **DOM:** Manipulate HTML elements
- **Drag-and-Drop:** Create effects that allow the viewer to drag-and-drop elements
- **Events:** Detect more advanced events and user actions
- **Forms:** Manipulate and validate Web forms
- **jQuery Extensions:** Change the behavior and interface of jQuery
- **Layout and User Interface:** Change the appearance of elements
- **Media:** Work with media such as Flash movies or video
- **Menus and Navigation:** Create advanced menu systems
- **Tables:** Change the way HTML tables work
- **Widgets:** Include reusable components, such as calendars and color pickers
- **Windows and Overlays:** Create pop-up window effects on your Web page

To get a plug-in, follow these steps:

1. **Browse to `plugins.jquery.com` and click through the categories until you locate the plug-in you want to use.**

2. **Locate the Releases table on the plug-in's information page and click the release that matches the version of jQuery you're using.**

   The recommended release is listed on the right side of the Releases table, as shown in Figure 10-2.

3. **Click the `Download` link and save the file to a location you'll remember on your computer.**

4. **Unzip the new file, and then save the `.js` file to the same directory on your Web server where your jQuery file is stored.**

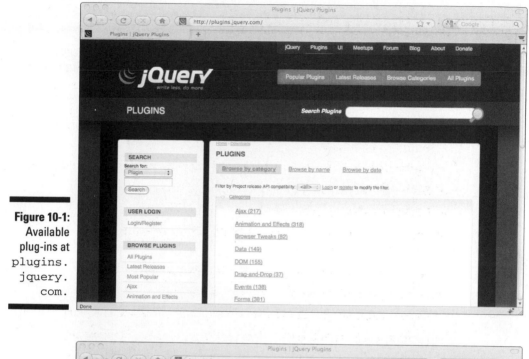

Figure 10-1:
Available
plug-ins at
plugins.
jquery.
com.

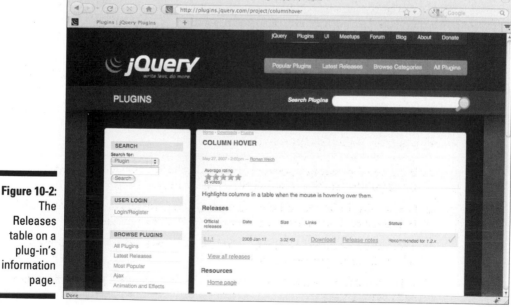

Figure 10-2:
The
Releases
table on a
plug-in's
information
page.

Testing Your First jQuery Plug-ins

In this section, you find out how to install and use three different plug-ins: the Snowfall plug-in, the Colorize plug-in for tables, and the Hovertip tooltip plug-in. The Snowfall plug-in creates the effect of animated snow falling on your Web page. Colorize is a plug-in that makes HTML tables easier to view by allowing visitors to click and highlight rows or columns in a table. Hovertip creates a small tooltip box that appears when a page element is hovered over with the mouse.

Making your page snow

The Snowfall plug-in is a simple, fun plug-in that creates an animated snowfall effect. You can apply the snow to a single element, such as an image, or to your entire page. To use the Snowfall plug-in, follow these steps

1. **Create a Web page containing the following code:**

```
<!DOCTYPE html PUBLIC "-//W3C//DTD XHTML 1.0 Strict//EN"
          "http://www.w3.org/TR/xhtml1/DTD/xhtml1-strict.dtd">
<html>
<head>
<title>My Test Page</title>
<script type="text/javascript" src="js/jquery-1.4.min.js"></script>
<script type="text/javascript">
$(document).ready(function(){

//Your code goes here.


});
</script>
</head>
<body style="background-color: #000;">
<div style="background-color: #AAA; width: 400px;height: 500px;">Is it
          snowing in here?</div>
</body>
</html>
```

This code creates a black page with a gray `<div>` element.

2. **Browse to `plugins.jquery.com/project/snowfall` and download the most recent Snowfall plug-in.**

3. **Unzip the plug-in, and then save it in the `js` directory on your Web server.**

4. **Locate this line in the code:**

```
<script type="text/javascript" src="js/jquery-1.4.min.js"></script>
```

and below it add this line:

```
<script type="text/javascript" src="js/snowfall.jquery.js"></script>
```

The filename for the plug-in in your code must match the plug-in you downloaded and saved to the `js` directory on your Web server.

5. **Replace `// Your code goes here.` with the following code:**

```
$(document).snowfall();
```

The `snowfall()` function is part of the Snowfall plug-in. This line of code tells the plug-in to make snow fall on the entire Web page.

6. **Save this file, and then view it in your browser.**

You see small white snowflakes falling on your page, as shown in Figure 10-3.

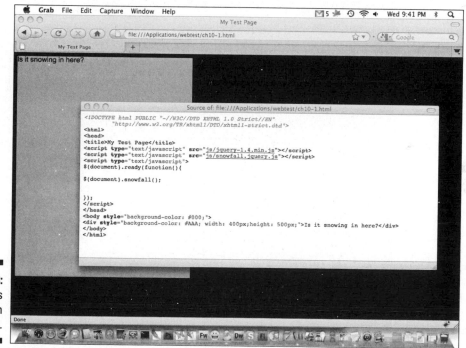

Figure 10-3: Snowflakes drift down the page.

The preceding example makes the entire page appear to snow. If you want to limit the plug-in to a specific area on the screen, do the following:

1. **Follow Steps 1–4 in the preceding example.**

2. **Replace `// Your code goes here.` with the following code:**

```
$('div').snowfall();
```

3. Save the file, and then view it in your browser.

The snowfall now shows up only in the <div> elements, as shown in Figure 10-4.

Plug-ins often have options. In the case of the Snowflake plug-in, you can change some of the default settings, such as the color of the flakes and the speed at which they fall. Here is a list of the options you can change and their default values:

- flakeCount: 35
- flakeColor: '#ffffff'
- minSize: 1
- maxSize: 3
- minSpeed: 2
- maxSpeed: 3

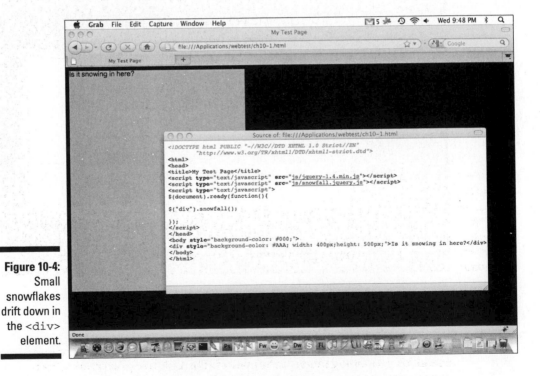

Figure 10-4:
Small snowflakes drift down in the <div> element.

To change the color and size of the flakes, do the following:

1. **Follow all the steps in the preceding example.**

2. **Replace `$('div').snowfall();`, with the following code:**

   ```
   $('div').snowfall({flakeColor:'#ff0000', maxSize: 20});
   ```

   The settings must be inside curly braces inside the `snowfall()` function. Separate each setting with a comma.

3. **Save this file, and then view it in your browser.**

   The snow now consists of small and large square blocks, as shown in Figure 10-5.

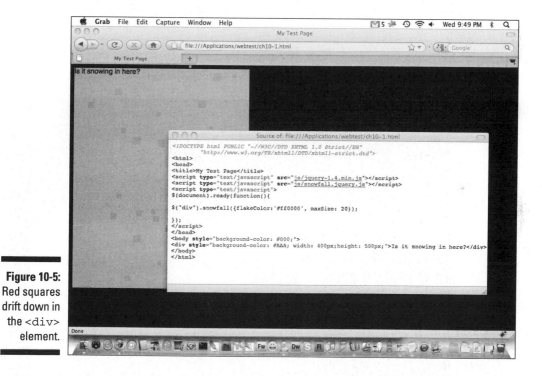

Figure 10-5: Red squares drift down in the `<div>` element.

Highlighting table rows and columns

Although HTML tables are not as popular as they once were, they're still useful for presenting tabular information. The Colorize plug-in for tables colors ever other row of a table and highlights a row when you click it. To use the Colorize plug-in, follow these steps:

1. **Create a Web page containing the following code:**

```
<!DOCTYPE html PUBLIC "-//W3C//DTD XHTML 1.0 Strict//EN"
            "http://www.w3.org/TR/xhtml1/DTD/xhtml1-strict.dtd">
<html>
<head>
<title>My Test Page</title>
<script type="text/javascript" src="js/jquery-1.4.min.js"></script>
<script type="text/javascript">
$(document).ready(function(){

//Your code goes here.

});
</script>
</head>
<body>
<table border=1>
            <tr><td>A</td><td>B</td><td>C</td><td>D</td></tr>
            <tr><td>E</td><td>F</td><td>G</td><td>H</td></tr>
            <tr><td>I</td><td>J</td><td>K</td><td>L</td></tr>
            <tr><td>M</td><td>N</td><td>O</td><td>P</td></tr>
            <tr><td>Q</td><td>R</td><td>S</td><td>T</td></tr>
</table>
</body>
</html>
```

This code creates a simple eight-celled table with a border.

2. **Browse to `plugins.jquery.com/project/Colorize` and download the most recent Colorize plug-in.**

3. **Unzip the plug-in, and then save it in the `js` directory on your Web server.**

4. **Locate this line in the code:**

```
<script type="text/javascript" src="js/jquery-1.4.min.js"></script>
```

and below it add this line:

```
<script type="text/javascript" src="js/jquery.colorize-2.0.0.js" ></script>
```

The filename for the plug-in in your code must match the plug-in you downloaded and saved to the `js` directory on your Web server.

5. **Replace `// Your code goes here.` with the following code:**

```
$('table').colorize();
```

The `colorize()` function tells the plug-in to add a colored background to every other row of your table.

6. **Save this file, and then view it in your browser.**

You see a table with colored rows. Click a row to highlight it, as shown in Figure 10-6.

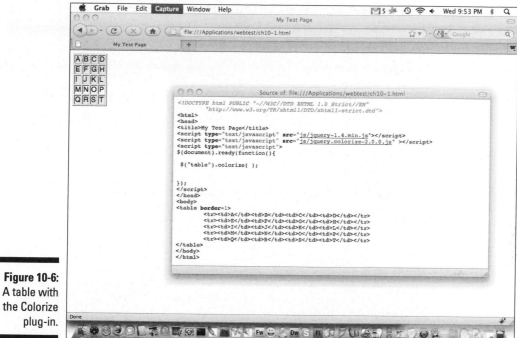

Figure 10-6:
A table with
the Colorize
plug-in.

As with the Snowfall plug-in, Colorize offers lots of options for customization. Consult the documentation on the plug-in Web page at `http://plugins.jquery.com/project/Colorize`.

Adding a tooltip

Tooltips are pop-up boxes or balloons that appear when you move the cursor over a specific spot on a Web page, such as a link or an image. The tooltip usually contains text describing the item the cursor is hovering over. Hundreds of tooltip plug-ins are available. The following example shows you how to install and use a basic tooltip plug-in called Hovertip:

1. **Create a Web page containing the following code:**

```
<!DOCTYPE html PUBLIC "-//W3C//DTD XHTML 1.0 Strict//EN"
         "http://www.w3.org/TR/xhtml1/DTD/xhtml1-strict.dtd">
<html>
<head>
<title>My Test Page</title>
<script type="text/javascript" src="js/jquery-1.4.min.js"></script>
<script type="text/javascript">
$(document).ready(function(){

//Your code goes here.
```

```
});
</script>
</head>
<body>
<a href="" id="mylink">Move your mouse over me</a>
<div class="hovertipContent">You are hovering over a link.</div>
</body>
</html>
```

This code contains a link and a `<div>` element. The text in the `<div>` element is displayed when a cursor hovers over the link.

2. **Save this file, and then view it in your browser.**

   Note that the text in the `<div>` element is visible, as shown in Figure 10-7. It will be hidden when you add the code to link in the plug-in.

3. **Browse to `code.google.com/p/hovertip/downloads/list` and download the most recent Hovertip file.**

4. **Unzip this file.**

   Note that this zip file contains both a `.js` file and a `.css` file.

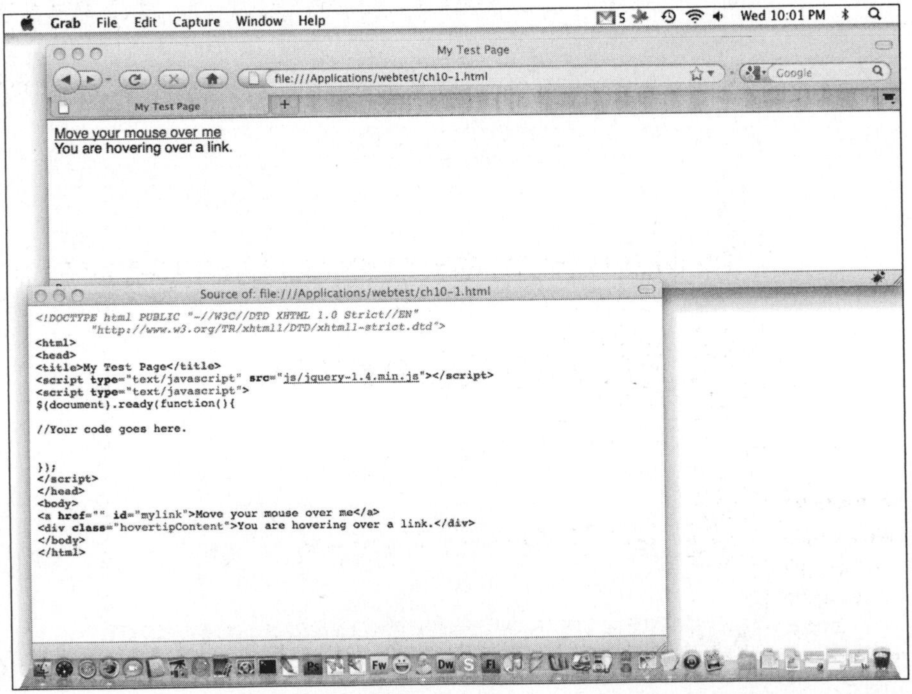

Figure 10-7:
The `<div>` element that will become the tooltip is currently visible.

5. **Save the Hovertip .js file to the js directory on your Web server, and save the Hovertip .css file to the css directory on your Web server.**

   If you don't have a css directory, you should create one in the same location as your js directory.

6. **Locate this line in the code:**

   ```
   <script type="text/javascript" src="js/jquery-1.4.min.js"></script>
   ```

   and below it add these lines:

   ```
   <script type="text/javascript" src="js/jquery.hovertip.min.js" ></script>
   <link rel=StyleSheet href="css/jquery.hovertip.css" TYPE="text/css">
   ```

7. **Replace // Your code goes here. with the following code:**

   ```
   $('#mylink').hovertip();
   ```

   The hovertip() method tells the plug-in to use the text in the <div> element that follows your link and display it as a tooltip.

8. **Save this file, and then view it in your browser.**

   When you mouse over the link, you see the text from the hidden <div> element displayed in a tooltip, as shown in Figure 10-8.

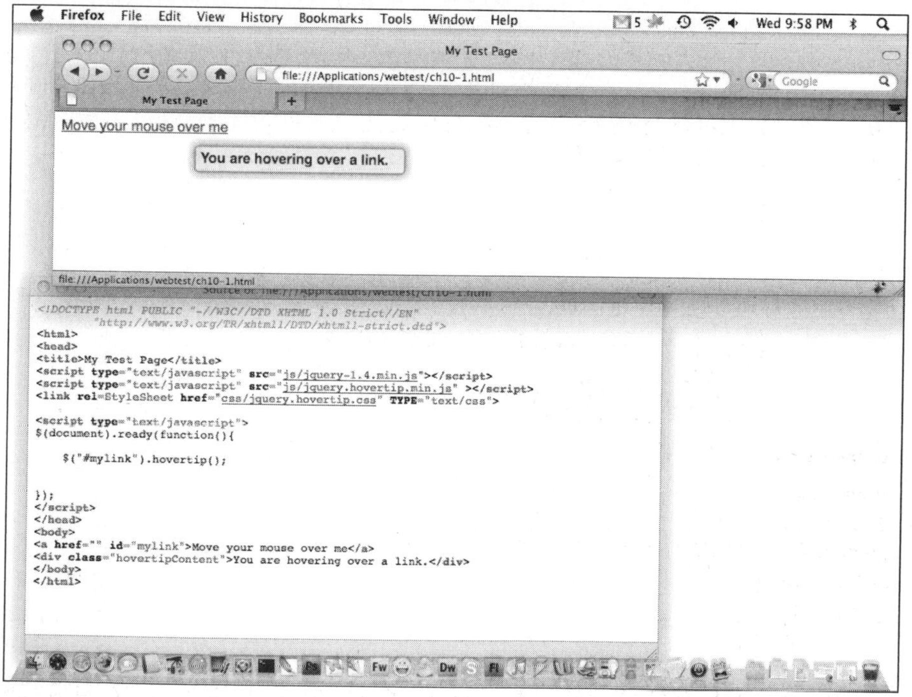

Figure 10-8:
A link with a simple tooltip.

One of the nice features about this plug-in is that it allows you to use HTML code in the tooltip. For example, if you want your tooltip to display an image, follow these steps

1. **Follow Steps 1–6 in the preceding example.**

2. **Locate this line in the code:**

   ```
   <div class="hovertipContent">You are hovering over a link.</div>
   ```

   and replace it with this line:

   ```
   <div class="hovertipContent">Here is an image of a house: <img src="images/
           home.gif /></div>
   ```

3. **Save this file, and then view it in your browser.**

   When you mouse over the link, you see the text and image from the <div> element displayed in a tooltip, as shown in Figure 10-9.

You can use any HTML code you want in the <div> element, and it will appear in the tooltip.

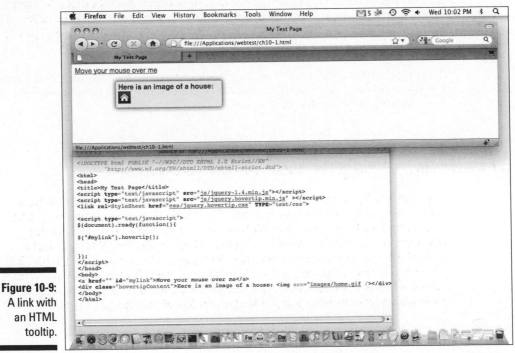

Figure 10-9:
A link with an HTML tooltip.

Chapter 11

Playing with Image Effects

*I*n the past, if you wanted to create an image gallery on the Web, you typically used thumbnail images and linked them to HTML pages containing a larger view of the image that was clicked. Now many Web sites that feature image-based content rely on jQuery to display those images dynamically. Instead of clicking a thumbnail and changing to another page, you can hover your cursor over an image to open a larger version.

That's just one of the creative ways you can present images using jQuery and jQuery plug-ins. This chapter describes popular jQuery plug-in techniques used to present images to visitors.

Creating a Lightbox with Colorbox

In photography, a lightbox is a glass pane with light below it that is used to view photographs on translucent film. The term *lightbox* has been extended to describe an image (or other Web content) displayed in the middle of a black frame. Generally, a visitor will click a link or thumbnail image, and a dark block will animate and cover the Web page. At the center of the block is a larger version of the image that the visitor clicked. Figure 11-1 shows a page before a link is clicked. Figure 11-2 shows a lightbox overlaying the original page with a translucent fill and a larger version of the image.

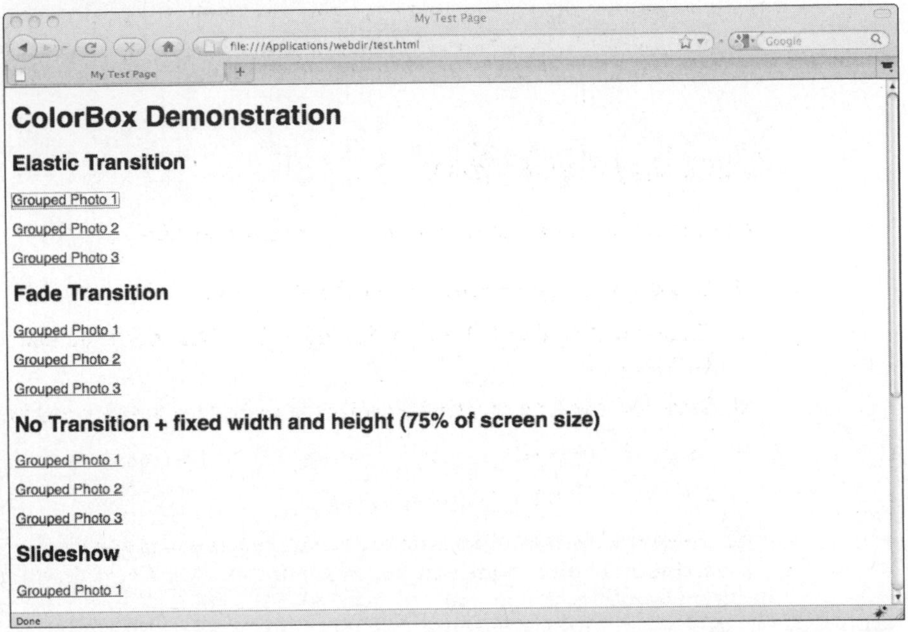
My Test Page
file:///Applications/webdir/test.html
Google
My Test Page
ColorBox Demonstration
Elastic Transition
Grouped Photo 1
Grouped Photo 2
Grouped Photo 3
Fade Transition
Grouped Photo 1
Grouped Photo 2
Grouped Photo 3
No Transition + fixed width and height (75% of screen size)
Grouped Photo 1
Grouped Photo 2
Grouped Photo 3
Slideshow
Grouped Photo 1
Done

Figure 11-1: A Web page with links to open lightboxes.

My Test Page
file:///Applications/webdir/test.html
Google
My Test Page
image 1 of 3
Done

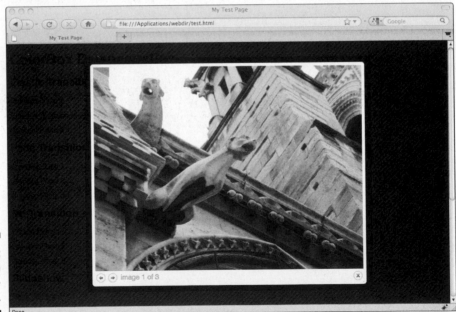

Figure 11-2: A Web page with a lightbox overlay.

Many lightbox plug-ins are available, but one of my favorites is Colorbox (colorpowered.com/colorbox), a robust plug-in built using jQuery. This section shows you how to install and use the Colorbox plug-in in a Web page.

Getting Colorbox

To get and install the Colorbox plug-in, follow these steps:

1. **Browse to colorpowered.com/colorbox.**

2. **Click the Download link on the left side of the page, as shown in Figure 11-3.**

3. **Save the file to a location you'll remember on your computer.**

4. **Unzip the new file.**

   This file contains several directories.

5. **Open the unzipped colorbox directory, and save the jquery. colorbox-min.js file to the same directory on your Web server as the jQuery file.**

6. **Navigate back to the unzipped colorbox directory and open the example1 directory. Save the colorbox.css file to the css directory on your Web server.**

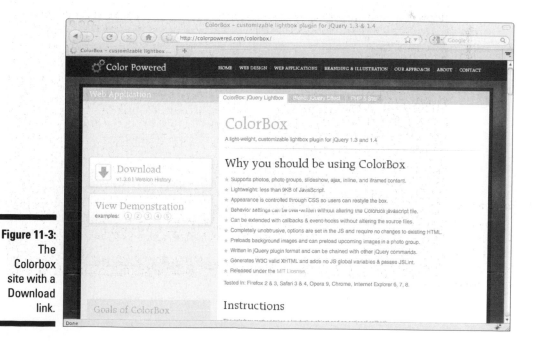

Figure 11-3:
The
Colorbox
site with a
Download
link.

If you don't have a `css` directory, you should create one in the same location as your `js` directory.

7. **Before leaving the `example1` directory in the `colorbox` zip file, locate the `example1/images` directory. Copy all the images in `example1/ images` to the `css` directory on your Web server.**

These are the images used by the Colorbox plug-in.

Before you begin creating your first Colorbox effect, you should have some image files handy. In the next few examples, I use a set of large images that I saved in the `content` directory on my Web server. My images are photos of Paris, so I've named them `paris1.jpg`, `paris2.jpg`, and so on.

Your Web server directory structure should consist of four directories, `js`, `css`, `images`, and `content`. Figure 11-4 shows the structure of the Web directory.

Figure 11-4:
The structure of the Web server directory.

Name	Date Modified	Size	Kind
ch11-1.html	Jan 27, 2010, 10:02 PM	4 KB	HTML...ument
▼ 📁 content	Today, 1:34 PM	--	Folder
paris1.jpg	Today, 1:28 PM	144 KB	JPEG image
paris2.jpg	Today, 1:29 PM	72 KB	JPEG image
paris3.jpg	Today, 1:33 PM	88 KB	JPEG image
paris4.jpg	Today, 1:33 PM	128 KB	JPEG image
paris5.jpg	Today, 1:33 PM	160 KB	JPEG image
paris6.jpg	Today, 1:33 PM	116 KB	JPEG image
paris7.jpg	Today, 1:34 PM	112 KB	JPEG image
paris8.jpg	Today, 1:34 PM	28 KB	JPEG image
▼ 📁 css	Today, 2:11 PM	--	Folder
colorbox.css	Dec 31, 2009, 4:53 PM	8 KB	Casca...ument
▼ 📁 images	Today, 2:14 PM	--	Folder
border.png	Jul 31, 2009, 1:40 AM	4 KB	Porta... image
controls.png	Jul 31, 2009, 1:43 AM	4 KB	Porta... image
▶ 📁 internet_explorer	Jan 13, 2010, 1:09 AM	--	Folder
loading_background.png	Jun 7, 2009, 12:19 PM	4 KB	Porta... image
loading.gif	Apr 29, 2009, 9:08 AM	12 KB	Graph...t (GIF)
overlay.png	Jul 31, 2009, 1:40 AM	4 KB	Porta... image
▶ 📁 images	Jan 10, 2010, 8:44 PM	--	Folder
▼ 📁 js	Today, 2:12 PM	--	Folder
jquery-1.4.min.js	Jan 17, 2010, 1:37 PM	72 KB	JavaSc...ment
jquery.colorbox-min.js	Jan 13, 2010, 12:56 AM	12 KB	JavaSc...ment

23 items, 162.95 GB available

Now that the files are organized on your Web server, you can link to them in your Web page and use the Colorbox plug-in.

Creating a basic image Colorbox

After you've saved and organized your files, you can create your first Colorbox effect. To create a simple Colorbox, follow these steps:

1. **Create a Web page containing the following code:**

```
<!DOCTYPE html PUBLIC "-//W3C//DTD XHTML 1.0 Strict//EN"
            "http://www.w3.org/TR/xhtml1/DTD/xhtml1-strict.dtd">
<html>
<head>
<title>My Test Page</title>
<script type="text/javascript" src="js/jquery-1.4.min.js"></script>
<script type="text/javascript">
$(document).ready(function(){

//Your code goes here.

});
</script>
</head>
<body>
<a href="content/paris1.jpg">Click me</a>
</body>
</html>
```

This code creates a simple page with a link to an image.

2. Locate this line in the code:

```
<script type="text/javascript" src="js/jquery-1.4.min.js"></script>
```

and *above* it add these lines:

```
<script type="text/javascript" src="js/ jquery.colorbox-min.js"></script>
<link type="text/css" media="screen" rel="stylesheet" href="css/colorbox.
        css" />
```

The filenames for your `js` and `css` plug-in files in your code must match the names you downloaded and saved to the `js` and `css` directories on your Web server. You also need to change the image name in the `<a>` element from `paris1.jpg` to the image name in your `content` directory.

3. Replace `// Your code goes here.` with the following code:

```
$('a').colorbox();
```

The `colorbox()` method is part of the Colorbox plug-in. This line of code tells the plug-in to respond to the `<a>` element on your page.

4. Save this file, and then open it in your browser.

When you click the link, the page is covered by a translucent animated background and your image appears in a lightbox, as shown in Figure 11-5.

This example uses text inside the `<a>` element to create a link that opens the lightbox. You can instead use an image as a link by replacing the link text with an `<img>` tag that points to a thumbnail image.

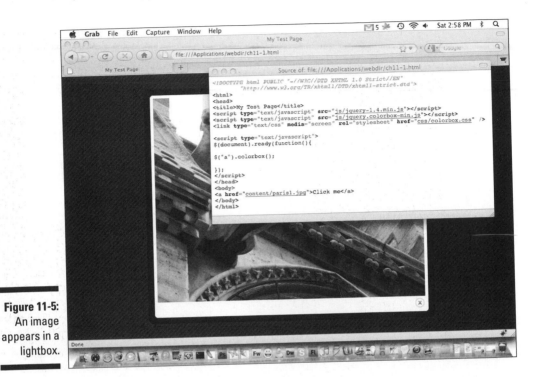

Figure 11-5:
An image
appears in a
lightbox.

Adding a title to a lightbox

You can also display a title under your image in the lightbox. Simply do the following:

1. **Follow Steps 1–3 in the preceding example.**

2. **Replace the line with the `<a>` link element with the following code:**

   ```
   <a href="content/paris1.jpg" title="Paris Rain Spout" >Click me</a>
   ```

   The `title` attribute in the image becomes the title.

3. **Save this file, and then open it in your browser.**

   The image now has a title, as shown in Figure 11-6.

Displaying a set of images in a lightbox

Colorbox can also display a set of images, with previous and next buttons appearing in the lightbox to view the images. To display a set of images in a lightbox, follow these steps:

Figure 11-6:
An image
with a title
in a lightbox.

1. **Create a Web page containing the final code from the preceding example:**

```
<!DOCTYPE html PUBLIC "-//W3C//DTD XHTML 1.0 Strict//EN"
          "http://www.w3.org/TR/xhtml1/DTD/xhtml1-strict.dtd">
<html>
<head>
<title>My Test Page</title>
<link type="text/css" media="screen" rel="stylesheet" href="css/colorbox.
          css" />
<script type="text/javascript" src="js/jquery-1.4.min.js"></script>
<script type="text/javascript" src="js/ jquery.colorbox-min.js"></script>
<script type="text/javascript">
$(document).ready(function(){

$('a').colorbox();
});
</script>
</head>
<body>
<a href="content/paris1.jpg" title="Paris Rain Spout" >Click me</a>
</body>
</html>
```

2. **Locate this line in the code:**

```
<a href="content/paris1.jpg" title="Paris Rain Spout" >Click me</a>
```

and change it to add the `rel` attribute with a value of `mygroup`:

```
<a rel="mygroup" href="content/paris1.jpg" title="Paris Rain Spout">Click
    me</a>
```

3. **Add additional `<a>` elements below the `<a>` element:**

```
<a rel="mygroup" href="content/paris2.jpg" title="Montmarte"></a>
<a rel="mygroup" href="content/paris3.jpg" title="Statue"></a>
<a rel="mygroup" href="content/paris4.jpg" title="Gargoyles"></a>
<a rel="mygroup" href="content/paris5.jpg" title="Blocks"></a>
```

Note that each link has the same `rel="mygroup"` attribute. You can set the `rel` attribute to any name, but all images that you want to group must have the same `rel` attribute. Also note that only the first `<a>` element has text (`Click me`) that creates a link between the open and closing `<a>` tags.

4. **Save this file, and then open it in your browser.**

When you click the link, you see previous and next arrow buttons in the lightbox, as shown in Figure 11-7.

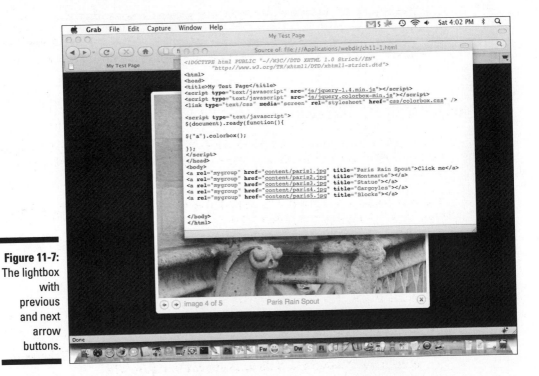

Figure 11-7:
The lightbox with previous and next arrow buttons.

Displaying a slideshow

You can turn a lightbox with multiple grouped images into a slideshow that plays automatically. To create a slideshow, do the following:

1. **Follow Steps 1–4 in the preceding example.**
2. **Replace this line:**

```
$('a').colorbox();
```

   with this:

```
$('a').colorbox({slideshow:true});
```

3. **Save the file, and then open it in your browser.**

   The images in the lightbox automatically scroll in a slideshow fashion.

Colorbox has many additional options and capabilities. Visit `colorpowered.com/colorbox` to find out how to

✔ Display HTML from another Web site in a lightbox

✔ Use other transition animations when the lightbox opens and closes

✔ Display videos or Flash movies in a lightbox

Creating an Image Gallery

Image galleries consist of a set of thumbnail images on a Web page. When you mouse over or click a thumbnail, a larger version of the image is displayed, usually on the same Web page.

In this section, you find out how to install and use the Galleria image gallery plug-in, which is shown in Figure 11-8.

Getting Galleria

To get and install the Galleria plug-in, do the following:

1. **Browse to `devkick.com/lab/galleria`.**
2. **Scroll down the page and locate the links to download the Galleria plug-in and Galleria CSS files, as shown in Figure 11-9.**

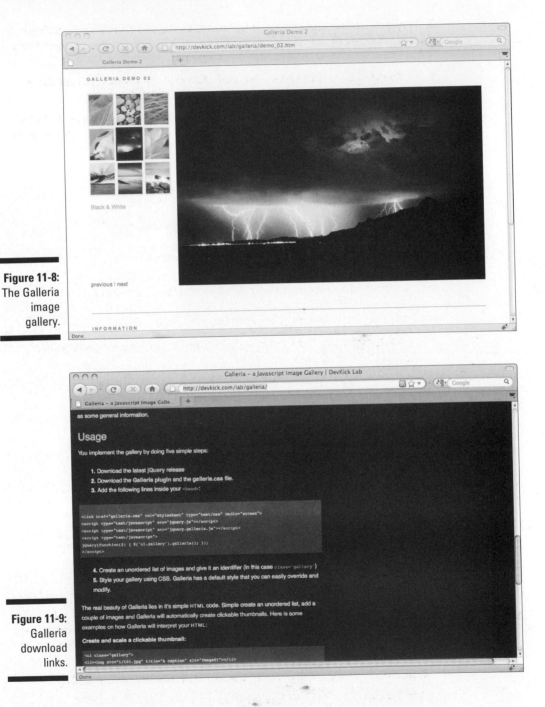

Figure 11-8:
The Galleria image gallery.

Figure 11-9:
Galleria download links.

3. **Right-click the Galleria plug-in link. Choose Save Link As and then save the `jquery.galleria.js` file to the `js` directory on your Web server.**

4. **Right-click the `galleria.css` link. Choose Save Link As and save `galleria.css` to the `css` directory on your Web server.**

As with Colorbox in the first section of this chapter, you need to have some images. In the following example, I use a set of large images saved in the `content` directory on my Web server.

Creating a basic image gallery

To create a simple Galleria image gallery, do the following:

1. **Create a Web page containing the following code:**

```
<!DOCTYPE html PUBLIC "-//W3C//DTD XHTML 1.0 Strict//EN"
          "http://www.w3.org/TR/xhtml1/DTD/xhtml1-strict.dtd">
<html>
<head>
<title>My Test Page</title>
<script type="text/javascript" src="js/jquery-1.4.min.js"></script>
<script type="text/javascript">
$(document).ready(function(){

//Your code goes here.

});
</script>
</head>
<body>
</body>
</html>
```

2. **Locate this line in the code:**

```
<script type="text/javascript" src="js/jquery-1.4.min.js"></script>
```

and below it add these lines:

```
<script type="text/javascript" src="js/jquery.galleria.js"></script>
<link type="text/css" media="screen" rel="stylesheet" href="css/galleria.
        css" />
```

The filenames for your `js` and `css` plug-in files in your code must match the names you downloaded and saved to the `js` and `css` directories on your Web server.

3. **Replace `// Your code goes here.` with the following code:**

```
$(function($) { $('ul.gallery').galleria(); });
```

4. **Place this code after the `<body>` tag in your page:**

```
<ul class="gallery">
<li><img src="content/paris1.jpg" title="Paris Water Spout"></li>
<li><img src="content/paris2.jpg" title="Montmarte" ></li>
<li><img src="content/paris3.jpg" title="Statue"></li>
<li><img src="content/paris4.jpg" title="Gargoyles"></li>
<li><img src="content/paris5.jpg" title="Blocks"></li>
</ul>
```

Note that each `<li>` element contains an `<img>` tag with the path to a gallery image. The `title` attribute specifies a title that will appear below the large image.

You need to change the image names in the `<li>` elements to the image names in your `content` directory.

5. **Save this file, and then view it in your browser.**

Galleria automatically generates thumbnails. When you click one, the large version of the image appears with the appropriate title below it, as shown in Figure 11-10.

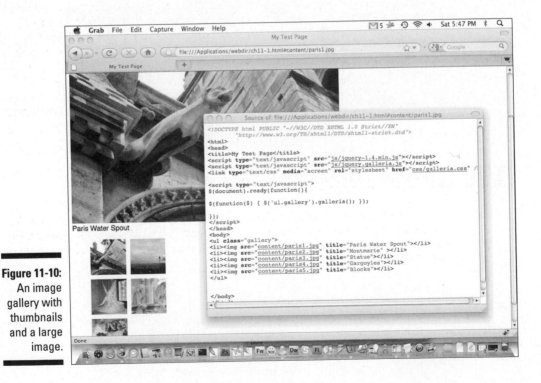

Figure 11-10: An image gallery with thumbnails and a large image.

Chapter 12

Jazzing Up Forms

· ·

· ·

A simple HTML form is powerful when connected to a backend processing script. You can gather information from your visitors and store or e-mail it. But basic HTML forms are just that, basic. They don't detect the information that is being entered. And there is no indication of what should be entered in a given field unless you add descriptive text.

Hundreds of great form enhancement plug-ins exist. The goal of this chapter is to introduce you to a sampling of how you can spruce up HTML forms with jQuery plug-ins.

Displaying Default Values

Figure 12-1 shows a basic HTML form with multiple fields. The Clearfield plug-in allows you to specify text that appears in each field and disappears when the user clicks the field. Figure 12-2 shows the same form in Figure 12-1 but using the Clearfield plug-in.

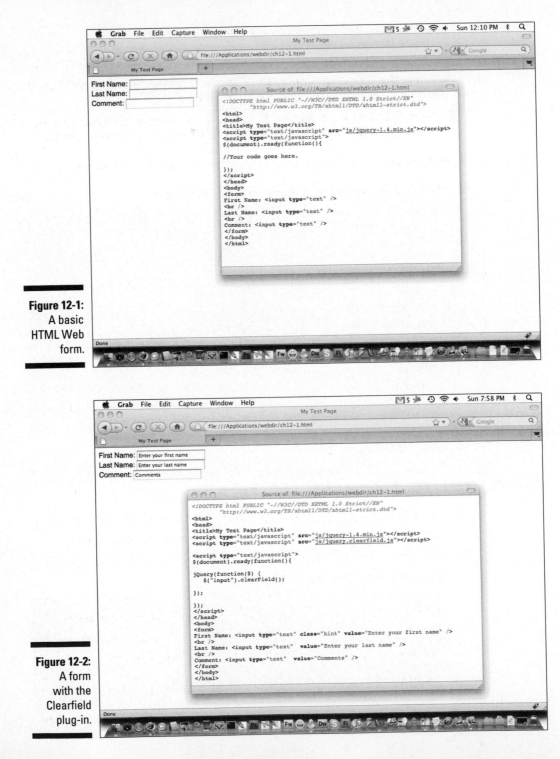

Figure 12-1:
A basic
HTML Web
form.

Figure 12-2:
A form
with the
Clearfield
plug-in.

To get and install the Clearfield plug-in, follow these steps:

1. Browse to `labs.thesedays.com/projects/jquery/clearfield`.

2. Locate the link to download the Clearfield plug-in on the right side of the page, as shown in Figure 12-3.

3. Right-click the Clearfield plug-in link and choose Save Link As. Save the `jquery.clearfield.js` file to the `js` directory on your Web server.

To add the Clearfield plug-in hints to your form fields, do the following:

1. **Create a Web page containing the following code:**

```
<!DOCTYPE html PUBLIC "-//W3C//DTD XHTML 1.0 Strict//EN"
        "http://www.w3.org/TR/xhtml1/DTD/xhtml1-strict.dtd">
<html>
<head>
<title>My Test Page</title>
<script type="text/javascript" src="js/jquery-1.4.min.js"></script>
<script type="text/javascript">
$(document).ready(function(){

//Your code goes here.

});
</script>
</head>
<body>
</body>
</html>
```

2. **Locate this line in the code:**

```
<script type="text/javascript" src="js/jquery-1.4.min.js"></script>
```

and below it add this line:

```
<script type="text/javascript" src="js/jquery.clearfield.js"></script>
```

3. **Replace** `// Your code goes here.` **with the following code:**

```
$('input').clearField();
```

4. **Place this code after the `<body>` tag:**

```
<form>
First Name: <input type="text" class="hint" value="Enter your first name"
        />
<br />
Last Name: <input type="text" value="Enter your last name" />
<br />
Comment: <input type="text" value="Comments" />
</form>
```

The text stored in the `value` attribute of each field will be displayed in the corresponding field until clicked by the user.

Figure 12-3:
The
Clearfield
plug-in
download
link.

5. **Save this file, and then view it in your browser.**

   Clearfield adds the text in the `value` attribute to the input fields of your form. When the user clicks a form field, the text disappears.

Validating Form Fields

One of the most useful enhancements to a Web form is adding validation. A *validated form field* means that the field is checked when the form is submitted to make sure that the correct information has been entered. Usually the person filling out the form receives notification when incorrect information is entered in a field. For example, a validated field asking for a first name should return a message when someone tries to enter numbers in that field. The form can't be submitted until the correct information is in all the fields.

The jQuery Validation plug-in is robust and easy to implement. To get and install the Validation plug-in, follow these steps:

1. **Browse to `plugins.jquery.com/project/validate`.**

2. **Download the latest version of the Validation plug-in zip file to a location you'll remember.**

3. **Unzip the Validation plug-in zip file.**

   The extracted file contains a number of directories and files, as shown in Figure 12-4.

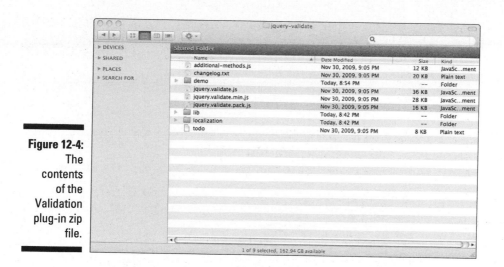

4. **Save a copy of the `jquery.validate.pack.js` file to the `js` directory on your Web server.**

To add the Validation plug-in to your page, follow these steps:

1. **Create a Web page containing the following code:**

```
<!DOCTYPE html PUBLIC "-//W3C//DTD XHTML 1.0 Strict//EN"
          "http://www.w3.org/TR/xhtml1/DTD/xhtml1-strict.dtd">
<html>
<head>
<title>My Test Page</title>
<script type="text/javascript" src="js/jquery-1.4.min.js"></script>
<script type="text/javascript">
$(document).ready(function(){

//Your code goes here.

});
</script>
</head>
<body>
</body>
</html>
```

2. **Locate this line in the code:**

```
<script type="text/javascript" src="js/jquery-1.4.min.js"></script>
```

and below it add this line:

```
<script type="text/javascript" src="js/ jquery.validate.pack.js"></script>
```

3. Replace `// Your code goes here.` with the following code:

```
$('#commentForm').validate();
```

4. Add the following code after the `<body>` tag:

```
<form  id="commentForm" >
First Name: <input  name="name" size="25" class="required" minlength="2" />
<br />
E-Mail: <input  name="email" size="25"  class="required email" />
<br />
URL: <input  name="url" size="25"  class="url" value="" />
<br />
Comment: <textarea id="ccomment" name="comment" cols="22"
          class="required"></textarea>
<br />
<input class="submit" type="submit" value="Submit"/>
 </form>
```

The first name field is required, as indicated by the `class="required"` attribute. The name must be at least two characters, as indicated by the `minlength="2"` attribute. The E-Mail field is required and must fit the pattern of an e-mail, with an @ sign and a period followed by a domain name, as indicated by the `class="required email"` attribute. The URL field isn't required, but if the user enters a URL, it must fit the correct pattern, for example, `http://abc.abc`. The URL pattern is controlled by the `class="url"` attribute.

5. Save this file, and then view it in your browser.

Validation checks for valid input controlled by the rules you set in your code. When bad data is entered, error messages appear to the right of invalid fields, as shown in Figure 12-5.

The preceding example barely scratches the surface of what the Validate plug-in can do. To find out about the Validation plug-in's additional options and customizations, check out `http://bassistance.de/jquery-plugins/jquery-plugin-validation`.

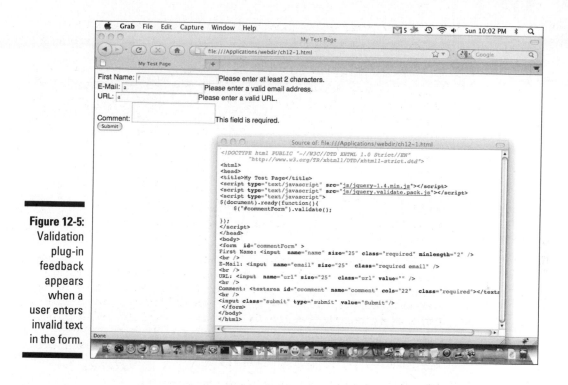

Figure 12-5:
Validation
plug-in
feedback
appears
when a
user enters
invalid text
in the form.

Creating a Date Picker

When users are supposed to enter a date on a form, they might enter a date in a variety of formats. For example, the date January 31, 2010 can be entered as 1/31/2010, Jan. 31 2010, 1-31-10, or even the European variation 31/1/2010. You can use validation to enforce a specific date format, but a friendlier solution is to offer your visitors a mini pop-up calendar from which to choose a date. Figure 12-6 shows an example of a jQuery calendar plug-in.

It only makes sense to use a calendar when the date you want your user to enter is within a few weeks before or after the current date. It's inconvenient for them to have to scroll forward or backward for months or years to select a date.

Date Input is a no-frills date picker plug-in that pops up when a visitor clicks a date field in a form. To get and install the Date Input plug-in, follow these steps:

1. **Browse to `plugins.jquery.com/project/date-input`.**

2. **Scroll down to the plug-in download link and download `date_input-1.2.1.zip` or the latest version of the plug-in.**

3. **Unzip the file.**

4. **Open the extracted `date_input` directory.**

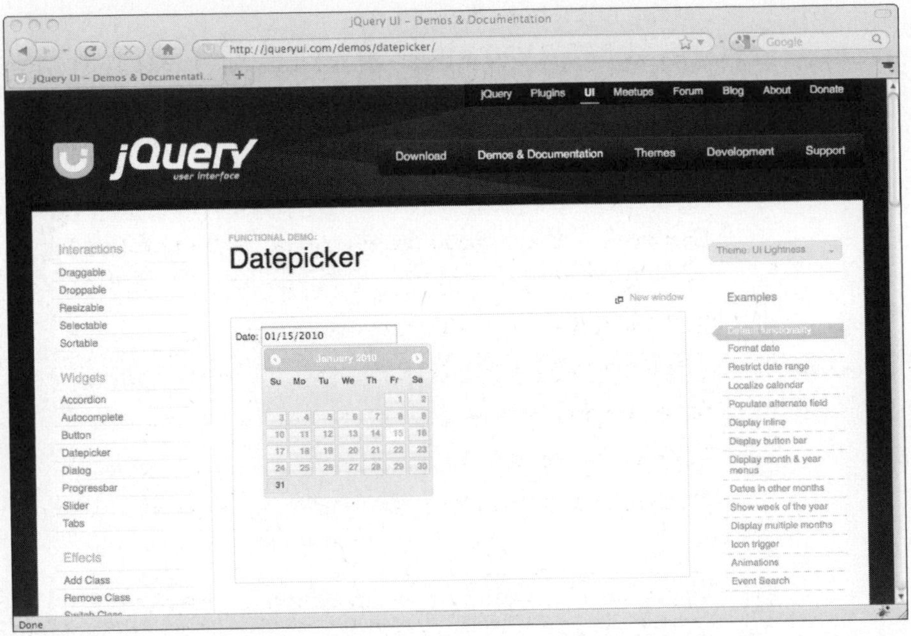

Figure 12-6:
A form with
a jQuery
calendar
plug-in.

5. **Save the `jquery.date_input.pack.js` file to the `js` directory on your Web server, and save `date_input.css` to the `css` directory on your Web server.**

To create a form with a date input field using the Date Input plug-in, do the following:

1. **Create a Web page containing the following code:**

```
<!DOCTYPE html PUBLIC "-//W3C//DTD XHTML 1.0 Strict//EN"
          "http://www.w3.org/TR/xhtml1/DTD/xhtml1-strict.dtd">
<html>
<head>
<title>My Test Page</title>
<script type="text/javascript" src="js/jquery-1.4.min.js"></script>
<script type="text/javascript">
$(document).ready(function(){

//Your code goes here.

});
</script>
</head>
<body>
</body>
</html>
```

2. **Locate this line in the code:**

```
<script type="text/javascript" src="js/jquery-1.4.min.js"></script>
```

and below it add these lines:

```
<script type="text/javascript" src="js/jquery.date_input.pack.js"></script>
<link type="text/css" media="screen" rel="stylesheet" href="css/date_input.css" />
```

3. **Replace `// Your code goes here.` with the following code:**

```
$('#datefield').date_input();
```

4. **Add the following code after the `<body>` tag:**

```
<input type='text' id='datefield' />
```

5. **Save this file, and then view it in your browser.**

6. **Click in the input box.**

   A calendar appears below the form field, as shown in Figure 12-7.

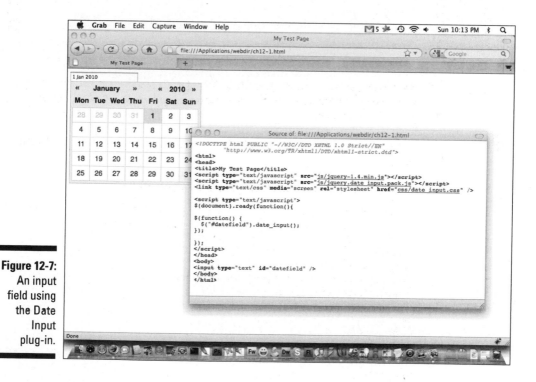

Figure 12-7:
An input
field using
the Date
Input
plug-in.

Chapter 13

Toying with Page Layout

*j*Query and jQuery plug-ins are great for giving you more control over the layout of your site, and this chapter shows you a few fun page layout tricks. You find out how to create an accordion menu that expands and contracts as items are clicked. You also see how to break up (or paginate) large, content-heavy Web pages into smaller chunks with automatically generated navigation links. Finally, you discover how to create a floating element that remains visible when you scroll down the page.

Creating an Accordion Menu

A *static menu* on a Web site consists of a set of links, typically across the top or on the left side of the page. An *accordion menu* presents the visitor with a list of links and sublinks that expand and contract when clicked. Figure 13-1 shows an accordion menu closed. Figure 13-2 shows a section of the same menu expanded after you click a menu item.

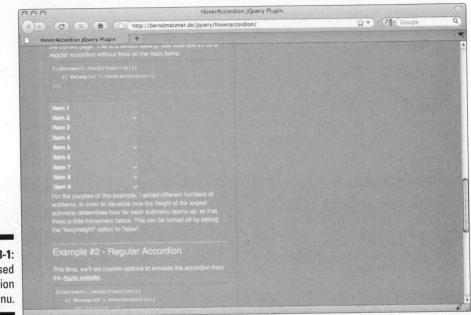

To get and install a simple accordion menu plug-in, follow these steps:

1. Browse to `www.unwrongest.com/projects/accordion`.

2. Locate the link to download the `jquery.accordion-1.3.zip` plug-in on the right side of the page, as shown in Figure 13-3.

3. Click and save the `jquery.accordion-1.3.zip` file.

4. Extract the zip file. Save the `jquery.accordion.source.js` file to the `js` directory on your Web server.

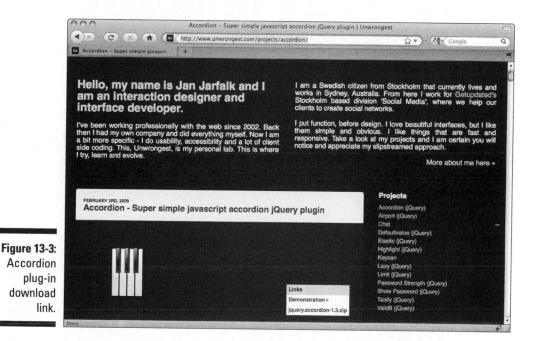

Figure 13-3: Accordion plug-in download link.

To use the accordion menu, do the following:

1. Create a Web page containing the following code:

```
<!DOCTYPE html PUBLIC "-//W3C//DTD XHTML 1.0 Strict//EN"
        "http://www.w3.org/TR/xhtml1/DTD/xhtml1-strict.dtd">
<html>
<head>
<title>My Test Page</title>
<script type="text/javascript" src="js/jquery-1.4.min.js"></script>
<script type="text/javascript">
$(document).ready(function(){
```

```
//Your code goes here.

});
</script>
</head>
<body>
</body>
</html>
```

2. Locate this line in the code:

```
<script type="text/javascript" src="js/jquery-1.4.min.js"></script>
```

and below it add this line:

```
<script src="js/jquery.accordion.source.js" type="text/javascript"
        charset="utf-8"></script>
```

3. Replace // Your code goes here. with the following code:

```
$('ul').accordion();
```

4. Place this code after the `<body>` tag:

```
<ul class="accordion">
  <li><a href="#a">First set</a>
    <ul>
      <li>
      <a href="#a"><a href="test.html">sublink 1</a></a></li>
      <li><a href="#a"><a href="test.html">sublink 2</a></a></li>
      <li><a href="#a"><a href="test.html">sublink 3</a></a></li>
      </li>
    </ul>
  </li>
  <li><a href="#b">Second set</a>
    <ul>
      <li>
      <a href="#b"><a href="test.html">sublink 1</a></a></li>
      <li><a href="#b"><a href="test.html">sublink 2</a></a></li>
      <li><a href="#b"><a href="test.html">sublink 3</a></a></li>
      </li>
    </ul>
  </li>
</ul>
```

Be careful not to miss any of the tags. Every `<ul>` tag and `<li>` tag has a matching `</ul>` tag or `</li>` tag, respectively.

You can download all the code in this book from www.dummies.com/go/jquery.

5. Save this file, and then view it in your browser.

The Accordion plug-in turns your unordered list element into a menu with an accordion effect, as shown in Figure 13-4. This current version is plain. In the next step, you apply CSS formatting to make it more impressive.

6. **Just before the `</head>` tag that closes the HEAD section, add the following CSS style code:**

```
<style>
.accordion { list-style-type: none; padding: 0; margin: 0 0 30px; border:
        1px solid #17a; border-top: none; border-left: none; }
.accordion ul { padding: 0; margin: 0; float: left; display: block; width:
        100%; }
.accordion li { background: #3cf; cursor: pointer; list-style-type: none;
        padding: 0; margin: 0; float: left; display: block; width:
        100%;}
.accordion li div { padding: 20px; background: #aef; display: block; clear:
        both; float: left; width: 360px;}
.accordion a { text-decoration: none; border-bottom: 1px solid #4df; font:
        bold 1.1em/2em Arial, sans-serif; color: #222; padding: 0 10px;
        display: block;}
.accordion li ul li { background: #7FD2FF; font-size: 0.9em; }
</style>
```

This CSS code changes the background colors, specifies borders, and controls the appearance of the text in menu, as shown in Figure 13-5.

Figure 13-4:
Menu created using the Accordion plug-in.

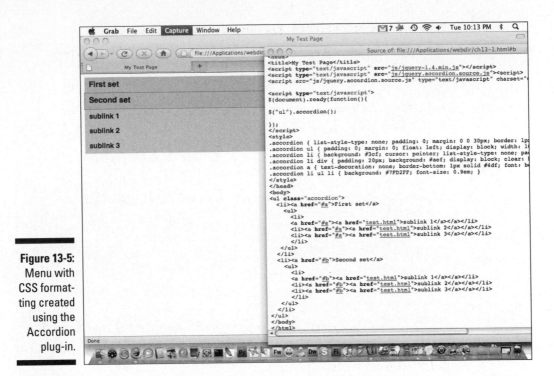

Figure 13-5:
Menu with
CSS format-
ting created
using the
Accordion
plug-in.

The demo on the Web page includes small graphics that indicate whether a
tab is opened or closed. Browse to `http://sandbox.unwrongest.com/`
`jquery.accordion` and choose View➪Source to take a closer look.

CSS code can be used to style most elements you manipulate with jQuery. If
you'd like to find out more about CSS, I recommend that you take a look at
HTML, XHTML and CSS All-In-One For Dummies, 2nd Edition, by Andy Harris
(Wiley).

Paginating Content

Suppose that you have a long page full of text. Your visitors might be willing
to scroll through all that text, but it's more elegant to display it as readable
chunks. You can break up the text by creating a bunch of Web pages and creating navigation links, but why not have a plug-in do the work for you?

To install the simple-to-use Pagination plug-in, follow these steps:

1. **Browse to `plugins.jquery.com/project/jquery-pagination`.**

2. **Locate the link to download the `paginator.js` file.**

3. **Click and save the file to the `js` directory on your Web server.**

To use the Pagination plug-in, do the following:

1. **Create a Web page containing the following code:**

```
<!DOCTYPE html PUBLIC "-//W3C//DTD XHTML 1.0 Strict//EN"
        "http://www.w3.org/TR/xhtml1/DTD/xhtml1-strict.dtd">
<html>
<head>
<title>My Test Page</title>
<script type="text/javascript" src="js/jquery-1.4.min.js"></script>
<script type="text/javascript">
$(document).ready(function(){

//Your code goes here.

});
</script>
</head>
<body>
</body>
</html>
```

2. **Locate this line in the code:**

```
<script type="text/javascript" src="js/jquery-1.4.min.js"></script>
```

and below it add this line:

```
<script src="js/paginator.js"></script>
```

3. **Replace `// Your code goes here.` with the following code:**

```
$('div').pagination();
```

4. **Place this code after the `<body>` tag:**

```
<div>
<p>A</p>
<p>B</p>
<p>C</p>
<p>D</p>
<p>E</p>
<p>F</p>
<p>G</p>
<p>H</p>
<p>I</p>
<p>J</p>
<p>K</p>
<p>L</p>
</div>
```

Feel free to fill up the <p> elements with any text you like.

5. **Save this file, and then view it in your browser.**

The Pagination plug-in turns the content in your <div> element into a set of sections with navigation links (see Figure 13-6).

You can include more than text in your <p> elements. Other HTML elements work as well, such as <img> and <div> tags.

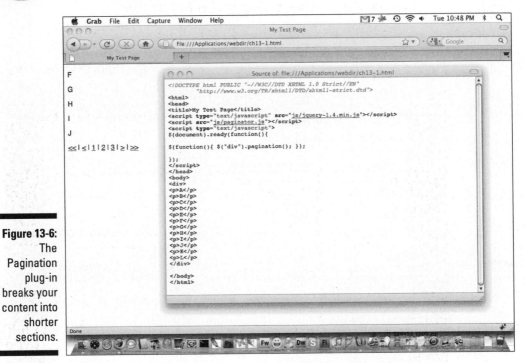

Figure 13-6:
The Pagination plug-in breaks your content into shorter sections.

Creating a Floating <div> Element

The Floating Div plug-in allows you to create a <div> element that always stays on the browser screen when someone scrolls down a long page. To see an example, look at `amirharel.com/labs/fo/float_demo.html`. The lyrics extend down the page; as you scroll, the embedded video scrolls down too.

To install the Floating Div plug-in, follow these steps:

1. **Browse to `plugins.jquery.com/project/floatobject`.**

2. **Locate the link to download the latest version of the plug-in.**

3. **Right-click and choose Save As.**

4. **Delete .txt in the filename (see Figure 13-7).**

   This file ends with the `.txt` file extension. You need to remove that extra extension so that the filename ends with `.js`.

5. **Save the renamed file to the `js` directory on your Web server.**

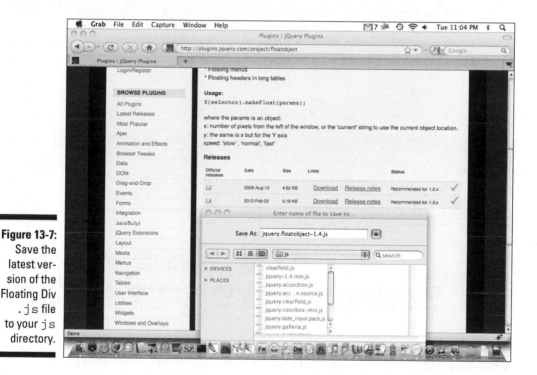

Figure 13-7:
Save the latest version of the Floating Div `.js` file to your `js` directory.

To create a floating element, follow these steps:

1. **Create a Web page containing the following code:**

```
<!DOCTYPE html PUBLIC "-//W3C//DTD XHTML 1.0 Strict//EN"
         "http://www.w3.org/TR/xhtml1/DTD/xhtml1-strict.dtd">
<html>
<head>
```

```
<title>My Test Page</title>
<script type="text/javascript" src="js/jquery-1.4.min.js"></script>
<script type="text/javascript">
$(document).ready(function(){

//Your code goes here.

});
</script>
</head>
<body>
</body>
</html>
```

2. **Locate this line in the code:**

```
<script type="text/javascript" src="js/jquery-1.4.min.js"></script>
```

and below it add this line:

```
<script src="js/jquery.floatobject-1.4.js"></script>
```

Make sure the name of the `.js` file matches the name of the file you saved in your `js` directory in Step 4 of the preceding exercise.

3. **Replace** `// Your code goes here.` **with the following code:**

```
$('#mydiv').makeFloat({x:'current',y:'current'});
```

This code selects the element with the `id` attribute of `mydiv`. The code keeps track of the current location of the selected element, and moves it to the same coordinates on the screen when the Web page is scrolled down.

4. **Place this code after the `<body>` tag:**

```
<div style="float:right;" id="mydiv">I'm floating</div>
```

5. **Add enough content to the page so that it becomes necessary to scroll down to see the bottom of the page.**

For example, you can cut and paste `<br />something<br />` again and again to fill up the page.

6. **Save this file, and then view it in your browser.**

The floating element is in the upper-right corner initially. When you scroll, the floating `<div>` element maintains its location on the screen even when the page is scrolled down (see Figure 13-8).

You can put any HTML element in the floating `<div>` element. You can also put in elements that have attached jQuery code and effects, such as an accordion menu.

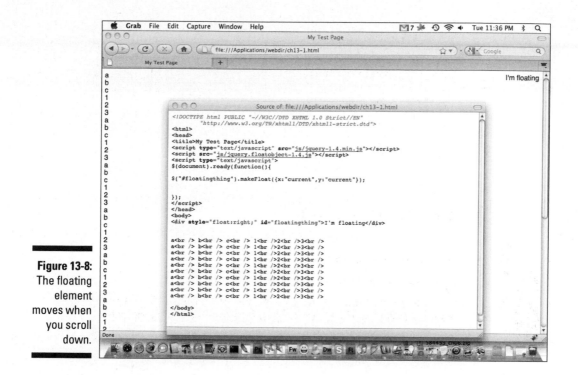

Figure 13-8:
The floating element moves when you scroll down.

Chapter 14

Incorporating a User Interface

. . . .

. . . .

Some jQuery plug-ins and widgets are extremely popular. The jQuery developer community has created a special library of code on top of the jQuery library that contains a collection of user interface widgets, interactions with elements, and special effects. The jQuery User Interface library also allows you to customize the appearance of the included widgets, controlling the colors and fonts.

In this chapter, you find out how to customize the jQuery User Interface library and use it in your pages. You select a predefined set of CSS styles and graphics known as a *theme,* customize it, install it, and then use selected interactions, effects, and widgets on your pages.

Using the jQuery User Interface

The jQuery User Interface (UI) Web site is at `http://jqueryui.com`. On this site, which is shown in Figure 14-1, you can download all the effects, widgets, and themes available through the jQuery UI.

Figure 14-1:
jQuery User
Interface
Web site.

The jQuery UI lets you interact with HTML elements in new ways. The available interactions are

- ✔ **Dragging:** Click an element and hold down the mouse button to drag the element around the page or inside another element on the page.

- ✔ **Dropping:** Drag and drop an element on a target element. The target element can change in response to the dragged element being dropped on it.

- ✔ **Resizing:** Resize an element by clicking and dragging its corners.

- ✔ **Selecting:** Select elements in a group by holding down the mouse button and dragging a selection box around them.

- ✔ **Sorting:** Sort elements in a list by dragging them to new locations in the list.

The jQuery UI also gives you a number of new effects. These are

- ✔ **Effects Core:** Extends internal jQuery effects; includes morphing and easing. These core effects are required by the additional effects in this list.

- ✔ **Blind:** Creates a roller blind animation on an element, causing the element to open or close from the bottom border of the element.

- ✔ **Bounce:** Bounces an element horizontally or vertically a specified number of times.

- ✔ **Clip:** Closes or opens an element from the bottom and top simultaneously.

- ✔ **Drop:** Moves the element in one direction and simultaneously hides it.

- ✔ **Explode:** Breaks the element apart into a specified number of pieces. Can also work in reverse, starting with exploded pieces converging to form the element.

- ✔ **Fold:** Collapses the element horizontally and then vertically.

- ✔ **Highlight:** Highlights the background of the element in a defined color for a custom duration.

- ✔ **Pulsate:** Pulsates the element by fading it in and out a specified number of times.

- ✔ **Scale:** Grows or shrinks the element.

- ✔ **Shake:** Shakes the element horizontally or vertically a specified number of times.

- ✔ **Slide:** Slides the element into or out of view.

- ✔ **Transfer:** Transfers an effect from one element to another.

You can see demonstrations of these effects at `jqueryui.com/demos/effect`.

All these effects are available to you when you download the jQuery UI.

Choosing Custom Download Options

Before you can use the jQuery UI library, you need to choose a theme. The theme controls the appearance of the widgets (for example, a date picker, an accordion menu, or tabs). The theme contains information about the appearance of widgets, including which font to use, what colors to use, and how to style the borders. You end up with a uniform appearance for all widgets used in your page.

Selecting a theme

You can download the jQuery UI library with your choice of theme. You can even customize a theme's colors and fonts. To select a theme, follow these steps:

1. **Click the Themes button at `jqueryui.com` or browse directly to `jqueryui.com/themeroller`.**

2. **In the ThemeRoller section of the page, click the Gallery tab (see Figure 14-2).**

   You see thumbnail images of calendars. Each represents a different theme and demonstrates what the calendar widget looks like in that theme.

3. **Click the UI darkness theme to select it.**

   In Figure 14-3, the sample widgets on the right change appearance to match the selected theme.

Figure 14-2:
The theme gallery with thumbnails.

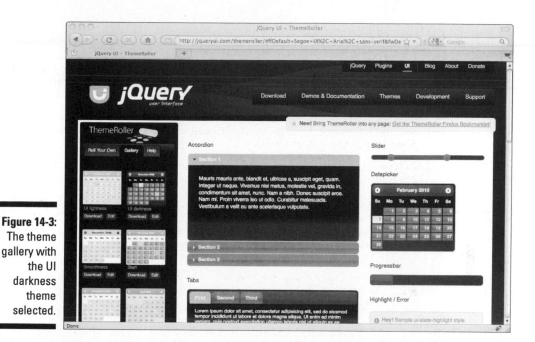

Figure 14-3:
The theme gallery with the UI darkness theme selected.

Customizing a theme

After you select a theme, you can customize many of its features, including colors, fonts, and even the roundness of the corners it uses for widget borders.

You can select and customize a theme in two ways:

- ✔ **Select the simple gray-and-white theme called Smoothness shown on the Themes page. Click the Roll Your Own tab of ThemeRoller.**
- ✔ **From the Gallery tab of ThemeRoller, click the Edit link under the theme you want to customize.**

As you customize a theme, keep an eye on the sample widgets on the right. Each change you make updates the widgets immediately, so you can preview your changes.

The Roll Your Own tab presents an accordion list of options that you can change, as shown in Figure 14-4.

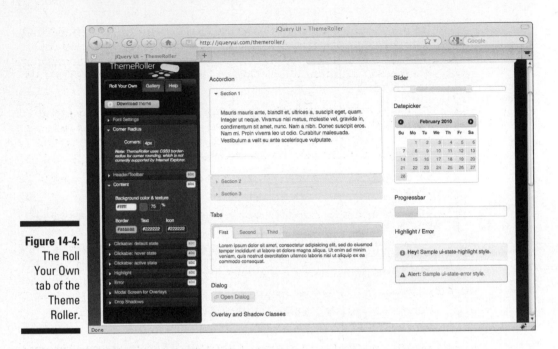

Figure 14-4:
The Roll
Your Own
tab of the
Theme
Roller.

Clicking each horizontal bar opens the set of options below it. Figure 14-4 shows the Corner Radius and Content sections expanded.

Don't be nervous about changing these settings. Playing with the sizes and colors and seeing the changes reflected in the widgets on the right helps you understand what you want for your settings when you download a custom theme.

The sections available for customization on the Roll Your Own tab are as follows:

✔ **Font Settings:** Controls the font face, weight, and size for the widget titles (for example, the titles Section 1, 2, and 3 under the Accordion widget).

✔ **Corner Radius:** Controls the roundness of the corners. The higher the number, the rounder the corners.

Just for fun, try setting this value to 200px. The boxes on the right become almost circular. Setting the value to 0px results in square corners.

✔ **Header/Toolbar:** Controls the appearance of your widget's header and toolbar. Figure 14-5 shows the color wheel that opens when you click the background color setting. The center of the color wheel controls the darkness or lightness of the color, and the wheel controls the hue (the actual color).

You can add a pattern to the header by clicking the small box to the right of the background color. In Figure 14-5, the header is set to a diagonal stripe pattern. You can also control the colors of the border, text, and icons in the Header/Toolbar section.

✔ **Content:** Controls the color, pattern, and font of the content in each widget.

✔ **Clickable: default, hover, and active state:** These states control how the clickable parts of the widget appear when they are selected and before and after a mouse cursor moves over them. For example, a tab is in the active state when it's the current top tab. Otherwise, tabs are in the default state and change to the hover state when moused over.

✔ **Highlight:** Controls the color, pattern, and font of the highlighted section of any widget. For example, the Highlight section controls the appearance of the current date in the calendar.

✔ **Error:** Controls the color, pattern, and font of error messages displayed by a widget.

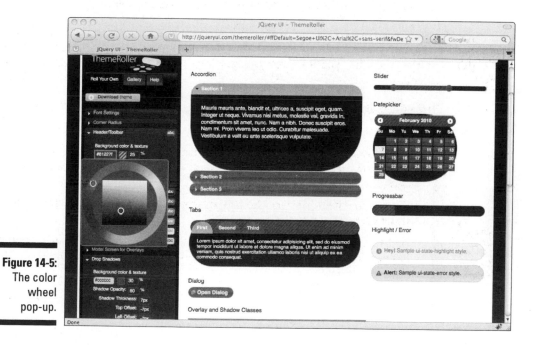

Figure 14-5:
The color wheel pop-up.

✔ **Modal Screen for Overlays:** Controls the color, pattern, and opacity of overlays, which are the translucent screens that cover the current Web page and display content in the center of the page.

✔ **Drop Shadows:** Controls the color, pattern, and opacity of overlays and the direction and thickness of the shadow.

To modify an existing theme, select the theme in the ThemeRoller Gallery tab and click the Edit link below it.

Downloading a theme

When you've selected the theme you want from the Gallery tab or modified a theme with the Roll Your Own tab, you need to download it:

✔ To download a theme from the Gallery with no changes, click the Download link under the theme of your choice.

✔ To download a theme you've customized with the Roll Your Own tab, click the Download Theme button at the top of the tab.

Both download options take you to the same place, the Build Your Download page, which is shown in Figure 14-6.

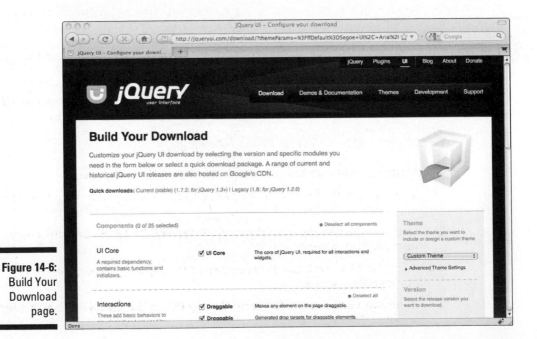

Figure 14-6:
Build Your
Download
page.

Building your download file

The Build Your Download page is where you put everything together. After you select a theme, you choose which widgets, effects, and interactions you want to include in your download file.

You choose or edit the theme first, before going to the Build Your Download page.

To create your download file, follow these steps:

1. **Choose or edit your theme and click the Download link or Download Theme button.**

   (See the preceding section, "Downloading a theme," for more information on selecting and customizing themes.) The Build Your Download page appears (refer to Figure 14-6). By default, the UI Core, Interactions, Widgets, and Effects options are selected.

2. **Select the interactions you want on your site.**

3. **Select the widgets you want on your site.**

4. **Select the effects you want on your site.**

5. **Click the Download button, which is on the right side of the screen.**

   You are prompted to save a .zip file containing your custom jQuery UI files. Save this file to a location you will remember.

You have already chosen your theme at this point, so it is included in the download.

The jQuery UI with your chosen options and theme has now been downloaded. Next, you need to install the contents of the zip file to your Web server.

To install the jQuery UI code, do the following:

1. **Unzip the file you downloaded in the preceding exercise.**

   You see several directories, including `css`, `development-bundle`, and `js`, as shown in Figure 14-7.

2. **Copy the files in the `css` directory of the zip file to the `css` directory on your Web server.**

3. **Copy the files from the `js` directory of the zip file to the `js` directory on your Web server.**

4. **Copy the `index.html` file from the zip file to the base HTML directory on your Web server.**

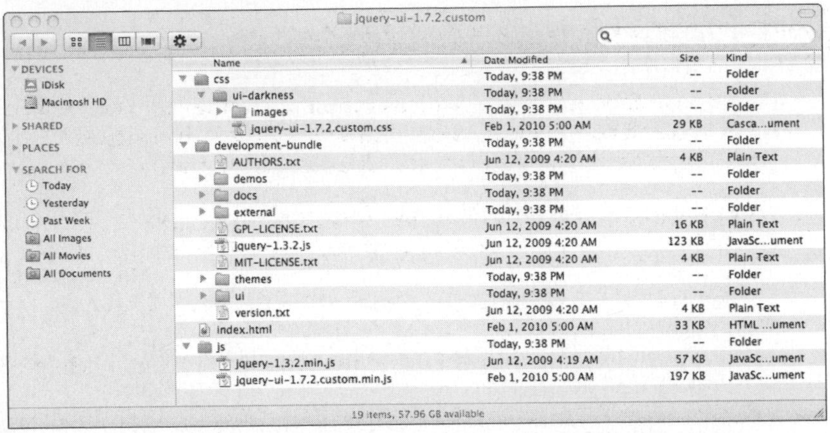

Figure 14-7:
The
unzipped file
containing
the jQuery
UI and a
custom
theme.

If you don't know the location of the `js` and HTML directories, refer to Chapter 1 for more information on the organization of a Web site.

5. **Open the `index.html` file on your Web browser.**

   You see the widgets that you selected using the theme settings you chose, as shown in Figure 14-8.

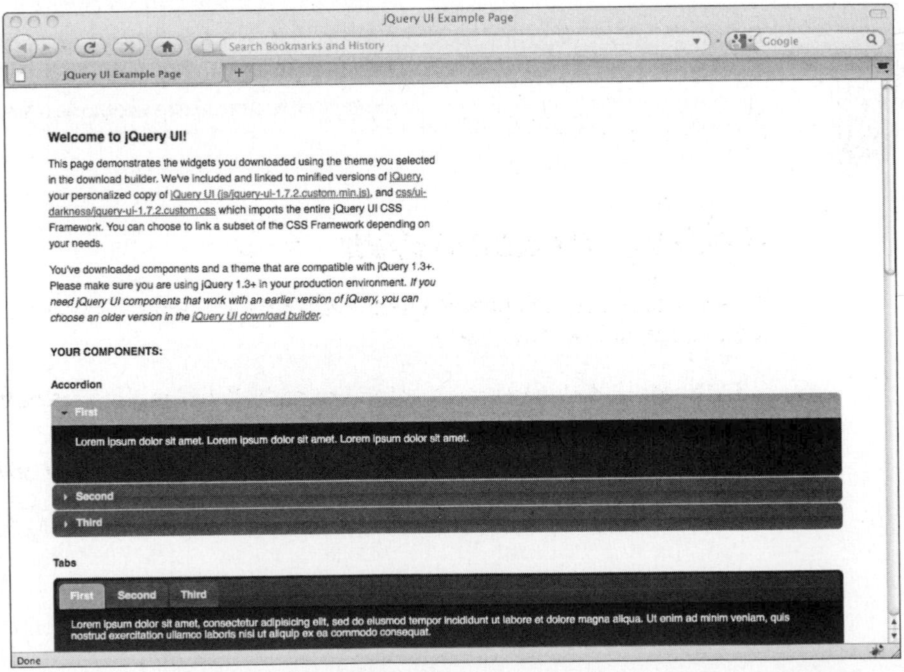

Figure 14-8:
The sample
`index.
html`
displays
widgets
with a cus-
tom theme.

Using jQuery UI Widgets

Your downloaded jQuery UI files contain the code you need to run the widgets you selected. This section shows you how to use several jQuery UI widgets. Type the following code for all examples in this chapter:

```
<!DOCTYPE html PUBLIC "-//W3C//DTD XHTML 1.0 Strict//EN"
                "http://www.w3.org/TR/xhtml1/DTD/xhtml1-strict.dtd">
<html>
<head>
<title>My Test Page</title>
<link type="text/css" href="css/ui-darkness/jquery-ui-1.7.2.custom.css"
                rel="stylesheet" />
<script type="text/javascript" src="js/jquery-1.4.min.js"></script>
<script type="text/javascript" src="js/jquery-ui-1.7.2.custom.min.js"></script>
<script type="text/javascript">
$(document).ready(function(){

//Your code goes here.

});
</script>
</head>
<body>
</body>
</html>
```

The links to the `css` files and `jquery-ui` files, such as `css/ui-darkness/ jquery-ui-1.7.2.custom.css`, have to match the filenames you stored in the `css` and `js` directories.

Adding an accordion

An accordion menu expands when you click a section. To create an accordion menu, follow these steps:

1. **Create a Web page containing the code listed at the beginning of this section.**

2. **Replace `// Your code goes here.` with the following code:**

   ```
   $('#accordion').accordion({ header: 'h3' });
   ```

3. **Add the following code after the <body> tag:**

```
<div id="accordion">
  <div><h3><a href="#">A</a></h3>
    <div>Text about A</div>
  </div>
  <div><h3><a href="#">B</a></h3>
    <div>Text about B.</div>
  </div>
  <div><h3><a href="#">C</a></h3>
    <div>Text about C.</div>
  </div>
</div>
```

4. **Save this file, and then open it in your browser.**

   You see an accordion menu.

Creating a datepicker

A datepicker is a small calendar that pops up so that you can click a specific date, To create a datepicker, follow these steps:

1. **Create a Web page containing the code listed at the beginning of this section.**

2. **Replace // Your code goes here. with the following code:**

```
$('#datepicker').datepicker({
inline: true
});
```

3. **Add the following code after the <body> tag:**

```
<div id="datepicker"></div>
```

4. **Save this file, and then open it in your browser.**

   You see a datepicker with your chosen theme, as shown in Figure 14-9.

Displaying tabs

To create a menu with tabs, follow these steps:

1. **Create a Web page containing the code listed at the beginning of this section.**

2. **Replace // Your code goes here. with the following code:**

```
$('#tabs').tabs();
```

3. **Add the following code after the `<body>` tag:**

```
<div id="tabs">
<ul>
<li><a href="#tab-a">A tab</a></li>
<li><a href="#tab-b">Another tab</a></li>
<li><a href="#tab-c">A third tab</a></li>
</ul><div id="tab-a">This is the first tab</div>
<div id="tab-b">This is the second tab</div>
<div id="tab-c">This is the third tab</div>
</div>
```

4. **Save this file, and then open it in your browser.**

You see tabs with your chosen theme, as shown in Figure 14-10.

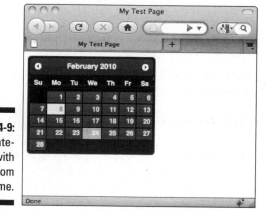

Figure 14-9:
A date-picker with a custom theme.

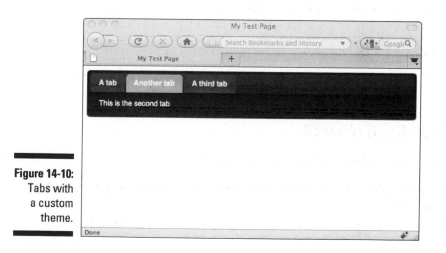

Figure 14-10:
Tabs with a custom theme.

Part V
Building AJAX Applications

The 5th Wave   By Rich Tennant

HORNER BROS.
MAKERS OF PREMIUM
BELLS & WHISTLES

"As a Web site designer I never thought I'd say this, but I don't think your site has enough bells and whistles."

In this part . . .

You may not have heard of AJAX, but you've probably seen it in use. Every time you go to a Web site and the content on the page updates without the page reloading, you can be sure that AJAX is being used. AJAX is a big deal right now, and clever jQuery plug-in developers know it.

The next two chapters offer you a taste of how jQuery and AJAX work together. The subject of AJAX is worthy of a book on its own; Part V is a friendly introduction. When you're finished reading this part, you'll know where to find the best AJAX plug-ins for jQuery.

Chapter 15

Understanding How AJAX Works with jQuery

In This Chapter

▶ Using AJAX functions

▶ Loading content from other Web pages

▶ Sending form data to the Web server

▶ Updating a Web page without reloading it

▶ Triggering code at specific times

*U*ntil fairly recently, when you searched for something on a Web page or filled out a form and clicked the Submit button, a new page loaded. Now with AJAX, you can build pages that let a visitor submit information or search without ever reloading the page. Instead, the results are dynamically displayed on the same Web page as the form. In this chapter, you get an introduction to AJAX.

Understanding AJAX

AJAX stands for asynchronous JavaScript and XML, a scary-sounding mix of technologies, but don't let the buzzwords scare you. Think of AJAX as a programming technique that combines several technologies. And remember, you're in luck because jQuery simplifies AJAX for you.

The basic idea behind AJAX is to allow a Web page to interact with the Web server and to send information to the current page and get information from the current page without the visitor ever leaving the page.

Using jQuery AJAX functions, you get data from and send data to other pages or programs on the Web server without having to create the AJAX code. jQuery does the hard part of getting and sending data dynamically for you.

AJAX on the Web

Here are some examples of where you may have seen AJAX in use on the Web:

✔ In a Yahoo! or Google e-mail account, AJAX sends you new e-mail notifications without leaving the mail page.

✔ When you use Twitter, you automatically get a notification when people you follow have tweeted. Clicking the notification loads these new tweets, again without you leaving the page.

✔ On Facebook, clicking a number of different links and options on the page changes the content on the page without sending you to a different page or reloading the current page.

✔ Yahoo! Maps and Google Maps dynamically update content as you scroll or zoom a map.

An additional benefit that jQuery offers is the ease with which you can make your AJAX communication happen in response to events. Instead of AJAX content showing up only when someone clicks something, you can use a jQuery event to make AJAX content appear to fade in when a visitor mouses over something on the page, for example. You see how to make AJAX interact with events later in this chapter.

Most chapters provide example code that you can save in a text file and view in a browser on your computer. You must test the examples in this chapter on a Web server because they are interacting with other pages or programs on the Web server.

This is a brief introduction to AJAX. Most AJAX applications depend on PHP, SQL, or another Web programming language or technology behind the scenes to manage the information being sent to or received from your Web page. The point of this chapter is to help you understand how data can be sent and received, not the manipulation of it behind the scenes.

Loading Data with AJAX

One of the simplest but most powerful uses of AJAX is grabbing information from Web pages, text files, or XML files and displaying it dynamically on your page.

Getting the contents of a text file

To display the contents of a text file on your Web page, follow these steps:

1. **Create a text file with the following text:**

```
This text is from my text file.
```

2. Save this file as `mytext.txt` on your Web server.

This file must be saved in the same directory on your Web server as the Web page you create in the next few steps.

3. Create a Web page containing the following code:

```
<!DOCTYPE html PUBLIC "-//W3C//DTD XHTML 1.0 Strict//EN"
          "http://www.w3.org/TR/xhtml1/DTD/xhtml1-strict.dtd">
<html>
<head>
<title>My Test Page</title>
<script type="text/javascript" src="js/jquery-1.4.min.js"></script>
<script type="text/javascript">
$(document).ready(function(){

//Your code goes here.

});
</script>
</head>
<body>
<div></div>
</body>
</html>
```

4. Replace `// Your code goes here.` with the following code:

```
$('div').load('mytext.txt');
```

5. Save this file, and then open it in your browser.

The text in the text file appears on your Web page, as shown in Figure 15-1.

Getting the contents of a Web page

You can also use AJAX to pull in the contents of a Web page.

To display the contents of another Web page on your page, do the following:

1. Create a Web page containing the following code:

```
<html>
<body>
<strong>This is from my Web page.</strong>
</body>
</html>
```

2. Save this file as `mywebpage.html` on your Web server.

As with the preceding example, this file must be saved in the same directory on your Web server as the Web page you create in the next few steps.

3. Create a Web page containing the following code:

```
<!DOCTYPE html PUBLIC "-//W3C//DTD XHTML 1.0 Strict//EN"
          "http://www.w3.org/TR/xhtml1/DTD/xhtml1-strict.dtd">
<html>
<head>
<title>My Test Page</title>
<script type="text/javascript" src="js/jquery-1.4.min.js"></script>
<script type="text/javascript">
$(document).ready(function(){

//Your code goes here.

});
</script>
</head>
<body>
<div></div>
</body>
</html>
```

4. **Replace // Your code goes here. with the following code:**

```
$('div').load('mywebpage.html');
```

5. **Save this file, and then open it in your browser.**

   The contents of the Web page file appears in the <div> element, as shown in Figure 15-2.

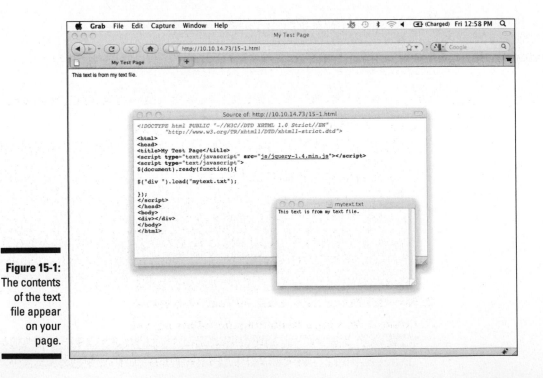

Figure 15-1:
The contents of the text file appear on your page.

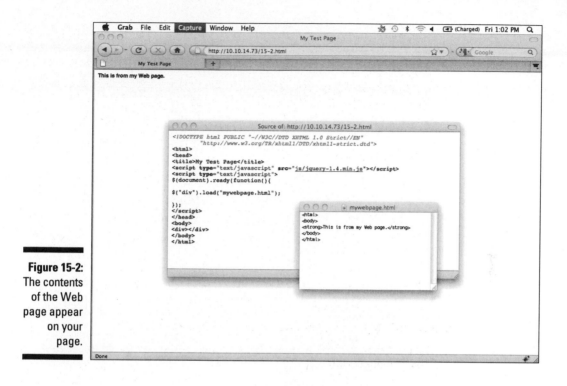

Figure 15-2:
The contents
of the Web
page appear
on your
page.

Getting part of a Web page

The preceding example grabbed all the contents of a Web page. The load()
function allows you to grab a selection instead.

To display selected content from a Web page on your page, do the following:

1. **Create a Web page containing the following code:**

```
<html>
<body>
<div id="monday">Content for Monday.</div>
<div id="tuesday">Content for Monday.</div>
<div id="wednesday">Content for Monday.</div>
<div id="thursday">Content for Monday.</div>
<div id="friday">Content for Monday.</div>
<div id="saturday">Content for Monday.</div>
<div id="sunday">Content for Monday.</div>
</body>
</html>
```

2. **Save this file as days.html on your Web server.**

3. **Create a Web page containing the following code:**

```
<!DOCTYPE html PUBLIC "-//W3C//DTD XHTML 1.0 Strict//EN"
        "http://www.w3.org/TR/xhtml1/DTD/xhtml1-strict.dtd">
```

```
<html>
<head>
<title>My Test Page</title>
<script type="text/javascript" src="js/jquery-1.4.min.js"></script>
<script type="text/javascript">
$(document).ready(function(){

//Your code goes here.

});
</script>
</head>
<body>
<div></div>
</body>
</html>
```

4. **Replace // Your code goes here. with the following code:**

```
$('div').load('days.html' #friday);
```

Only the content in days.html with the id friday is selected and displayed in the <div> element on your page.

5. **Save this file, and then open it in your browser.**

The selected content in the Web page file appears in the <div> element,
as shown in Figure 15-3.

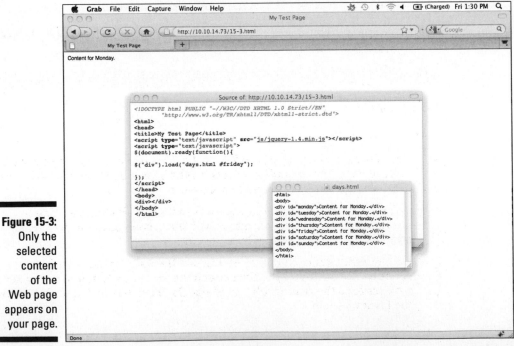

Figure 15-3:
Only the
selected
content
of the
Web page
appears on
your page.

Sending Data with AJAX

Traditional Web forms work as follows:

1. A visitor fills out the form fields.

2. The visitor clicks the Submit button.

3. The browser sends the data from the form fields to a file on the Web server that contains code, such as PHP.

4. This code does something with the information, such as e-mailing it or saving it to a database.

5. The code sends a new Web page to the visitor's browser.

With AJAX, the process changes to the following:

1. A visitor fills out the form fields.

2. The visitor clicks the Submit button.

3. AJAX techniques send the data from the form fields to a file on the Web server that contains code.

4. This code does something with the information, such as e-mailing it or saving it to a database.

5. The AJAX code receives a response from the processing code and updates the current Web page without reloading it.

You can use the jQuery `post()` function to send and receive data. A simple `post()` function looks like this:

```
$.post( url, data, success())
```

Here are the parts of the `post()` function:

- ✔ `$.post`: Begin the function.

- ✔ `url`: Contains the path to the file on the Web server to which you want to send data. For example, the path might be to a PHP file that will e-mail form data to you when a visitor submits it.

- ✔ `data`: Contains the data you want to send to the Web server. The information a visitor enters into a Web form, such as name and e-mail address, can be part of the data element.

- ✔ `success`: Contains code that executes if the data was sent to the `url` successfully. For example, the code in the `success()` function can send a message to the person who filled out the form, letting him or her know the form was sent.

Using other AJAX functions

In this chapter, you find out how to send data from a form to a PHP file on a Web server for further processing. Other jQuery AJAX functions let you execute code before sending data, after receiving data, when something goes wrong with the data transfer, or when the data is successfully sent or received.

AJAX involves the processing of data with Web server languages (such as PHP, .NET, and SQL) and technologies. For more information and examples of their use, visit `api.jquery.com/category/ajax`.

Here's an overview of some of jQuery AJAX functions:

✔ **ajax()**: Performs an AJAX request. This function can send and receive data from the Web server using either GET or POST.

✔ **ajaxComplete()**: Contains code to be executed when an AJAX request is completed.

✔ **ajaxError()**: Contains code to be executed if an AJAX request causes an error.

✔ **ajaxSend()**: Contains code to be executed before an AJAX request is sent.

✔ **ajaxStart()**: Contains code to be executed when an AJAX request begins.

✔ **ajaxStop()**: Contains code to be executed after all AJAX requests have stopped.

✔ **ajaxSuccess()**: Contains code to be executed when an AJAX request completes successfully.

✔ **get()**: Performs an AJAX request. This function can send and receive data from the Web server using GET.

✔ **getScript()**: Loads a JavaScript file from the Web server.

✔ **load()**: Loads data from the Web. For example, load data from a text file or HTML file. As in the first example in this chapter, the loaded data can be displayed inside an element on the current page.

✔ **post()**: Performs an AJAX request. This function can send and receive data from the Web server using POST.

✔ **serialize()**: Grabs the values from a Web form and turn them into a single string of data to send using get(), post(), or ajax() function.

Do the following to create a basic Web form that uses AJAX to send code to a PHP script:

1. **Create a Web page containing the following code:**

   You must have a Web server that can process PHP code for these steps to work.

```
<!DOCTYPE html PUBLIC "-//W3C//DTD XHTML 1.0 Strict//EN"
          "http://www.w3.org/TR/xhtml1/DTD/xhtml1-strict.dtd">
<html>
<head>
<title>My Test Page</title>
<script type="text/javascript" src="js/jquery-1.4.min.js"></script>
<script type="text/javascript">
```

```
$(document).ready(function(){

//Your code goes here.

});
</script>
</head>
<body>
<form id="testform">
Email: <input type="text" name="email" />
<br />
First Name: <input type="text" name="fname" />
<br />
Last Name: <input type="text" name="lname" />
<br />
<input type="button" name="submit" id="submit" value="Submit" />
</form>
</body></html>
```

2. **Save this file to your Web server.**

   This code creates a simple Web form that asks for an e-mail address, first name, and last name (see Figure 15-4).

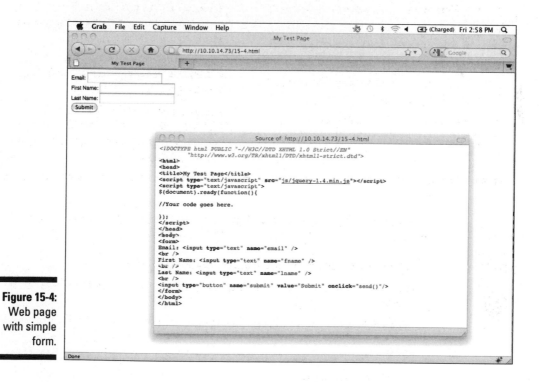

Figure 15-4:
Web page
with simple
form.

3. Replace `// Your code goes here.` **with the following code:**

```
$("#testform").submit(function(){
//Code after form submitted
})
```

This code is triggered when the visitor clicks the Submit button on the form. The AJAX code will go inside this function.

4. Replace `// Code after form submitted` **with the following code:**

```
$.post( "test.php",
$("#testform").serialize(),
function(data){
        alert(data);
});
return false;
```

The `$.post` jQuery function uses the POST method to send data to a PHP file.

You can use the jQuery `get()` function in the same way as `post()`. POST and GET are two techniques for sending form data to Web servers To learn more about Web programming, GET, POST, and Web server processing of data sent by a form, check out *HTML, XHTML, & CSS For Dummies* by Ed Tittel and Jeff Noble.

The `serialize()` function is a handy jQuery function that puts all the values of a submitted form in an query string.

Finally, the `alert(data)` command displays the data submitted in the form in a pop-up box. Seeing your data in a pop-up alert box is good for testing but unnecessary and annoying when you are using PHP code to process the form data.

5. Create the `test.php` **file with the following code:**

```
<?php
print_r($_POST);
?>
```

This PHP code displays the information sent by the jQuery `post()` function. If you weren't using AJAX, the data from the form would print on a blank page. But instead, the AJAX function displays the data in an alert box on the current page.

6. Open the Web page in your browser. Enter data in the form fields and click the Submit button.

You see an alert box containing the form data that was sent to the PHP file, as shown in Figure 15-5.

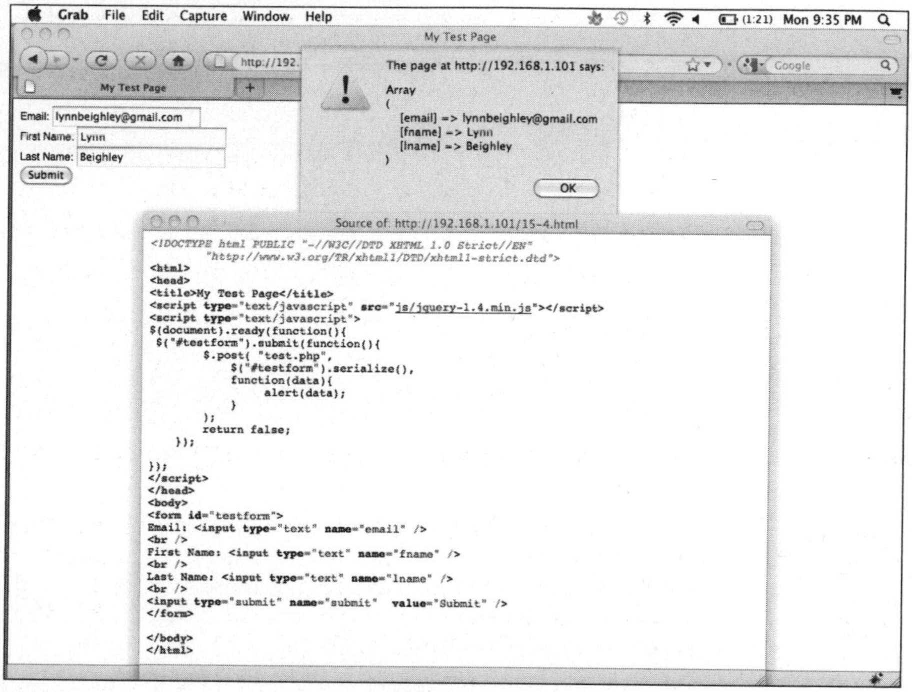

Figure 15-5:
Web page
with form
data
submitted to
a PHP form
with AJAX.

You can extend the code from the this example in a number of ways. You can
use an alert to display a success message when the form is submitted. Or display a success message after the form is submitted by using a `<div>` element
on the Web page. You can also hide the form after it has been submitted
using jQuery hide methods.

Chapter 16

Using AJAX Plug-ins

Chapter 15 introduces you to jQuery AJAX functions. You find out how to load content from other Web pages and send and receive data from code files or scripts on your Web server. The AJAX functions allow you to execute code before and after AJAX requests, as well as when requests succeed or fail. But as with all jQuery functions, each AJAX function does a relatively small role. To build a robust AJAX Web application requires a great deal of coding.

As with jQuery plug-ins discussed previously in this book, the work of building robust AJAX-based applications already exists in the form of jQuery AJAX plug-ins, free extensions to the jQuery library that create AJAX effects with a minimal amount of effort on your part to install and use them.

This chapter introduces you to several jQuery plug-ins that use AJAX techniques, tells you where to get them, and shows you how to use them.

How AJAX jQuery Plug-ins Work

As with all jQuery plug-ins, AJAX plug-ins work in much the same way as jQuery. When you find a plug-in you want to use, you download a .js file and save it to a directory on your Web server. In your Web page, you include the path to that file. (For an overview of how jQuery plug-ins work, see Chapter 10.)

Unlike other jQuery plug-ins, however, AJAX plug-ins often need other code files on the Web server. AJAX exists to allow the transfer of data from and to a Web server without the current page reloading, and the code that receives the data and returns data back to the current page usually exists in additional files on the Web server.

Most chapters provide example code that you can save in a text file and view in a browser on your computer. The examples in this chapter must be tested on a Web server because they are interacting with other pages or programs on the Web server.

Using AJAX File Uploader

A common practice is to allow visitors to a Web page to upload a file to the Web server. With AJAX, the upload occurs without the Web page reloading. Instead, a success or failure message is displayed. Even nicer, most jQuery file uploaders include a progress bar so the user can see the progress of the upload.

A number of excellent jQuery AJAX file uploaders are available. A simple one to install is called AJAX Upload; its home page is located at `http://valums.com/ajax-upload` (see Figure 16-1).

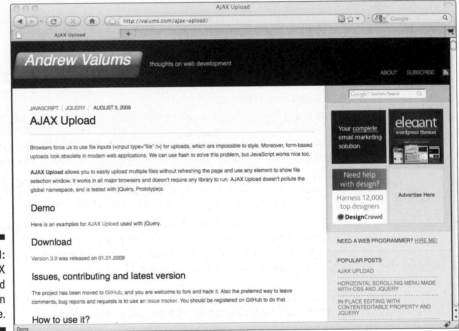

Figure 16-1:
AJAX
Upload
plug-in
home page.

To install and use AJAX Upload, do the following:

1. **Create a Web page containing the following code:**

```
<!DOCTYPE html PUBLIC "-//W3C//DTD XHTML 1.0 Strict//EN"
        "http://www.w3.org/TR/xhtml1/DTD/xhtml1-strict.dtd">
<html>
```

```
<head>
<title>My Test Page</title>
<script type="text/javascript" src="js/jquery-1.4.min.js"></script>
<script type="text/javascript">
$(document).ready(function(){

//Your code goes here.



});
</script>
</head>
<body>
<input type="button" id="upload_button" value="Upload">
</body>
</html>
```

This code creates a page with a button.

2. **Browse to `valums.com/ajax-upload` and download the most recent version of the plug-in.**

3. **Unzip this plug-in and save the `ajaxupload.js` file in the `js` directory on your Web server.**

4. **Locate this line in the code:**

```
<script type="text/javascript" src="js/jquery-1.4.min.js"></script>
```

and below it add this line:

```
<script type="text/javascript" src="js/ajaxupload.js"></script>
```

The filename for the plug-in in your code must match the plug-in you downloaded and saved to the `js` directory on your Web server.

5. **Replace `// Your code goes here.` with the following code:**

```
new AjaxUpload('#upload_button', {action: 'upload.php'});
```

The `AjaxUpload()` function is part of the AJAX Upload plug-in. This line of code tells the plug-in to tie the element with the id of `upload_button` to the plug-in. When the visitor clicks the button, a file browse dialog box appears, as shown in Figure 16-2.

After the user selects a file to upload, the file information is sent to the PHP `upload.php` script, which handles the actual upload.

The `upload.php` script is just a placeholder for any code you want to use to handle the file upload itself.

The download file for the AJAX Upload plug-in includes not only a number of samples but also PHP code that you can use in your application. This file, called `upload-handler.php`, is in the `server-side` directory.

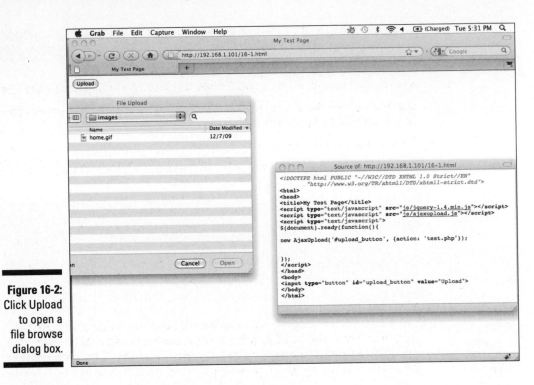

Figure 16-2:
Click Upload
to open a
file browse
dialog box.

Rotating Dynamic Content

The Rich HTML Ticker plug-in displays content that changes every few minutes. Think of the plug-in as a rotating billboard. The plug-in pulls chunks of content into your Web page from an HTML page on your Web server, as shown in Figure 16-3.

To install and use the Rich HTML Ticker plug-in, do the following:

1. **Create a Web page containing the following code:**

```
<!DOCTYPE html PUBLIC "-//W3C//DTD XHTML 1.0 Strict//EN"
        "http://www.w3.org/TR/xhtml1/DTD/xhtml1-strict.dtd">
<html>
<head>
<title>My Test Page</title>
<script type="text/javascript" src="js/jquery-1.4.min.js"></script>
<script type="text/javascript">
$(document).ready(function(){
});
</script>
</head>
<body>
<div id="myhtmlticker" class="tickerstyle">
</div>
```

```
</body>
</html>
```

2. **Browse to www.javascriptkit.com/script/script2/ richhtmlticker.shtml and locate the link to richhtmlticker.js.**

3. **Right-click the link and select Save As. Then save richhtmlticker.js in the js directory on your Web server.**

4. **Locate this line in the code:**

```
<script type="text/javascript" src="js/jquery-1.4.min.js"></script>
```

and below it add these lines:

```
<script type="text/javascript" src="js/richhtmlticker.js">
/***************************************************
* Rich HTML Ticker- by JavaScript Kit (www.javascriptkit.com)
* This notice must stay intact for usage
* Visit JavaScript Kit at http://www.javascriptkit.com/ for full source
        code
***************************************************/
</script>
```

The author of this plug-in requests that you include credit if you use the plug-in on your own site by adding the preceding comments to your code. Add the comments before the closing </script> tag. The comments are visible only when someone views the source code of your page.

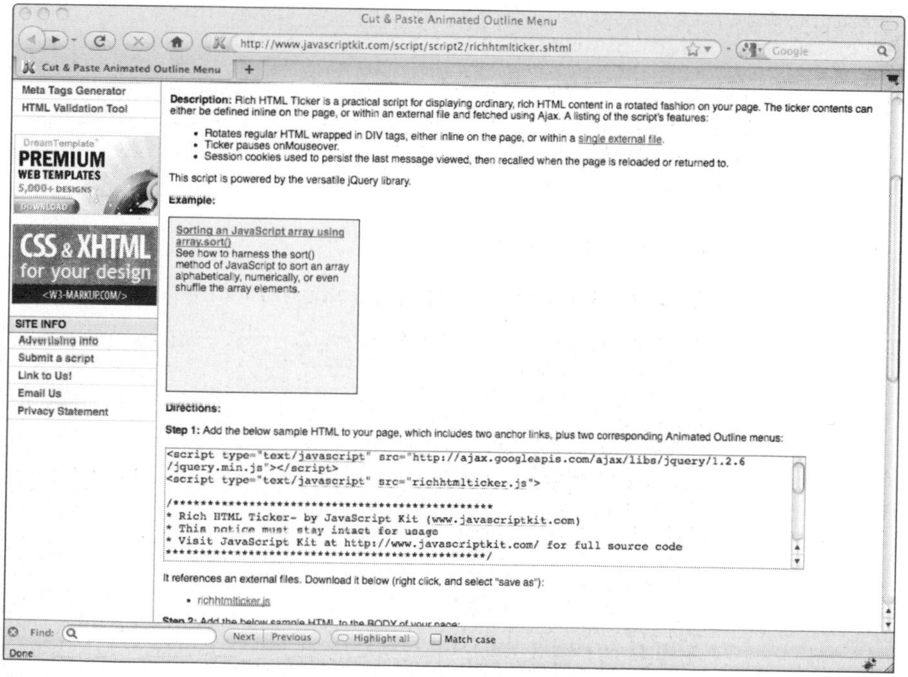

Figure 16-3:
The Rich HTML Ticker plug-in changes the content after a specified interval.

![Screenshot of the Rich HTML Ticker page at javascriptkit.com showing the Cut & Paste Animated Outline Menu browser window with description, example, and directions for the ticker script.]

5. **In your text editor, open the file you saved in Step 3.**

6. **Scroll down to the last function in this file, `richhtmlticker.`**
   `define()`, shown next:

```
richhtmlticker.define({
id: "myhtmlticker", //main ticker DIV id
msgclass: "messagediv", //CSS class of DIVs containing each ticker message
msgsource: "inline", //Where to look for the messages: "inline", or "path_
            to_file_on_your_server"
rotatespeed: 3000, //pause in milliseconds between rotation
animateduration: 1000 //duration of fade animation in milliseconds
})
```

7. **Change the code**

```
msgsource: "inline",
```

   to read

```
msgsource: "mycontent.html",
```

   The `mycontent.html` file will contain the dynamic content that you
   want to display.

8. **Save the `richhtmlticker.js` file.**

9. **Create a Web page containing the following code:**

```
<!DOCTYPE html PUBLIC "-//W3C//DTD XHTML 1.0 Strict//EN"
            "http://www.w3.org/TR/xhtml1/DTD/xhtml1-strict.dtd">
<html>
<body>
<div class="messagediv">
First content
</div>
<div class="messagediv">
Second content
</div>
<div class="messagediv">
Third content
</div>
</body>
</html>
```

10. **Save this file as `mycontent.html`.**

    This file contains all the content. Each `<div>` element will be displayed
    in turn on the page you created in Step 1.

    You can use any HTML code you want within the `<div>` elements in the
    `mycontent.html` file. You can also add as many `<div>` blocks as you
    want.

11. **Open in a browser the file you created in Step 1.**

    Each `<div>` element in `mycontent.html` is displayed, one at a time, as
    shown in Figure 16-4.

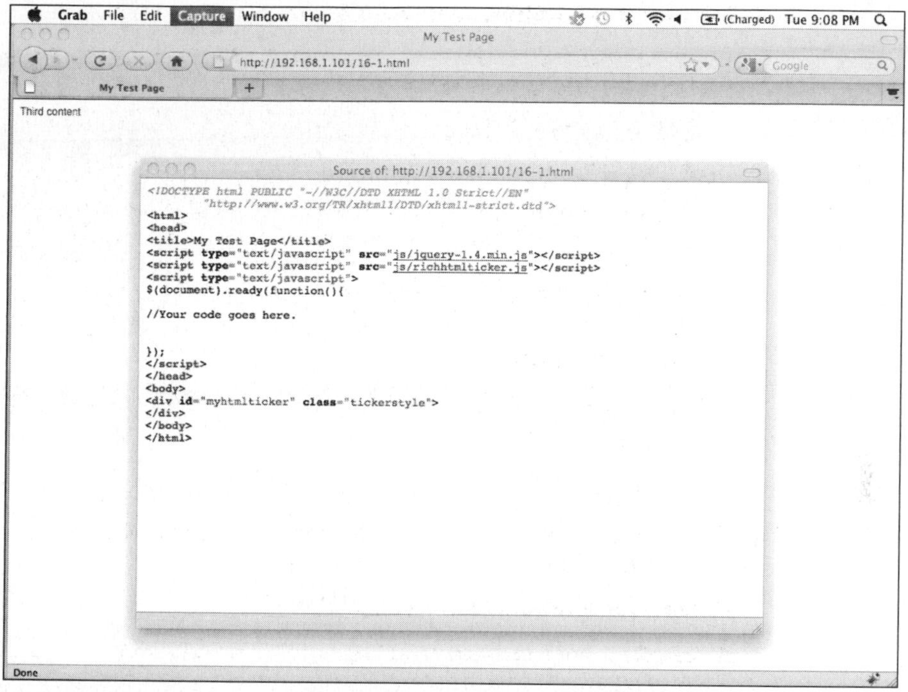

Figure 16-4:
The Rich
HTML
Ticker
plug-in
displays
content
from `my`
`content.`
`html.`

Take another look at the code from `richhtmlticker.js` in Step 6:

```
richhtmlticker.define({
id: "myhtmlticker", //main ticker DIV id
msgclass: "messagediv", //CSS class of DIVs containing each ticker message
msgsource: "inline", //Where to look for the messages: "inline", or "path_to_
                file_on_your_server"
rotatespeed: 3000, //pause in milliseconds between rotation
animateduration: 1000 //duration of fade animation in milliseconds
})
```

You have three options you may want to modify:

✔ **msgsource:** Control where the content comes from. You can put the `<div>` code in a separate file, as you did in the preceding steps, or in the main file.

✔ **rotatespeed:** Control how long each `<div>` element containing content is visible.

✔ **animateduration:** Control the speed of the animation.

You can also use CSS style to control the appearance of the scrolling content. The demo at www.javascriptkit.com/script/script2/richhmlticker. shtml uses the following code to create a yellow box with a border that encloses the dynamic content, as shown in Figure 16-5.

```
<style type="text/css">
.tickerstyle{width:200px; height:180px; border:1px solid black;
             background:lightyellow; padding:8px; overflow:hidden;}
.messagediv{display: none;background:lightyellow}
</style>
```

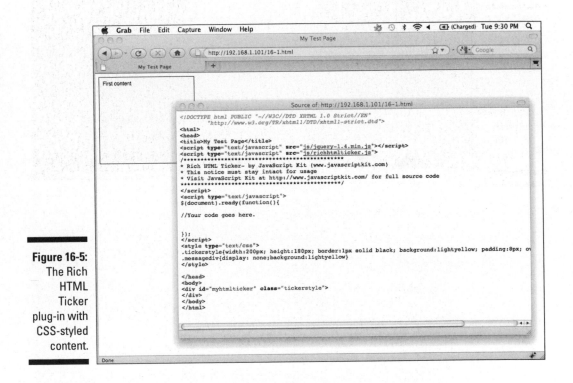

Figure 16-5:
The Rich HTML Ticker plug-in with CSS-styled content.

Creating AJAX Pop-Up Windows

In Chapter 15, you use the jQuery load function to load part or all of another Web page into the current page. The jmpopups plug-in allows you to load another Web page as a lightbox-style pop-up window over the current page. You can load multiple pop-ups at the same time (see Figure 16-6).

To create a page with an AJAX pop-up window using the jmpopups plug-in, do the following:

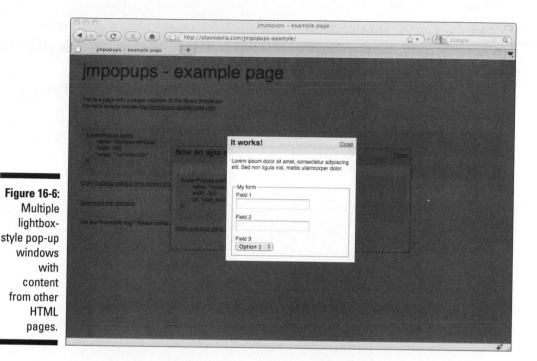

Figure 16-6:
Multiple
lightbox-
style pop-up
windows
with
content
from other
HTML
pages.

1. Create a Web page containing the following code:

```
<!DOCTYPE html PUBLIC "-//W3C//DTD XHTML 1.0 Strict//EN"
           "http://www.w3.org/TR/xhtml1/DTD/xhtml1-strict.dtd">
<html>
<head>
<title>My Test Page</title>
<script type="text/javascript" src="js/jquery-1.4.min.js"></script>
<script type="text/javascript">

//Your code goes here.

</script>
</head>
<body>
<a href="javascript:;" onclick="ajaxPopup()">Open popup</a>

</body>
</html>
```

This code creates a page with a link that will open the AJAX pop-up
window.

2. Browse to `code.google.com/p/jmpopups` and download the most
recent version of the plug-in.

3. Unzip the plug-in and save the `jquery.jmpopups-0.5.1.js` file in
the `js` directory on your Web server.

Your version of this file may differ. Keep track of the actual filename and use it in the following step.

4. **Locate this line in the code:**

```
<script type="text/javascript" src="js/jquery-1.4.min.js"></script>
```

and below it add this line:

```
<script type="text/javascript" src="js/jquery.jmpopups-0.5.1.js"></script>
```

The plug-in filename in your code must match the plug-in you down-loaded and saved to the js directory on your Web server.

5. **Replace // Your code goes here. with the following code:**

```
$.setupJMPopups({
screenLockerBackground: "#000000",
screenLockerOpacity: "0.5"
});

function ajaxPopup() {
$.openPopupLayer({
name: "myPopup",
width: 300,
url: "mypopup.html"
});
}
```

The setupJMPopups() function contains two options that control the appearance of the screen when the pop-up opens. The ajaxPopup() function specifies how wide to make the pop-up and where to find the content. In this example, the content comes from the mypopup.html page we create and save in the next step.

6. **Create a Web page named mypopup.html and use a text editor to add the content that you want to appear in the pop-up window. Save the page to your Web server.**

7. **Open the page you created in Step 1, and then click the Open pop-up link.**

A pop-up window appears containing the content from mypopup.html.

Figure 16-7:
Content
from a
second
HTML page
appears in
a pop-up
window.

Part VI

Integrating jQuery with Content Management Systems

The 5th Wave   By Rich Tennant

"Evidently he died of natural causes following a marathon session animating everything on his personal Web site. And no, Morganstern — the irony isn't lost on me."

In this part . . .

Creating HTML pages on your own can be tedious. As an alternative, many people turn to Content Management Systems to help them build and manage robust Web sites quickly and easily. You've probably heard of at least one of the three most popular Content Management Systems: Drupal, Joomla, and WordPress. And better yet, they're free.

All three software applications can use the jQuery library and even some jQuery plug-ins. In the next three chapters, you find how to use jQuery with each one and where to find compatible jQuery plug-ins for each.

Chapter 17

Cool Image Effects with jQuery and Drupal

In This Chapter
▶ Finding jQuery Drupal modules
▶ Including jQuery effects in Drupal posts
▶ Using the Thickbox jQuery plug-in with Drupal
▶ Installing and enabling jQuery modules in Drupal

Drupal is a popular, free software application that you use to build and manage a Web site and the content you post to it. Drupal also allows you to use modules, or add-ons, that extend the functionality of your Web site. Some of these modules incorporate jQuery plug-ins.

This chapter shows you how to find and use several jQuery-based Drupal modules devoted to fancy image effects.

This chapter does not provide you with information about setting up a Drupal Web site. Instead, the focus is on adding jQuery-based Drupal modules to your existing Drupal site. To get a Drupal site up and running, check out my *Drupal For Dummies*.

Investigating Drupal Modules

Before you can use a jQuery-based Drupal module, you have to find, download, and install it. This section shows you how.

Finding Drupal modules

When looking for new Drupal modules, the best place to go is `http://drupal.org`. To find modules that use jQuery, follow these steps:

1. **Browse to `drupal.org`, which is shown in Figure 17-1.**

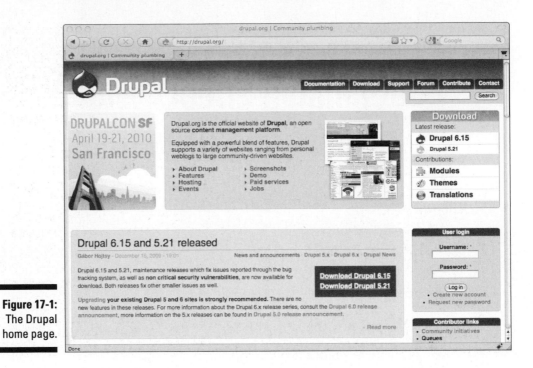

Figure 17-1:
The Drupal
home page.

2. **Click the Modules link, on the right side of the page.**

3. **In the Search Modules section on the right, type** jQuery **in the search box and then click Submit.**

   The screen displays a list of jQuery-based Drupal modules, as shown in Figure 17-2.

You can view the most popular modules by clicking the Usage Statistics link in the Sort by menu on the right side of the page. Click the link once to display the list in the most-popular-first order. Click the link again to reverse the order.

Downloading Drupal modules

Before you can use jQuery-based Drupal modules with images, you need images on your Drupal site. The easiest way to include images on a Drupal site is to use the Image module. The Image module isn't part of the default Drupal installation. Several jQuery Drupal modules require the Image module to function, so you need to download and install it on your Drupal Web site. The Drupal module needs to be downloaded to your computer, uploaded to your Web server, extracted, enabled, and configured.

To download the Image module, follow these steps:

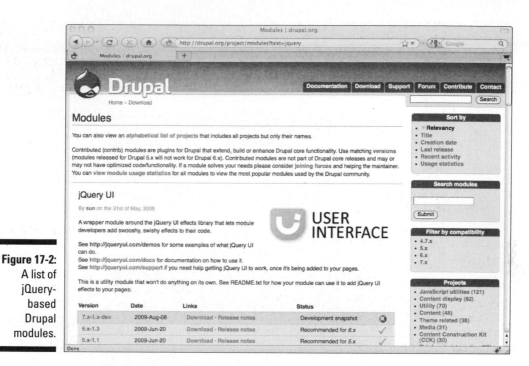

Figure 17-2:
A list of
jQuery-
based
Drupal
modules.

1. **Browse to `drupal.org/project/image`.**

2. **Scroll down the page to find the download links, shown in Figure 17-3.**

3. **Click the link to download the Image module, and save it to a directory you will remember.**

   The module is downloaded as a single compressed `.tar.gz` file.

   As of this writing, the most current version of the Image module for Drupal 6 is 6.x-1.0-beta5. Feel free to download the more recent version of the Image module.

4. **Log in to the control panel on your ISP's Web site.**

   The control panel is a Web page that lists various Web applications that allow you to control your Web site.

   If you're comfortable using FTP software, you can connect directly to your Web server with the FTP login and password provided by your ISP. If you go this route, extract the module on your local computer and use your FTP application to upload the extracted `Images` directory to the Web server's `module` directory under your Drupal installation.

5. **Click the link to a file manager, such as File Manager or File Manager Pro.**

   You need a file manager so that you can select the `.tar.gz` file and put it in the `module` directory on your Web server. After you click the file manager, you will see a screen that displays the files on your Web server.

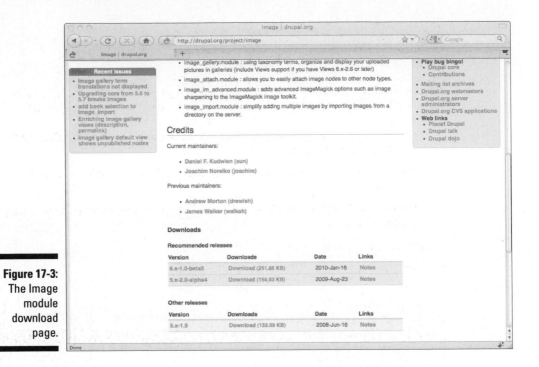

Figure 17-3:
The Image
module
download
page.

6. **Click the single folder or directory named `html`, `www`, or `htdocs`.**

   There may be several directories, but the one for your Web site should be easy to spot. Look for the directory containing several subdirectories including `modules`, `scripts`, `sites`, and `themes`. This area is where all your Web pages belong, and where you installed Drupal.

7. **Click the `modules` directory.**

8. **Click the Upload link in your file manager.**

   You see an upload form with a Browse button.

9. **Click Browse and select the `.tar.gz` file you downloaded in Step 3. Click Upload.**

   The compressed file containing the module is now on your site in the correct folder and ready to be extracted.

10. **Click the `.tar.gz` module to select the file.**

    You see a list of files stored inside your compressed file, all selected.

11. **Leave the selection set to Uncompress All, and then click the Go button.**

12. **Select the original `.tar.gz` module file on your Web server and delete it.**

Enabling the Image and Image Gallery modules

After you have uploaded and extracted the Image module, it will show up in Drupal's list of modules. To enable the Image module, follow these steps:

1. **Log in to your Drupal site as administrator, and choose Administer⇨ Site Building⇨Modules.**

   The Image module is made up of several modules, as you can see in Figure 17-4.

2. **Select the Enabled check box next to the Image module and the Image Gallery module.**

3. **Click Save configuration.**

   The new modules are activated.

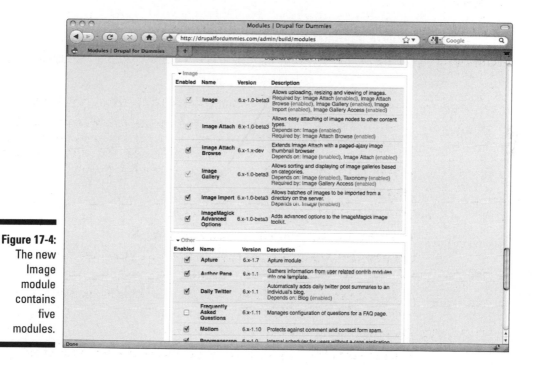

Figure 17-4: The new Image module contains five modules.

Before you can create image effects with jQuery, you need to create a Drupal image gallery and upload images to your Drupal site. To accomplish these task, follow these steps:

1. **Log in to your Drupal site as administrator, and choose Administer⇨ Content Management⇨Image Galleries.**

2. **Click the Add Gallery tab.**

   The Add Gallery form appears, as shown in Figure 17-5.

3. **For Gallery Name, enter a short, descriptive title.**

4. **For Description, enter a few sentences that describe the images you will be storing in the gallery.**

5. **Click Save.**

The Image Gallery module allows you to create as many galleries as you want. Simply repeat the preceding steps to add additional galleries.

Adding images to your gallery

Now that you've created your galleries, you can add images to them. To add an image to your new gallery, do the following:

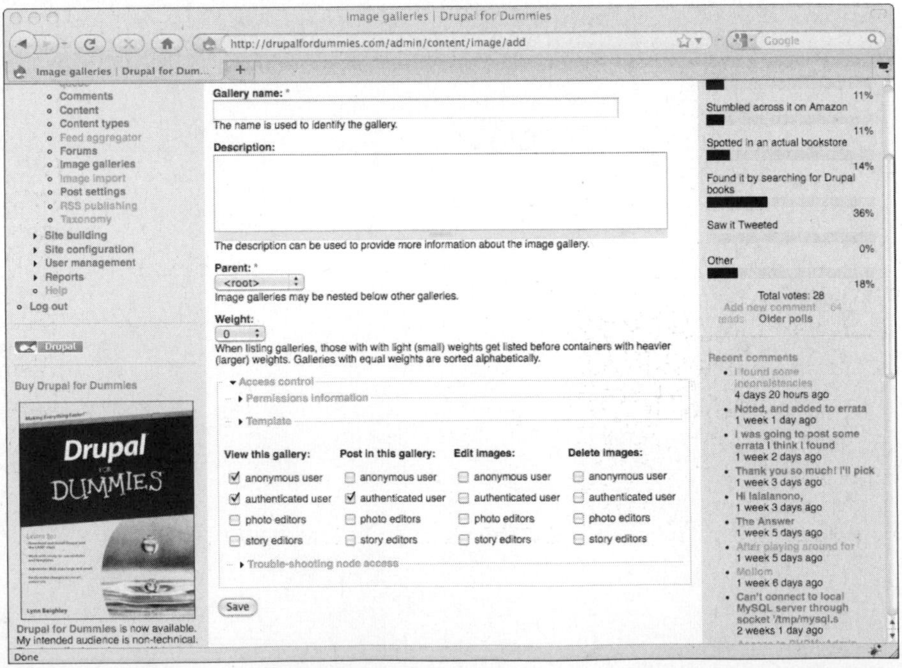

Figure 17-5:
Add gallery
form to
create a
new image
gallery.

1. **Log in to your Drupal site as administrator, and choose Create Content⇨Image.**

   The Create Image form appears, as shown in Figure 17-6.

2. **Enter a title for your image in the Title field.**

3. **Select one of the galleries you created in the preceding example from the Image Galleries drop-down list.**

4. **Click the Image text box or the Browse button and select the file you want to upload.**

5. **If you want to add more information about this image, type it in the Body field.**

6. **Click Save.**

   Your image is placed in your image gallery. You can add more images to this gallery, or other galleries you've created, by repeating these steps.

To view your new image gallery, browse to your Drupal site, *yourwebsite name*.com/image. For example, mine is located at drupalfordummies.com/ image.

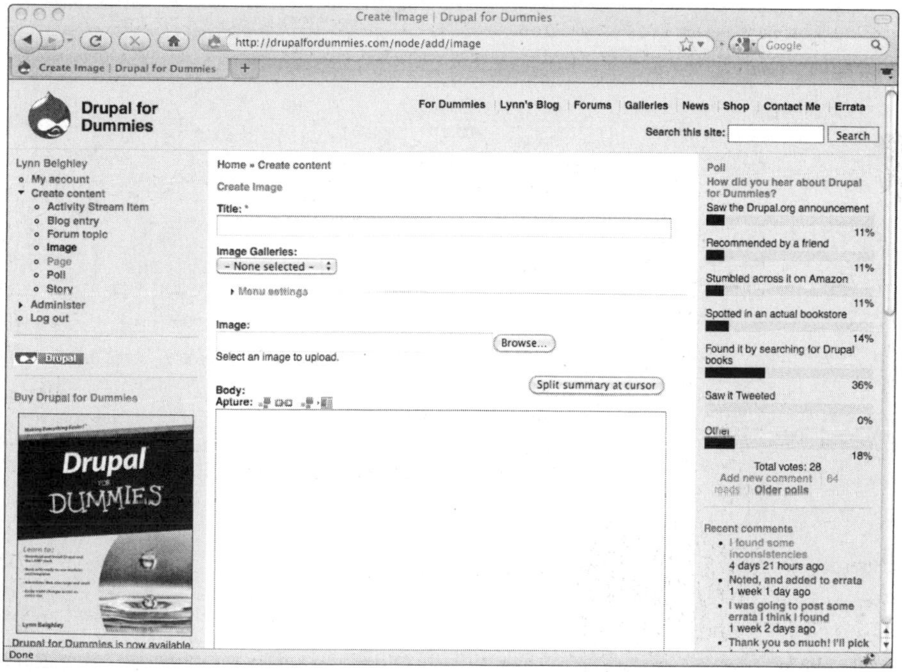

Figure 17-6:
Add an
image to
your
gallery with
the Create
Image form.

Creating Image Effects in Drupal

With the Image and Image Gallery modules now in place, you can add additional jQuery-based image modules so you can add jQuery effects to your images. A simple but impressive jQuery module to start with is Thickbox, which you can see at jquery.com/demo/thickbox. Thickbox is an easy-to-use, jQuery-based lightbox, as shown in Figure 17-7.

This section shows you where to get Thickbox and how to install and use it with your Drupal images.

Getting the Thickbox jQuery module for Drupal

The Thickbox module is available on the drupal.org Web site. To download this file, do the following:

1. **Browse to drupal.org/project/thickbox.**

2. **Follow Steps 2–12 in the "Downloading Drupal modules" section, previously in this chapter.**

Enabling Thickbox

1. **Log in to your Drupal site as administrator, and choose Administer⇨ Site Building⇨Modules.**

   The Thickbox module is under the Other section on the page, as shown in Figure 17-8.

2. **Select the Enabled option next to the Thickbox module.**

3. **Click Save configuration.**

   Thickbox is now enabled.

Figure 17-7:
The Thickbox module allows you to create a lightbox overlay for an image.

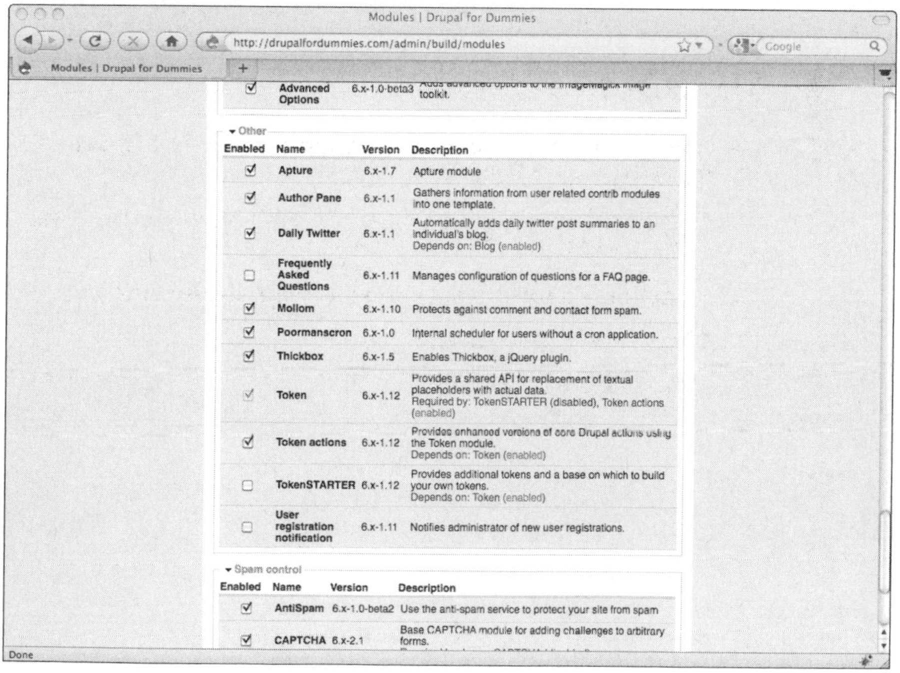

Figure 17-8:
The Thickbox module on the Modules page.

Using Thickbox with your Image Gallery

To add the Thickbox jQuery module to your Image Gallery, do the following:

1. **Log in to your Drupal site as administrator, and choose Administer⇨ Site Configuration⇨Thickbox.**

   The Thickbox configuration page appears, as shown in Figure 17-9.

2. **Select the Enabled for Image Nodes option under the Image Module Options section.**

3. **Select Original from the Image derivative drop-down list.**

4. **Click Save Configuration.**

   The Thickbox plug-in appears when you click an Image Gallery image. You can see an example of this action by clicking one of the thumbnail images in the Image Gallery at `drupalfordummies.com/image` (see Figure 17-10).

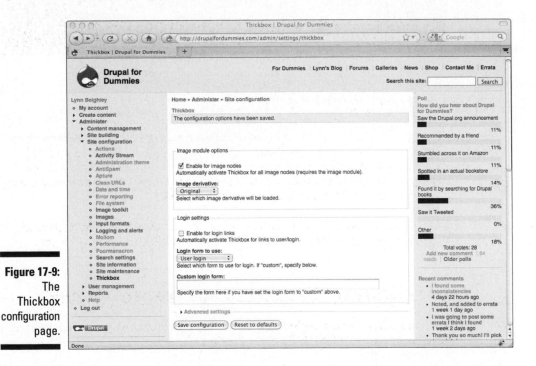

Figure 17-9: The Thickbox configuration page.

Figure 17-10:
The
Thickbox
jQuery
plug-in
appears
when a
thumbnail
image is
clicked.

Integrating jQuery in Drupal

The preceding example used one of the many jQuery modules available for Drupal. But suppose you want to create a simple jQuery effect on an HTML element — as you do in Chapters 5, 6, and 7 — on your Drupal site? Drupal manages your site's content and navigation for you, so you can't easily create an HTML page and integrate it into your Drupal site.

First, you need your Drupal content set up to include jQuery code. Second, the jQuery library has to be included in your page with a `<script>` tag.

Configuring Drupal to recognize jQuery

To ensure that you can include jQuery code in your Drupal-generated content, such as pages and stories, do the following:

1. **Log in to your Drupal site as administrator, and choose Administer⇨ Site Configuration⇨Input Formats.**

2. **Select the Full HTML option.**

3. **Click the Set Default Format button.**

Now each time you post content, you can include jQuery code as well and Drupal will interpret it correctly. But you still need to make sure the path to the jQuery library is included.

Including the jQuery library in Drupal content

By default, Drupal installs a copy of jQuery. It's not the most recent version of jQuery, but in general most of the code in this book will work with the included version. But even though the jQuery code is installed, it isn't included in the HTML code of Drupal-generated pages and stories you create. An additional step is necessary to include the jQuery library in your pages.

A handy Drupal module called jQuery Update keeps your version of jQuery current. You can download this module from `drupal.org/project/ jquery_update`. To install and enable the jQuery Update module, follow the steps for installing and enabling the Image module, presented in the "Downloading Drupal modules" and the "Enabling the Image and Image Gallery modules" sections.

To make sure the current jQuery library is included, do the following:

1. **Choose Administer⇨Site Building⇨Themes.**

2. **Locate and note the name of the currently enabled theme.**

3. **Log in to your control panel on your ISP's Web site.**

4. **Click the link to a file manager.**

5. **Click the single folder or directory named `html`, `www`, or `htdocs`.**

6. **Click the `themes` folder.**

7. **Locate and open the folder that has the same name as your current Drupal theme, which you identified in Step 2.**

8. **Open the `.info` file inside the `theme` folder and use a text editor to add this line to the end:**

   ```
   scripts[] = jquery.js
   ```

   The `.info` file contains a number of lines that control how the theme will be displayed. Figure 17-11 shows the `.info` file for the Bluemarine theme with the `scripts` line added.

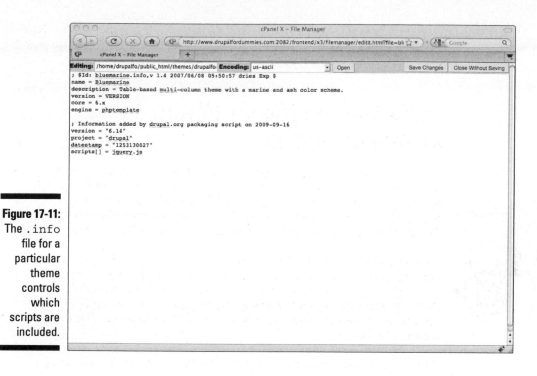

Figure 17-11:
The `.info` file for a particular theme controls which scripts are included.

9. **Save the modified `.info` file.**

   When you include jQuery code in your page or story, the code will execute correctly.

You can now include any jQuery effect in your page or story. For example, create a story on your Drupal site with the following code:

```
<p>
   This text will fade out if you click it.
</p>
<script>
   $('p').click(function () {
   $('p').fadeOut('slow');
   });
</script>
```

When you preview or view this content on your site, it will behave as expected, with the text in the paragraph fading from view when you click it (see Figure 17-12).

Figure 17-12:
You can
include
jQuery
code in
your Drupal
stories and
pages.

Chapter 18

Integrating jQuery and Joomla!

Chapter 17 discussed using jQuery with Drupal. Like Drupal, Joomla! is a free software application that helps you build and manage a Web site and its content. And Joomla!, like Drupal, can be enhanced with the addition of extensions, some of which incorporate jQuery plug-ins. Unlike Drupal, however, Joomla! does not support jQuery by default. Joomla! uses a different JavaScript library that makes integrating jQuery code in a Joomla! site more difficult than in Drupal.

This chapter shows you how to install an extension that helps you overcome the code conflicts between jQuery and the JavaScript library that Joomla! uses. You also discover where to find and incorporate several jQuery-based Joomla! extensions.

This chapter does not provide information about setting up a Joomla! Web site. Instead, you add jQuery-based Joomla! extensions to an existing Joomla! site. To get a Joomla! site up and running, check out *Joomla! For Dummies* by Steve Holzner and Nancy Conner.

Understanding How jQuery Works with Joomla!

Suppose that you want to create a simple jQuery effect on an HTML element, as you do in Chapters 5, 6, and 7. Joomla! manages your content, but you can't use jQuery with Joomla! without some initial setup. First, you need to install the jQuery library and then you need to call it in your code.

Configuring Joomla! to recognize jQuery

You're in luck. A handy plug-in for Joomla! called SC jQuery installs a version of jQuery and allows you to use it. Here's how to get and install SC jQuery:

1. **Browse to http://snellcode.com/downloads.**

   You can avoid Steps 1–4 and install the plug-in directly from the snellcode.com site if, in the field below the Install from URL section, you enter the entire URL: http://snellcode.com/releases/plg_system_scjquery.zip.

2. **Click the SC jQuery menu bar on the right side of the page.**

   The SC jQuery section expands, as shown in Figure 18-1.

3. **Click the Download plg_system_scjquery.zip button, and save the file to a location you will remember.**

4. **Browse to your Joomla! site's control panel, and choose Extensions⇨Install/Uninstall.**

   The Extension Manager appears, as shown in Figure 18-2.

Figure 18-1:
The home page for the SC jQuery Joomla! plug-in.

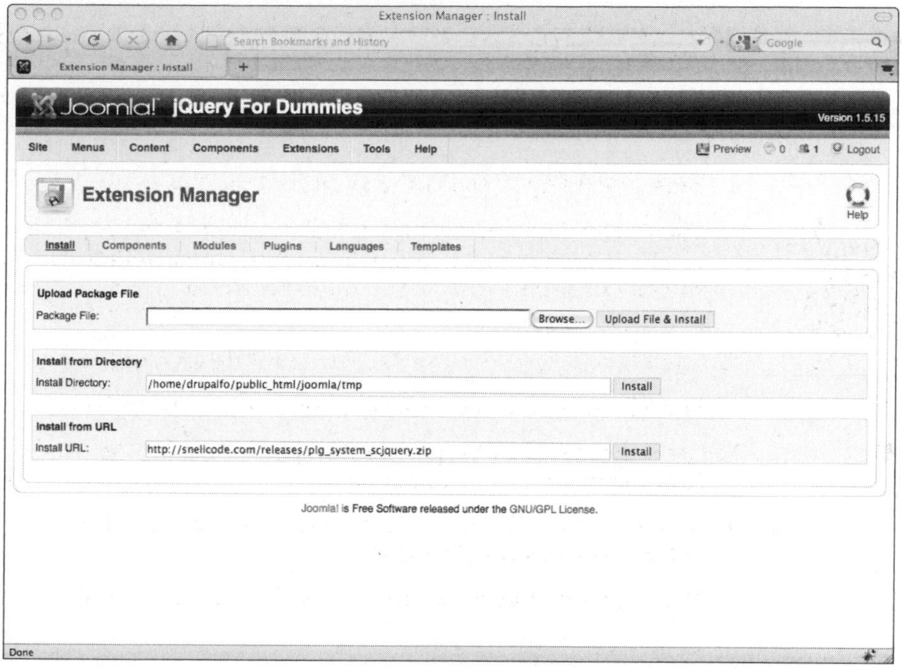

Figure 18-2:
The Joomla!
Extension
Manager.

5. **Click the Browse button below the Upload Package File section, and select the `plg_system_scjquery.zip` file.**

6. **Choose Extensions⇨Plugin Manager.**

   You see a list of all installed Joomla! plug-ins, including the one you just installed. You still need to enable the new SC jQuery plug-in.

7. **Browse through the list and locate the SC jQuery plug-in. Click the small red x icon under the Enabled column for the SC jQuery plug-in, as shown in Figure 18-3.**

   Click Next if necessary to display the second page.

Accessing jQuery from Joomla!

When you add a new post to your Joomla! site, you create a Joomla! *article*. To use jQuery code in your Joomla! articles, you must put the code inside the following code:

```
jQuery(function($) {
//Your jQuery code goes here.
});
```

To create a simple jQuery fade effect when a <p> element is clicked in a Joomla! article, follow these steps:

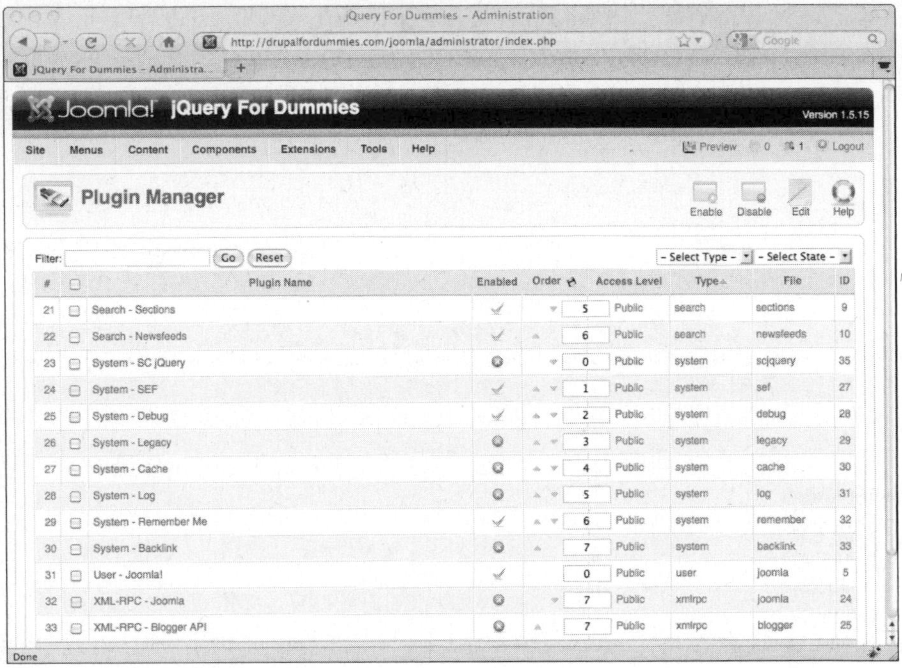

Figure 18-3:
Enable SC
jQuery by
clicking the
small red x
icon to the
right.

1. **Browse to your Joomla! site's control panel, and then choose Content↪Article Manager.**

   The Article Manager appears, as shown in Figure 18-4.

2. **Click the green New button in the Article Manager menu bar.**

   The New Article page appears, as shown in Figure 18-5.

   If you see the text editor shown in Figure 18-5, and you type jQuery code in the form, Joomla! will treat your code as text, not as code. You need to enter it as HTML code, which you do next.

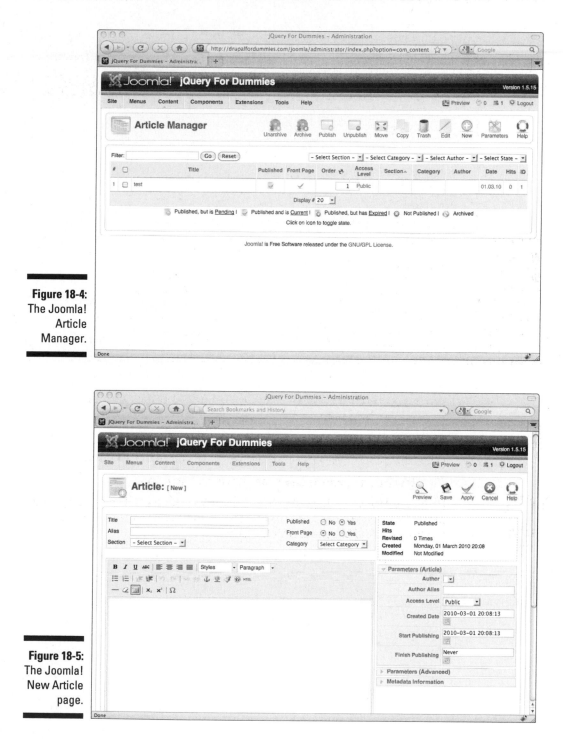

Figure 18-4:
The Joomla!
Article
Manager.

Figure 18-4:
The Joomla!
Article
Manager.

Figure 18-5:
The Joomla!
New Article
page.

3. **Click the blue word** *HTML*.

   The HTML editor opens, and you can enter `<script>` tags and jQuery code, as shown in Figure 18-6.

4. **Type the following code in the HTML source editor:**

   ```
   This is a jQuery test.
   <p>If you click on this paragraph you'll see it just fade away.</p>
   <script type="text/javascript">

    jQuery(function($) {

    $('p').click(function () {
     $('p').fadeOut('slow');
     });

    });
   </script>
   ```

5. **Click the Update button.**

6. **Enter a title for your page and publish it as you would any Joomla! article.**

   When you view the article on your Joomla! site, clicking the text in the `<p>` element causes the element to fade away. Reload to see the effect again.

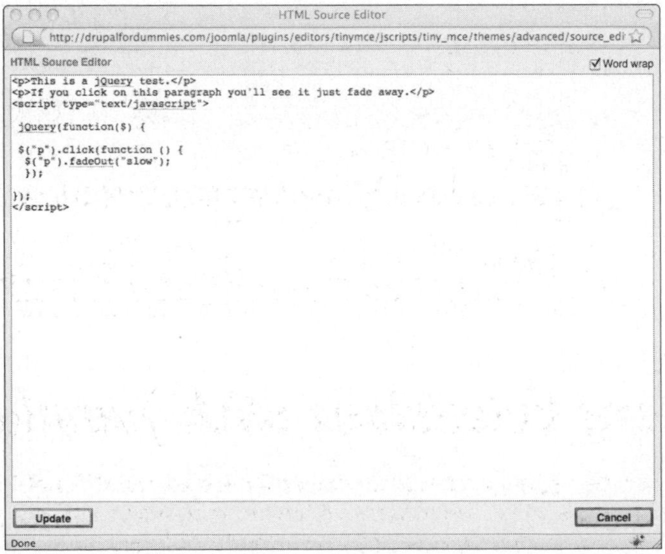

Figure 18-6:
The HTML
editor.

Finding jQuery Extensions for Joomla!

The best place to find jQuery extensions for Joomla! is `joomla.com`. To find extensions that use jQuery, do the following:

1. **Browse to `extensions.joomla.com` (see Figure 18-7).**

2. **Type** jQuery **in the search box in the top-right of the page, and then press Enter.**

   A list of extensions ordered by user rating is displayed.

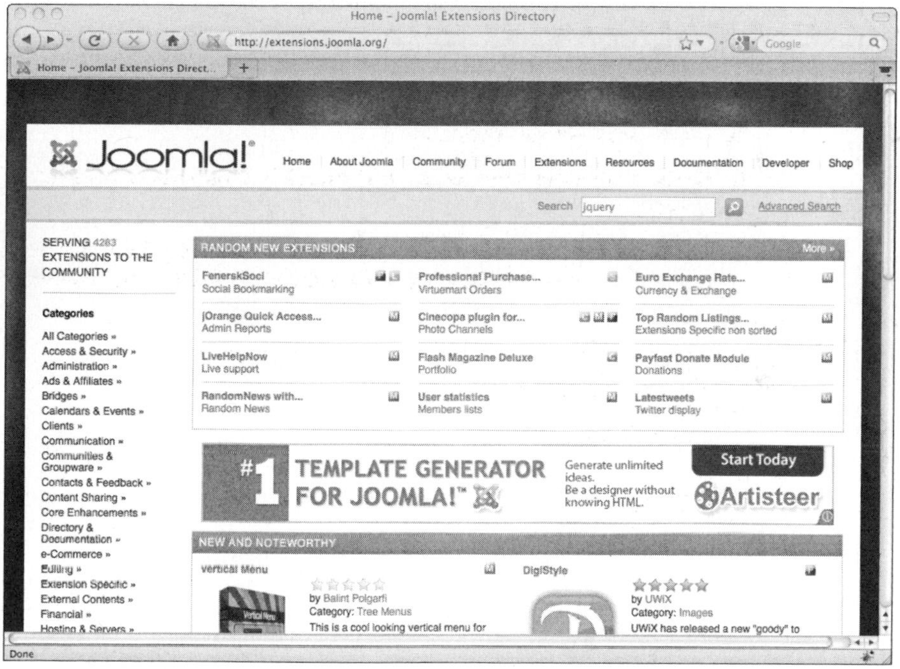

Figure 18-7:
The Joomla!
Extensions
page.

Using jQuery Extensions with Joomla!

After you locate a jQuery extension, you still need to install, enable, and configure it. This section demonstrates how to install and use two jQuery Joomla! extensions: an image gallery and a Twitter plug-in.

Creating an image gallery

The first jQuery-based plug-in for Joomla! is a simple image gallery called, appropriately, Very Simple Image Gallery. To download and enable the Very Simple Image Gallery extension, do the following:

1. **Browse to www.bretteleben.de/lang-en/joomla/very-simple-image-gallery.html.**

   REMEMBER

   You can avoid Steps 1–3 and install the plug-in directly if you enter in the field below the Install from URL section the entire URL to the zip file: `http://www.bretteleben.de/attachments/080_plugin_vsig_1.5.5.zip`.

2. **Scroll down the page and click the link to download `plugin_vsig_1.5.5.zip`.**

   The link is located about halfway down the page, as shown in Figure 18-8.

3. **Save the `plugin_vsig_1.5.5.zip` file to a location you will remember.**

4. **Browse to your Joomla! site's control panel, and choose Extensions⇨ Install/Uninstall.**

5. **Click the Browse button below the Upload Package File section, and then select the `plugin_vsig_1.5.5.zip` file.**

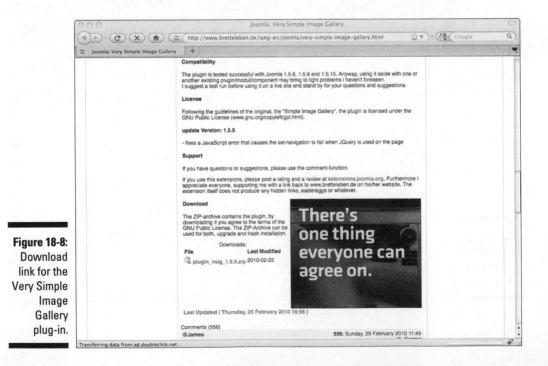

Figure 18-8: Download link for the Very Simple Image Gallery plug-in.

6. **Choose Extensions⇨Plugin Manager.**

   You see a list of all installed Joomla! plug-ins. You still need to enable the new plug-in.

7. **Click the small red x icon under the Enabled column for the Very Simple Image Gallery plug-in.**

   You may have to click the Next link at the bottom of the list to find the plug-in.

Now you can create your first image gallery. To do so, follow these steps:

1. **Browse to your Joomla! site's control panel, and choose Site⇨Media Manager.**

   The Media Manager appears, as shown in Figure 18-9.

2. **Click the stories folder on the left side.**

3. **Type a name for a new folder in the text field on the right, below the Files section.**

   In Figure 18-9, I typed the name mygallery.

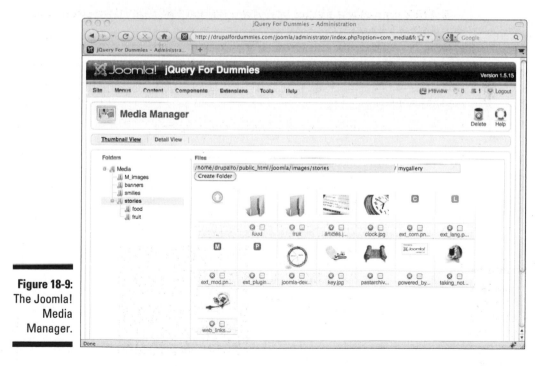

Figure 18-9: The Joomla! Media Manager.

4. **Click the Create Folder button.**

   Your new folder now appears in the folder list on the left in the `stories` folder.

5. **Select your new folder and scroll to the bottom of the page to the Upload File form, which is shown in Figure 18-10.**

6. **Click Browse, select the image file you want to upload, and click Open. Then click Start Upload.**

7. **Repeat Step 6 until you have uploaded all the images you want in your gallery.**

   Now that your images are loaded into your folder, you need to display your gallery in an article.

8. **Choose Content⇨Article Manager. Edit or create a new article where you want your article to appear.**

9. **In the New Article or Edit Article page, add the following code to your article where you want your gallery to appear (see Figure 18-11):**

   ```
   {vsig}mygallery{/vsig}
   ```

10. **Click the Save button to save your article.**

    Your gallery now appears in the article, as shown in Figure 18-12.

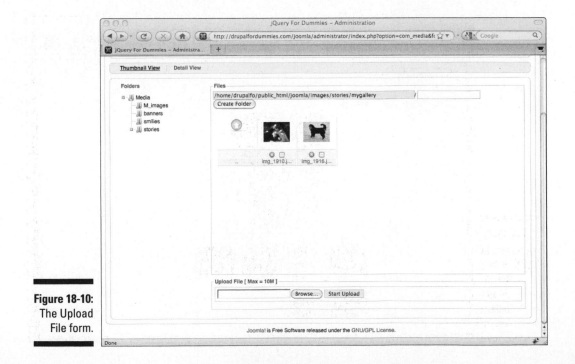

Figure 18-10: The Upload File form.

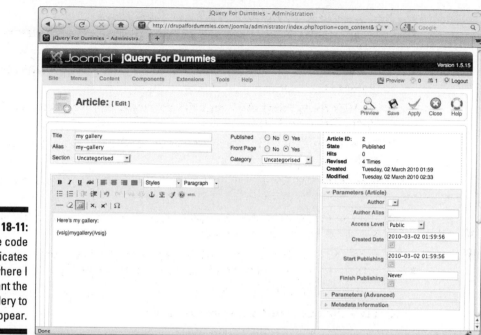

Figure 18-11:
The code
indicates
where I
want the
gallery to
appear.

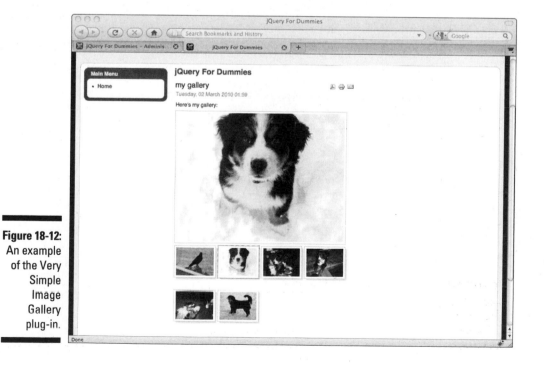

Figure 18-12:
An example
of the Very
Simple
Image
Gallery
plug-in.

Displaying tweets from Twitter on your Joomla! page

Another nifty jQuery-based extension for Joomla! is called jTweet, which displays your tweets from Twitter.com on your Joomla! site. To download and enable the jTweet extension, do the following:

1. **Browse to `joomlabamboo.com/joomla-extensions/free-joomla-extensions/jtweet-free-joomla-twitter-module`.**

2. **Scroll down the page and click the link to download `JB_jTweet_J1.5_v1.5.2.zip`. Then save the file to a directory you will remember.**

   The Download link is located at the bottom right, as shown in Figure 18-13.

3. **Browse to `www.joomlabamboo.com/joomla-extensions/free-joomla-extensions/jb-library-plugin-a-free-joomla-jquery-plugin` and download the JB Library plug-in.**

4. **Browse to your Joomla! site's control panel.**

5. **Choose Extensions⇨Install/Uninstall.**

Figure 18-13: Download link for jTweet.

6. **Click the Browse button below the Upload Package File section and upload one of the two .zip files you just downloaded. Then upload the other one.**

7. **Choose Extensions⇨Plugin Manager.**

   You see a list of all installed Joomla! plug-ins. You still need to enable the new plug-in.

8. **Click the small red x icon under the Enabled column for the JB Library plug-in.**

   You may have to click the Next link at the bottom of the list to find the plug-in.

9. **Choose Extensions⇨Module Manager.**

10. **Click the small red x icon under the Enabled column for the jTweet extension.**

You need to add your Twitter information to this module. To do so, follow these steps:

1. **Browse to your Joomla! site's control panel.**

2. **Choose Extensions⇨Module Manager, and click the jTweet extension.**

   The Edit Module settings for jTweet appears, as shown in Figure 18-14.

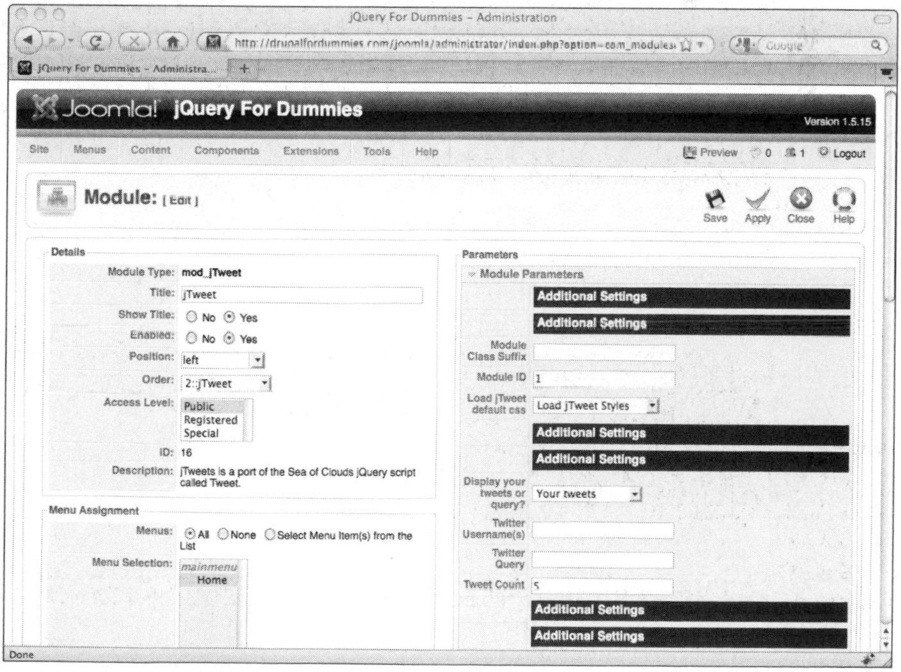

Figure 18-14: The settings for the jTweet extension.

TIP

A number of settings are available in the Edit Module settings for jTweet. Check out www.joomlabamboo.com/joomla-extensions/free-joomla-extensions/jtweet-free-joomla-twitter-module to find out more.

3. **In the Twitter Username(s) field on the right, type your Twitter username.**

4. **Click the Save button.**

   Your tweets now appear on your Joomla! site, as shown in Figure 18-15.

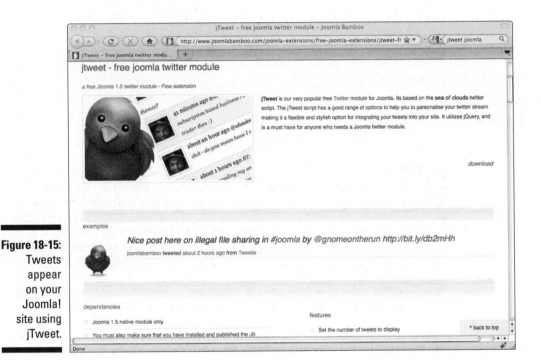

Figure 18-15:
Tweets
appear
on your
Joomla!
site using
jTweet.

Chapter 19

Building Better Blogs with jQuery and WordPress

*W*ordPress is a free software application that helps you build and manage a Web site, typically one that features a blog. WordPress manages the content you post to it, automatically archiving old entries. Like Drupal and Joomla!, WordPress can be enhanced with the addition of plug-ins, some of which incorporate jQuery. WordPress also supports jQuery by default, making it relatively easy to use jQuery code in your posts.

This chapter shows you how to use jQuery code in your WordPress site and how to locate and use some impressive jQuery-based WordPress plug-ins.

This chapter does not provide information about setting up a WordPress Web site. Instead, the focus is on adding jQuery-based WordPress extensions to your existing WordPress site. To get a WordPress site up and running, check out *WordPress For Dummies,* 3rd Edition, by Lisa Sabin-Wilson.

Making jQuery Work with WordPress

By default, WordPress installs a copy of jQuery. But even though the jQuery code is installed, it isn't included in the template code of WordPress posts and pages. You have to explicitly include the jQuery code.

To include jQuery in your WordPress pages, do the following:

1. Browse to your WordPress administration panel and log in.

2. **Click to expand the Appearance menu on the left, as shown in Figure 19-1.**

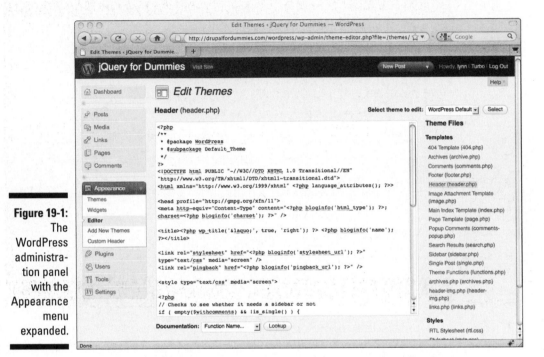

Figure 19-1:
The
WordPress
administra-
tion panel
with the
Appearance
menu
expanded.

3. **Click the Editor link.**

   The WordPress editor appears with a list of files on the right.

4. **Click the Header (header.php) file link on the right.**

   The `header.php` file opens in the editor.

5. **Locate this line in the `header.php` file:**

   ```
   <head profile="http://gmpg.org/xfn/11">
   ```

   and add the following code directly below it:

   ```php
   <?php wp_enqueue_script("jquery"); ?>
   <?php wp_head(); ?>
   ```

   This code calls the jQuery library that was installed with WordPress (see Figure 19-2). Because this jQuery call occurs in the Header file, jQuery will now be included on all site pages for this WordPress theme.

   The second line, `<?php wp_head(); ?>`, is probably already in the `<head>` section of the Header file. If it is, you can leave it out here, but it doesn't hurt anything if it appears twice.

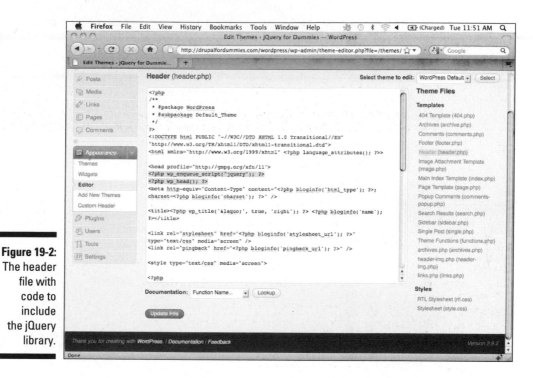

Figure 19-2:
The header
file with
code to
include
the jQuery
library.

6. **Scroll down the page and click the Update File button to save your changes.**

You can now include any jQuery effect in your post. For example, to add a fade out effect when a paragraph is clicked, do the following:

1. **Browse to your WordPress administration panel and log in.**

2. **Click to expand the Posts menu on the left, as shown in Figure 19-3.**

3. **Click Add New.**

    The WordPress Add New Post page appears.

    If you type jQuery code in the form with the Visual tab selected, WordPress will treat your code as text, not as code. You need to enter the code as HTML code. You need to enter the code in the HTML editor, which you do next.

4. **Click the HTML tab.**

    The HTML editor appears, so you can enter `<script>` tags and jQuery code.

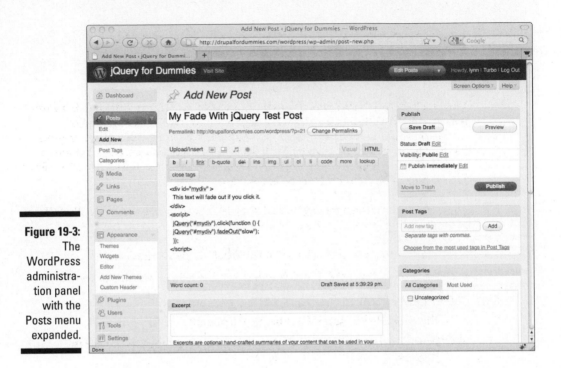

Figure 19-3:
The
WordPress
administra-
tion panel
with the
Posts menu
expanded.

5. **Enter the following code in the text box:**

```
<p>
  This text will fade out if you click it.
</p>
<script>
  jQuery("p").click(function () {
  jQuery("p").fadeOut("slow");
  });
</script>
```

Note that the preceding code uses the word jQuery instead of the $ shorthand that you may be accustomed to. Anywhere in your code where you need $ to call jQuery, use the jQuery keyword instead!

6. **Enter a title for your post and publish it as you would any WordPress article.**

When you view your post on your WordPress site, clicking the text in the <div> element causes the element to fade away. Reload to see it again.

Finding WordPress jQuery-Based Plug-ins

You can find WordPress jQuery-based plug-ins by searching the administration panel on your WordPress site or by browsing to the Extend section of `http://wordpress.org`. The easiest method is using the administration panel. The downside, however, is that you won't get as many results when you search the administration panel as you will from the Extend section. For that reason, I present both techniques here.

To locate and install a jQuery-based WordPress plug-in using your WordPress administration panel, do the following

1. **Browse to your WordPress administration panel and log in.**

2. **Click to expand the Plugins menu on the left, as shown in Figure 19-4.**

3. **Click Add New.**

   The WordPress Install Plugins page appears.

4. **Type** jQuery Colorbox **in the Search box, and then click Search Plugins.**

   You are presented with a list of results.

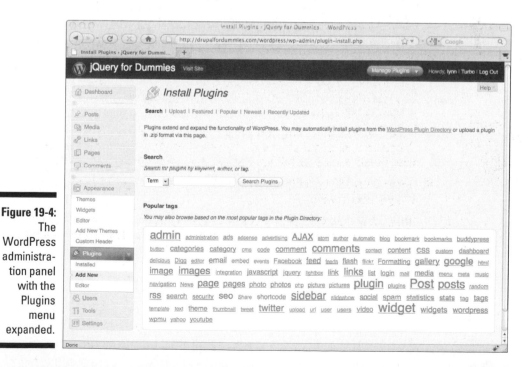

Figure 19-4:
The WordPress administration panel with the Plugins menu expanded.

5. **Click the Install link to the right of the jQuery Colorbox plug-in.**

   A window pops up with an Install Now button at the upper right, as shown in Figure 19-5.

6. **Click Install Now.**

   The Colorbox plug-in is installed.

To locate and install a jQuery-based WordPress plug-in at wordpress.org, do the following:

1. **Browse to wordpress.org/extend/plugins. Enter the words jQuery Colorbox in the Search box, and then click Search Plugins (see Figure 19-6).**

2. **Click the jQuery Colorbox plug-in, click the link to download the plug-in, and then save the file to a directory you will remember.**

   This plug-in is downloaded as a single zip file.

3. **Log in to the control panel on your ISP's Web site.**

4. **Click the link to a file manager.**

5. **Click the single folder or directory named html, www, or htdocs. Click the wp-content directory, and then click the plugins directory inside it.**

   The plugins directory is where you will upload your plug-in.

6. **Click the upload link in your file manager.**

   You see an upload form with a Browse button.

7. **Click Browse, and select the Colorbox zip file you downloaded. Click Upload.**

   The compressed Colorbox zip file is now on your site in the correct folder, ready to be unzipped.

8. **Click the Colorbox zip file to select it.**

   You see a list of files stored inside your compressed file, all selected.

9. **Make sure the Uncompress All option is selected, and then click the Go button.**

10. **Select the original Colorbox plug-in zip file on your Web server and delete it.**

Figure 19-5: Plug-in detail page with Install Now button on the upper right.

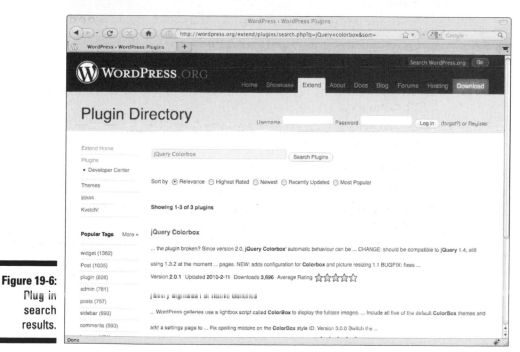

Figure 19-6: Plug-in search results.

Colorbox is installed, but it still needs to be activated. To activate Colorbox, follow these steps:

1. **Browse to your WordPress administration panel and log in.**

2. **Click to expand the Plugins menu on the left, as shown in Figure 19-7.**

3. **Click the Installed link.**

   The Manage Plugins page appears.

4. **Locate the jQuery Colorbox plug-in in the list and click its Activate link.**

   The plug-in is installed, and you can now use it in your posts.

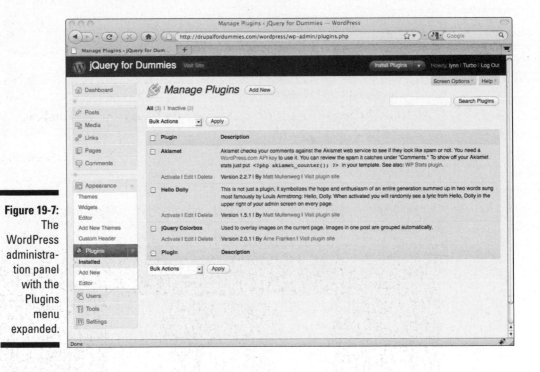

Figure 19-7:
The WordPress administration panel with the Plugins menu expanded.

Using the Colorbox jQuery Plug-in with WordPress

To use Colorbox with images in your posts, follow these steps:

1. **Browse to your WordPress administration panel and log in.**

2. **Click to expand the Media menu on the left.**

3. **Click Add New, and then upload an image to your WordPress media library.**

4. **Click to expand the Posts menu on the left.**

5. **Click Add New to create a new post.**

6. **Click the Add an Image button next to Edit/Insert.**

   An Add an Image pop-up appears.

7. **Click the Media Library tab, and then click the Show link next to the image you want in your post.**

8. **Click the Insert Into Post button, near the bottom of this window.**

9. **Publish your post.**

   Your image now appears in a Colorbox when it is clicked, as shown in Figure 19-8.

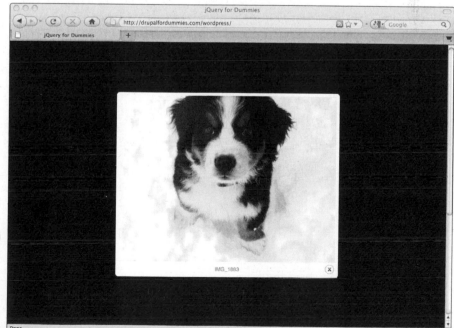

Figure 19-8:
Image displayed in a jQuery Colorbox.

Part VII
The Part of Tens

The 5th Wave   By Rich Tennant

"We're here to clean the code."

In this part . . .

You've added some amazing jQuery effects, plugins, and widgets to your sites, but you're ready for more. Each chapter in this part consists of ten tips or Web sites that give you information, connect you with other users, and point you at more great jQuery plug-ins. You're ready to build something truly amazing with a little more help from jQuery.

Chapter 20

Ten Don't-Miss Plug-ins

As you've seen in previous chapters, your site can be enhanced with hundreds of free jQuery plug-ins available for download. I particularly like ones that help you control your content and make your site more user friendly, such as image carousels to manage lots of images, tab or page controls to break long texts into shorter bits, pop-up tool tips for links, and drop-down menus. In this chapter, I point out several useful or interesting ones and give you an overview of what they do.

The plug-ins mentioned in this chapter are just the starting point. Literally hundreds more are just as useful. The point of this chapter is to sample a few categories of plug-ins to give you a better understanding of what you can do with plug-in extensions to jQuery.

I haven't included instructions on how to install these plug-ins because they already come with clear documentation for installation and use. Refer to that documentation if you choose to use any of these.

uploadify

http://www.uploadify.com/

If you have a Web site where you want to allow users to upload files, uploadify can handle this task for you.

It's seldom a good idea to let people you don't know upload files to your Web server. And even trusting the user isn't enough because a user might upload a malicious file without realizing it. Make sure you have code in place to check any uploaded files for viruses before you do anything with the files.

The uploadify plug-in gives you several options for the upload form that the user sees. You can have a single file upload or a multifile upload with a browse button and progress bar, as shown in Figure 20-1, or you can customize the button and bar. You can make your users click an upload link or press a button when they're ready, or you can configure uploadify to automatically upload after the users select files.

To create a page with a basic uploadify script that allows a user to upload a single file, follow these steps:

1. **Go to `http://www.uploadify.com/download` and download the latest version of the uploadify plug-in.**

   As of this writing, the latest version is 2.1.0.

2. **Save the `uploadify.zip` file to a location you will remember.**

3. **Unzip the file.**

   The unzipped file expands into a directory containing a number of files, including several you need to move in the next two steps.

4. **Save the `swfobject.js` and `jquery.uploadify.v2.1.0.min.js` files to the same directory on your Web server where you have your copy of jQuery.**

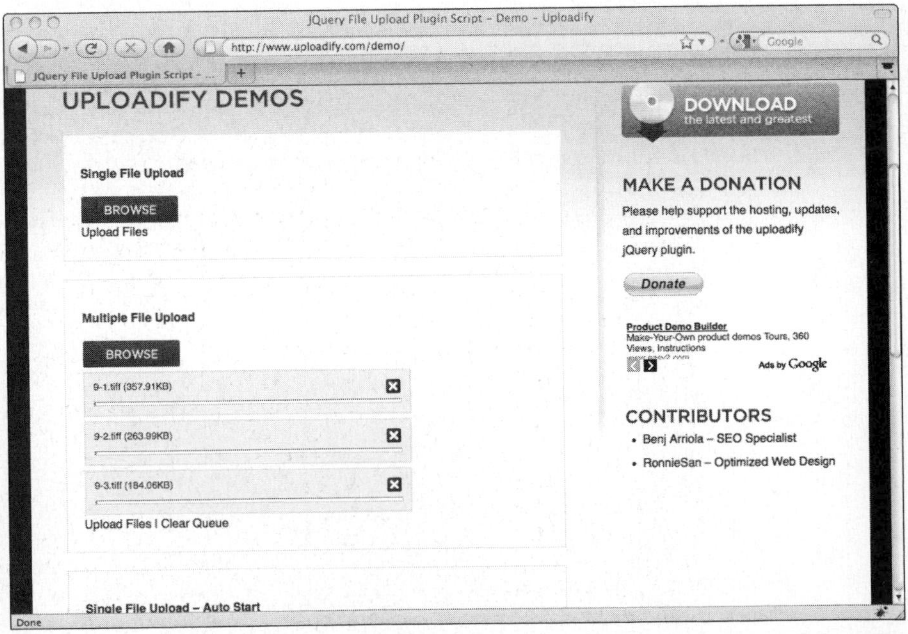

Figure 20-1:
Uploadify plug-in interface with three files in the queue and progress bars.

The directory containing JavaScript (.js) files is typically in a directory called js. For the sample code to work, your file structure needs to look like the following in your Web directory (the directory on your Web server containing your HTML files):

> your_uploadify_file.html
>
> cancel.png
>
> uploadify.swf
>
> js (a directory)
>
> css (a directory)
>
> uploads (a directory)

5. **Save the default.css and uploadify.css files to your css directory.**

6. **Create a directory where you want to eventually save the uploaded files.**

   In the example, I named it uploads.

7. **Copy the uploadify.swf and cancel.png files to the base Web directory where your HTML file will be.**

8. **Create a Web page with the following code and save it to your Web server.**

   If you don't feel like typing the code, you can download it from www.dummies.com/go/jquery:

```
<html> <head>
<link href="css/default.css" rel="stylesheet" type="text/css" />
<link href="css/uploadify.css" rel="stylesheet" type="text/css" />
<script type="text/javascript" src="js/jquery-1.3.2.min.js"></script>
<script type="text/javascript" src="js/swfobject.js"></script>
<script type="text/javascript" src="js/jquery.uploadify.v2.1.0.min.js"></
        script>
<script type="text/javascript">
$(document).ready(function()
{        $("#uploadify").uploadify({
         'uploader'        : 'uploadify.swf',
         'script'          : 'scripts/yourfiletoprocessuploads.php',
         'cancelImg'       : 'cancel.png',
         'folder'          : 'uploads',
         'queueID'         : 'fileQueue',
         'auto'            : true,
         'multi'           : true        });
});
</script></head><body>
<div id="fileQueue"></div>
<input type="file" name="uploadify" id="uploadify" />
<p><a href="javascript:jQuery('#uploadify').uploadifyClearQueue()">Cancel
        All Uploads</a>
</p></body></html>
```

You can change any settings inside the `uploadify` block. For example, to put the uploaded files in a directory other than one named `uploads`, change the setting next to `folder`. Also, if you intend to do something with the files after they are uploaded, change the `script` setting to an appropriate filename and path. The one I use in this example is just a placeholder.

jCarousel

http://sorgalla.com/jcarousel/

Do you want to display images on a Web page but also leave room for more content? The nifty jCarousel plug-in lets you specify a set of images to display in a box that the user can scroll through by clicking arrow buttons, as shown in Figure 20-2.

You can configure whether jCarousel should display images horizontally or vertically. You can control how many images scroll at once when the arrow is clicked and can even make it scroll automatically after a specific number of seconds that you choose. jCarousel also comes with two skins to choose between. A *skin* is a set of images and a CSS file that controls the appearance of jCarousel.

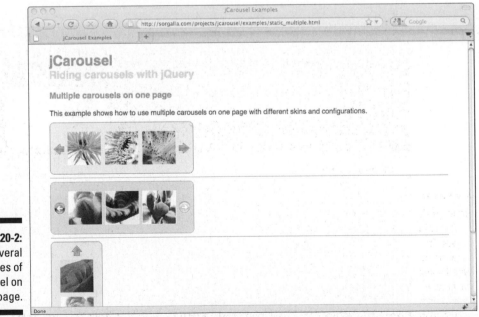

Figure 20-2:
Several examples of jCarousel on one page.

Most plug-ins include examples, and jCarousel is no exception. Simply open the `static_start.html` file in the `examples` directory in your browser to see how jCarousel works.

jCarousel is simple to implement. You can use the `static_start.html` file and edit it with the correct paths to your JavaScript and CSS files, typically your `js` and `css` folders on your Web server. Then place your images in a block of code such as the following:

```
<ul id="mycarousel" class="jcarousel-skin-tango">
<li><img src="yourimage1.gif" width="75" height="75" alt="" /></li>
<li><img src="yourimage2.gif" width="75" height="75" alt="" /></li>
<li><img src="yourimage3.gif" width="75" height="75" alt="" /></li>
</ul>
```

qTip

http://craigsworks.com/projects/qtip

The qTip plug-in lets you add a pop-up bubble containing text, called a tooltip, whenever someone hovers a cursor over a link on your Web page (see Figure 20-3).

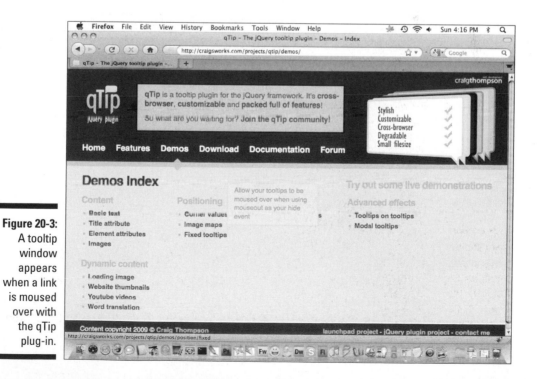

Figure 20-3: A tooltip window appears when a link is moused over with the qTip plug-in.

The qTip download consists of a zip file containing some text files with basic information and the `jquery.qtip-1.0.0-rc3.min.js file`, which contains the code for the plug-in. The best place to begin is to view the demos page and read the provided documentation.

jQuery pager

`http://rikrikrik.com/jquery/pager/`

No doubt you've seen Web pages with lots and lots of text, requiring you to scroll down the page and risk losing track of your location. jQuery pager gives you an easy way to break up long blocks of text into smaller sections that your visitors can page through, as shown in Figure 20-4.

To use the jQuery pager plug-in, install it in the same directory as jQuery. Begin with the example page, making sure to change the `jQuery` and pager JavaScript file paths to the correct paths on your Web server.

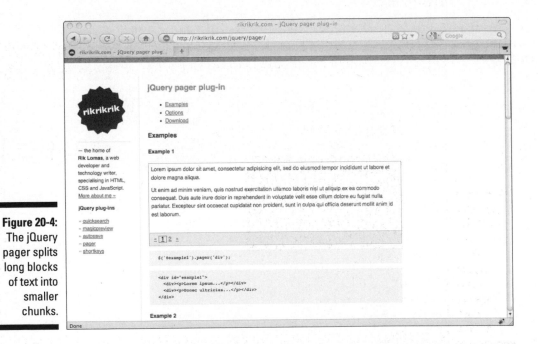

Figure 20-4: The jQuery pager splits long blocks of text into smaller chunks.

You need to split your text into chunks and surround each chunk with a
`<div>` element, which creates the pages. Each tabbed page of text will be
inside a pair of `<div>` tags. The entire set of pages will also be surrounded
by a pair of `<div>` tags. For example, your code might look like the following:

```
<div id="pagertext">
  <div>This is the text I want in the first page.</div>
  <div>The second page should contain this text</div>
</div>
```

jQuery Flash

```
http://jquery.lukelutman.com/plugins/flash/
```

If you have the Flash program, you can save a Flash (`.swf`) file to a Web page
automatically. But if you don't have Flash, it can be a bit of a pain figuring out
how to post an `.swf` file on your Web page — unless you have the jQuery
Flash plug-in. Figure 20-5 shows the Flash plug-in being used to display a
Flash movie.

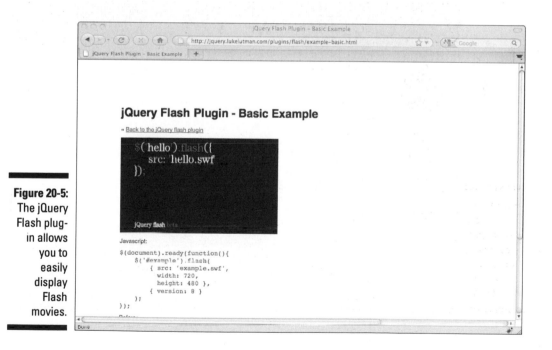

Figure 20-5:
The jQuery
Flash plug-
in allows
you to
easily
display
Flash
movies.

Download and save the JavaScript for the plug-in to your `js` directory. Then place the following script block in your HTML page where you want the movie to appear:

```
<script type="text/javascript">
$(document).ready(function(){
$('#example').flash({
        src: 'example.swf',
        width: 360,
        height: 215 },
        { version: 8 }); });
</script>
```

You need to provide a height, width, and Flash version number for the movie.

toggleElements

http://jquery.andreaseberhard.de/toggleElements/

Similar to the preceding plug-in, jQuery pager, the toggleElements plug-in hides content until a user clicks a link to expand it. But instead of a horizontal presentation of links, toggleElements gives you a sliding window effect. When you click an arrow next to a title bar, the text and images in the block slide down (see Figure 20-6).

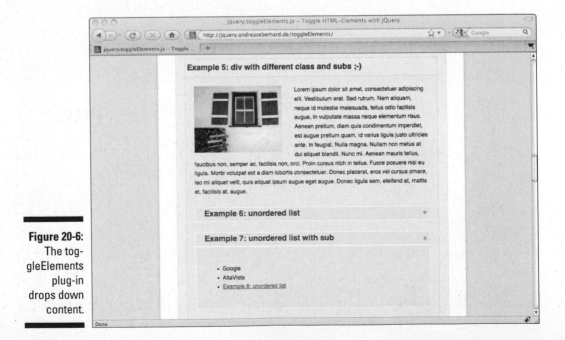

Figure 20-6:
The toggleElements plug-in drops down content.

The author provides clear instructions for the setup of this plug-in at the bottom of the page (scroll down to see the instructions).

Coda-Slider 2.0

```
http://www.ndoherty.biz/2009/10/coda-slider-2/
```

The Coda-Slider plug-in, like the jQuery pager mentioned earlier, presents a block of content in a horizontal series of tabbed blocks (see Figure 20-7).

However, Coda-Slider is sleeker than its pager cousin, with lots of bells and whistles. You can set it to automatically scroll through your tabbed blocks and can even give it special effects, such as a rubbery bounce when the blocks shift. Visit the demos page at `http://www.ndoherty.biz/demos/coda-slider/2.0/` and try the special effects for yourself.

By now it should not come as a surprise that the more polished and elaborate the jQuery plug-in, the more work is required to get it running and the more pieces there are to install. No matter what the complexity, your first, best bet is to view the demos and check out the source code in the examples. Feel free to test the plug-in by playing with the example code on your own Web server while you figure it out and make it your own.

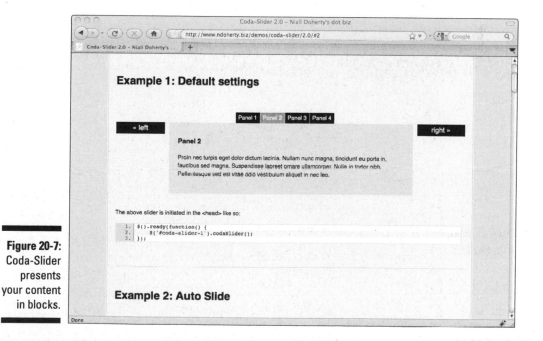

Figure 20-7: Coda-Slider presents your content in blocks.

pagination

`http://plugins.jquery.com/project/pagination`

If you want to present a long list, the pagination plug-in may be what you need. It's similar to jQuery pager, but it gives your content a more list-like feel with a robust numbering system that appears at the top of your content block, as shown in Figure 20-8.

The pagination plug-in gives you plenty of options, such as:

✔ Number of items per page to display

✔ Number of pagination links shown

✔ Number of start and end points

✔ Label for Previous button

✔ Label for Next button

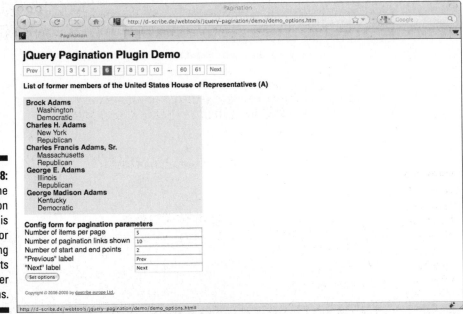

Figure 20-8:
The pagination plug-in is great for breaking long lists into shorter sections.

Humanized Messages for jQuery

http://binarybonsai.com/2007/10/15/humanized-messages-
for-jquery/

The Humanized Messages plug-in is fun and useful. Try a demo, as shown
in Figure 20-9, at http://binarybonsai.com/misc/humanmsg/ to get a
sense of how the program works.

When a user clicks an element on your page, you can prominently display a
custom message in response. Perhaps you might provide amusing feedback,
or serve up flash cards, or present fortune-teller–style content.

The responses require a bit of code, but a look at the source code behind
the demo page should give you a clearer understanding of how to set it
up. You can also visit http://code.google.com/p/humanmsg/wiki/
UsingHumaneMessages to view a guide on installing and using this plug-in.

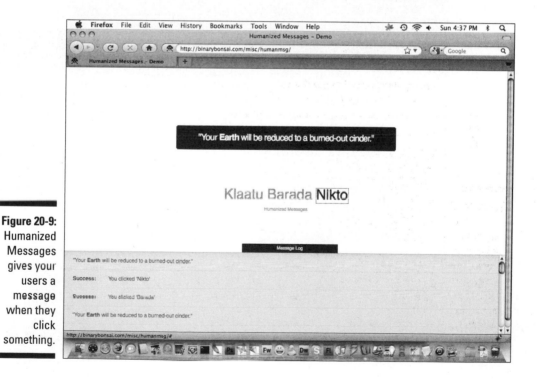

Figure 20-9:
Humanized
Messages
gives your
users a
message
when they
click
something.

Single Drop Down Menu

http://www.codenothing.com/archives/jquery/single-drop-down-menu/

The Single Drop Down Menu plug-in creates drop-down submenus when you mouse over a category. For example, when you mouse over the Home link in Figure 20-10, three menu options drop down below it.

Make sure your drop-down menus make sense. For example, if you have an upper-level menu called Company Info, you probably don't want to have drop-down link to Photos of My Dog.

You can download the zipped plug-in at http://www.codenothing.com/archives/jquery/single-drop-down-menu/#download.

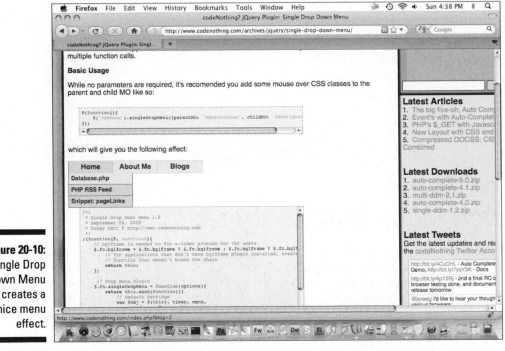

Figure 20-10:
Single Drop
Down Menu
creates a
nice menu
effect.

Chapter 21

Ten Design and Code Tricks

· ·

In This Chapter

▶ Detecting the visitor's browser

▶ Animating the background of your Web page

▶ Changing the size of text

▶ Turning off the right-click menu

▶ Getting the newest version of jQuery

▶ Creating a slide panel

▶ Adding a special effect to disappearing elements

▶ Saving time with a jQuery cheat sheet

▶ Making any element clickable

▶ Simplifying document.ready code

· ·

*M*any Web sites offer jQuery tips and tricks. This chapter provides a sampling of some of the most useful ones.

Detecting Browser Types

Not all Web browsers are created equal. A Web page viewed in Internet Explorer might look very different when displayed in Firefox. This is why it's useful to be able to detect which browser the visitor to your Web page is using, and display different CSS or HTML code depending on the browser. The code in the following example displays an alert box with information about the browser (see Figure 21-1).

```
<html>
<head>
<title>My Test Page</title>
<script type="text/javascript" src="js/jquery-1.4.min.js"></script>
<script type="text/javascript">
$(document).ready(function(){
if( $.browser.safari )
alert('The browser is Safari');
if ($.browser.msie && $.browser.version > 6 )
alert('The browser is IE6 or later');
if ($.browser.mozilla && $.browser.version >= '1.8' )
alert('The browser is Firefox 2 or later');
});
</script>
</head>
<body>
</body>
</html>
```

You can find this code and more jQuery tricks at www.catswhocode.com/blog/8-awesome-jquery-tips-and-tricks.

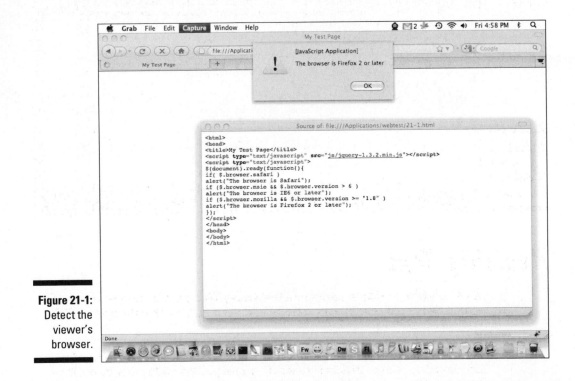

Figure 21-1:
Detect the
viewer's
browser.

Animating a Background Image

The tip in the preceding section came from www.catswhocode.com. That site also has a tutorial that shows you how to animate a background image on a Web page. The tutorial is located at www.catswhocode.com/blog/ animated-background-image-with-jquery. Animating a background image is an impressive trick; you can see a demo at www.codingkitty. com/demo/animated-background. In the demo, the image of clouds at the top of the Web page appears to move across the screen (see Figure 21-2).

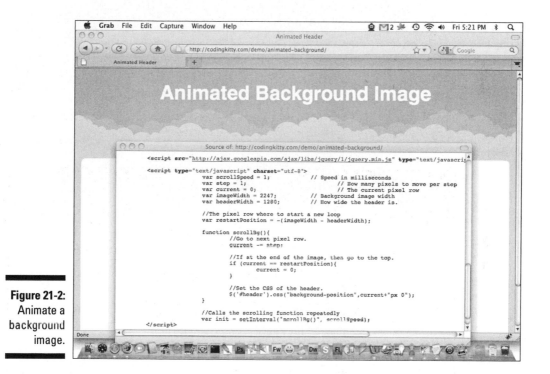

Figure 21-2:
Animate a
background
image.

Resizing Text

A nice feature to offer visitors to a text-heavy Web page is links to resize the text. jQuery gives you an easy way to add links that control the size of Web page text (see Figure 21-3).

You can find code to add resize text links to your Web page at www.shopdev. co.uk/blog/text-resizing-with-jquery. This code adds three links: Increase, Decrease, and Reset. Clicking Increase makes the text larger, Decrease makes it smaller, and Reset restores the text to the size it was when the Web page was first loaded.

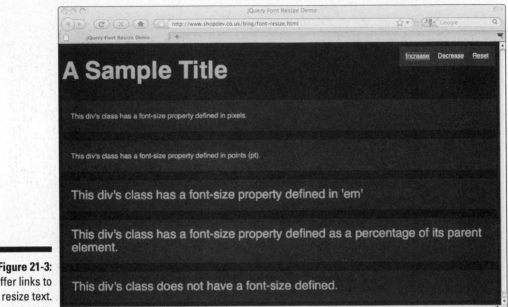

Figure 21-3:
Offer links to resize text.

Disabling the Right-Click Menu

By default, users can right-click your Web page and get a variety of menu options, as shown in Figure 21-4.

You can disable this menu by using the following code:

```
<html>
<head>
<title>My Test Page</title>
<script type="text/javascript" src="js/jquery-1.4.min.js"></script>
<script type="text/javascript">
$(document).ready(function(){
$(document).bind('contextmenu',function(e){
return false;
});
});
</script>
</head>
<body>
 A context menu will not open if you right-click this page.
</body>
</html>
```

This trick is from www.queness.com/post/126/useful-and-handy-jquery-tips-and-tricks.

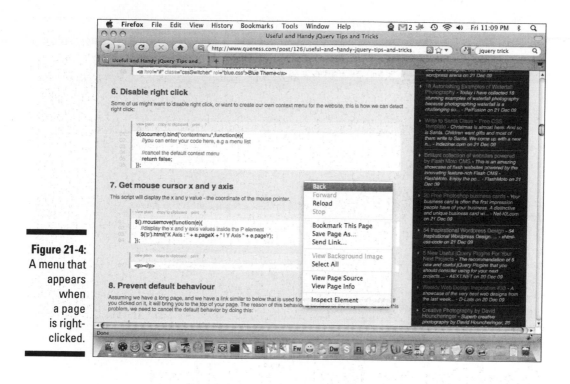

Figure 21-4:
A menu that appears when a page is right-clicked.

Loading jQuery from Google

All the code examples in this book use the following line to load the jQuery library:

```
<script type="text/javascript" src="js/jquery-1.4.min.js"></script>
```

This code calls the jQuery library from the `js` directory on your Web server. The article at www.tvidesign.co.uk/blog/improve-your-jquery-25-excellent-tips.aspx#tip1 recommends that you call the jQuery code from a copy of jQuery stored on Google's machines. To call jQuery from Google's Web server, replace the preceding code with

```
<script type="text/javascript" src="http://ajax.googleapis.com/ajax/libs/
          jquery/1.4/jquery.min.js"></script>
```

The `src` attribute is replaced with the location of the current version of the JQuery library on Google's server.

The Google repository keeps copies of older versions of the jQuery library, which means that even though the current version of jQuery might be later than 1.4, the old version is still available. This means you don't have to worry about your code breaking while you switch to the latest version of jQuery.

There are several good reasons to load jQuery from Google:

- **Loading jQuery from Google saves bandwidth.** Because the code is hosted on Google's Web server, not yours, visitors are hitting those machines and not your machine.

- **jQuery loads faster from Google.** Odds are that Google's Web server is faster than your server, so the jQuery library downloads more quickly.

- **jQuery may already be loaded.** If your visitors have been to any other sites that call jQuery from the Google Web server, they will already have jQuery loaded, making your Web page load more quickly.

Creating a Simple Slide Panel

You can find a nice tutorial for creating a sliding panel at www.webdesigner wall.com/tutorials/jquery-tutorials-for-designers. This simple panel slides open when a visitor clicks the tab at the bottom of the panel, as shown in Figure 21-5.

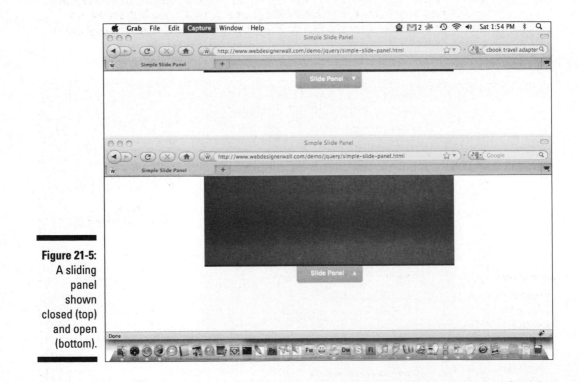

Figure 21-5:
A sliding panel shown closed (top) and open (bottom).

The jQuery code to create the panel is short and simple, as follows:

```
$(document).ready(function(){
$('.btn-slide').click(function(){
$('#panel').slideToggle('slow');
$(this).toggleClass('active');
});
});
```

This effect requires CSS styles and elements with specific IDs or classes. Your best bet is to browse to the demo page at www.webdesignerwall.com/ demo/jquery/simple-slide-panel.html and choose View⇨Source.

Creating a Disappearing Effect

You can create a simple `<div>` element with a button that closes it using a fading or disappearing effect. To see a demonstration, visit www.webdesigner wall.com/demo/jquery/simple-disappear.html. The tutorial at www. webdesignerwall.com/tutorials/jquery-tutorials-for-designers shows you how to create a nice-looking panel with a close button. When you click the close link (see Figure 21-6), the panel fades out, and any other panels below it move up.

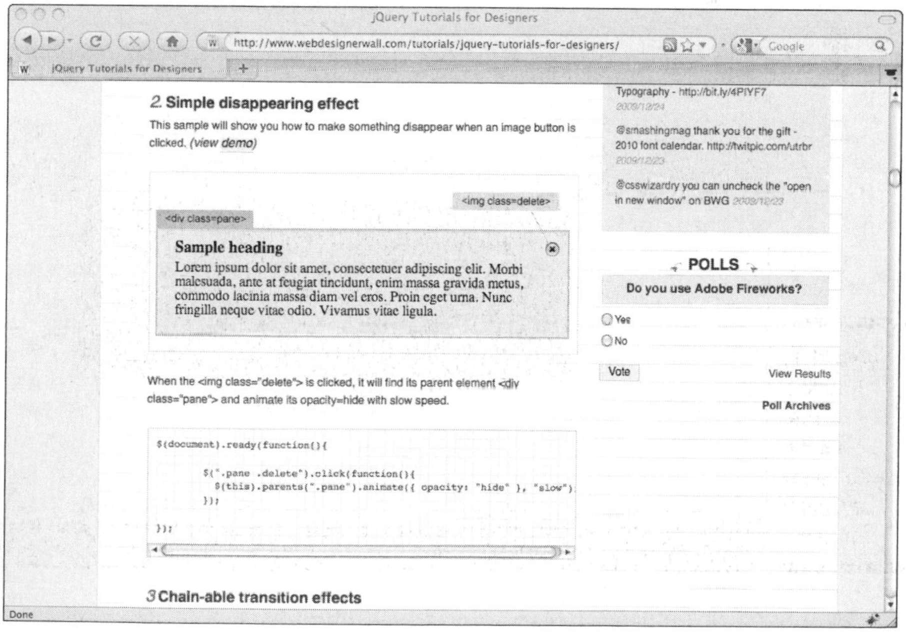

Figure 21-6:
The panel disappears when the close button is clicked.

The jQuery code to create a simple disappearing panel is as follows:

```
$(document).ready(function(){
$('.pane .delete').click(function(){
$(this).parents('.pane').animate({ opacity: 'hide' }, 'slow');
});
});
```

This code slowly fades the panel until it is invisible. The effect requires CSS styles and elements with specific IDs or classes. For further instructions, view the tutorial on the www.webdesignerwall.com site.

Using a jQuery Cheat Sheet

When you are working with jQuery and can't remember the correct syntax, it's great to have a cheat sheet handy. The www.javascripttoolbox.com/jquery/cheatsheet site offers a cheat sheet of the current jQuery version in several formats, as shown in Figure 21-7.

The best site to visit to find the current version of jQuery is always jquery.com.

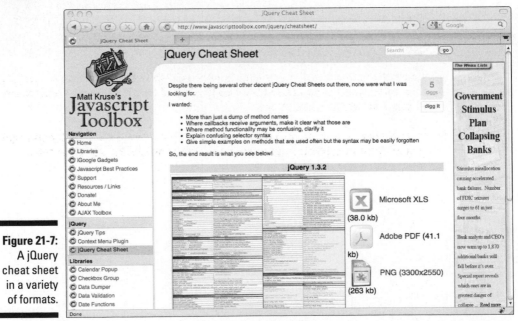

Figure 21-7: A jQuery cheat sheet in a variety of formats.

Making Elements Clickable

You can make any HTML element clickable with the following simple code trick from www.tripwiremagazine.com/2009/11/more-jquery-and-general-javascript-tips-to-improve-your-code.html. The following code selects <li> elements and makes them clickable, rather than just the <a> link inside each:

```html
<html>
<head>
<title>My Test Page</title>
<script type="text/javascript" src="js/jquery-1.4.min.js"></script>
<script type="text/javascript">
$(document).ready(function(){

$('ul li').click(function(){
  window.location=$(this).find('a').attr('href'); return false;
});
});
</script>
</head>
<body>
<ul>
  <li><a href="link1.html">Go somewhere</a></li>
  <li><a href="link2.html">Go somewhere else</a></li>
</ul>
</body>
</html>
```

This code creates a Web page with a list (see Figure 21-8). When you test this code, notice that clicking the bullet to the left of each link also acts as a link and takes you to the linked page.

You can select any element you want, not simply <li> elements, by changing the selector code. To find out more about using selectors, see Chapter 3.

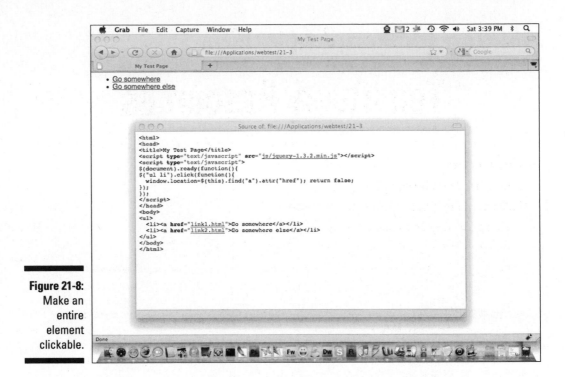

Figure 21-8:
Make an
entire
element
clickable.

Streamlining document.ready Code

You can simplify your $(document).ready() code with this handy tip from www.geekology.co.za/blog/2009/10/12-tips-improve-your-jquery-code. The standard code used to execute your jQuery functions when the page loads is

```
$(document).ready(function (){
//Your code goes here
});
```

Instead, you can save a few keystrokes and use the following instead:

```
$(function (){
//Your code goes here
});
```

Chapter 22

Ten jQuery Resources

*H*ere are ten great online resources to help you discover even more about jQuery.

jQuery Web site

jquery.com

Your first, best source for all things jQuery is the official jQuery Web site. The most recent version of the jQuery library and the most current documentation are always here.

 Each time the jQuery library is updated, the version number of the file changes. To avoid having to change the jQuery filename in the script lines on all your Web pages to reflect this filename change, always rename the latest jQuery `.js` file to something like `jquery-latest.js` and use a matching call to this file in your script code:

```
<script type="text/javascript" src="js/jquery-latest.js"></script>
```

The latest version of the jQuery library can be downloaded by clicking the Download jQuery button at the upper right of the Web page, which is shown in Figure 22-1.

Figure 22-1:
The official
jQuery Web
site.

jQuery on Wikipedia

`en.wikipedia.org/wiki/JQuery`

The technical content on the jQuery Wikipedia Web page (see Figure 22-2) is dense, but great information is buried in the article. The Wikipedia page provides you with

- ✔ A quick refresher when you forget some of the syntax basics.
- ✔ An up-to-date record of the latest releases and planned future releases of the jQuery library.
- ✔ The latest news about jQuery.
- ✔ A set of reference links to additional information about jQuery.

Figure 22-2:
The
Wikipedia
entry for
jQuery.

jQuery for Absolute Beginners Video Series

```
blog.themeforest.net/screencasts/jquery-for-absolute-
beginners-video-series/
```

With that long URL, navigating to the site shown in Figure 22-3 is a bit of a pain, but the content makes the site worth visiting. If you learn by seeing, check out this series of video tutorials.

Each video begins with a commercial you have to sit through. The tutorial is clear with easy-to-follow jQuery code and instructions. The topics are

- Day 1: Downloading the Library
- Day 2: Fade, Slide, and Show Methods
- Day 3: The Animate Method
- Day 4: Advanced Selectors
- Day 5: Creating and Removing Elements
- Day 6: The `toggle()` and `toggleClass()` Methods

✔ Day 7: The `hover()` Methods

✔ Day 8: Image Slides

✔ Day 9: Resizing Text

✔ Day 10: Intro to AJAX: Using the Load Method

✔ Day 11: Fun Image Hovering

✔ Day 12: Advanced Tooltips

✔ Day 13: Submitting Information to a Database Asynchronously

✔ Day 14: Implementing Your First Plug-in

✔ Day 15: Building a jQuery Style-Switcher

Figure 22-3:
jQuery for
Absolute
Beginners
Web site.

Visual jQuery

visualjquery.com

It's easy to forget the exact name of a jQuery function that you want to use.
The Visual jQuery site is a cheat sheet for all the jQuery functions, with an
easy-to-navigate interface, as shown in Figure 22-4.

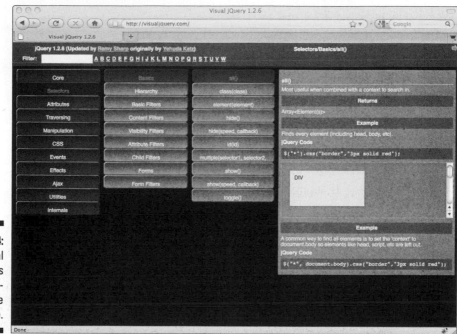

Visual jQuery does not use the most up-to-date version of the jQuery library. Although the majority of the information on the site is correct, some functions have changed. The final authority for everything jQuery is always `jquery.com`.

Use jQuery

`usejquery.com/category/Background`

If you find yourself in need of inspiration, look no further than Use jQuery. This self-styled showcase of jQuery sites presents hundreds of nifty Web sites with interesting jQuery treatments. The showcased sites are broken down into a category list on the right side of the page for easier browsing, as shown in Figure 22-5.

Categories of showcased jQuery applications include:

- Ajax
- DOM Manipulation
- Drag 'n Drop

- ✔ Fading
- ✔ Forms
- ✔ Lightbox
- ✔ Navigation
- ✔ Popup
- ✔ Preload
- ✔ Slider
- ✔ Slideshow
- ✔ Tabs
- ✔ Text Replacement
- ✔ Tooltip
- ✔ User Interface
- ✔ Validation

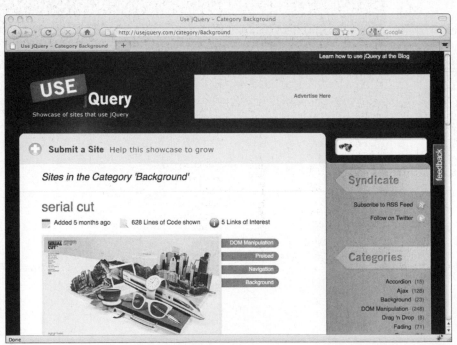

Figure 22-5:
Use jQuery
showcases
Web sites
creatively
using
jQuery.

jQuery Plug-ins

`plugins.jquery.com/`

When you need a specific plug-in, the place to begin looking is the plug-ins section of the official jQuery Web site. The only problem with the site is that you may have a tough time choosing a plug-in because there are so many. Plug-ins are organized by category (see Figure 22-6), are searchable, and are browsable.

Each plug-in has a link to a detail page, with download links and an overview of the plug-in's behavior. Most plug-in detail pages have a link to a demonstration of the plug-in.

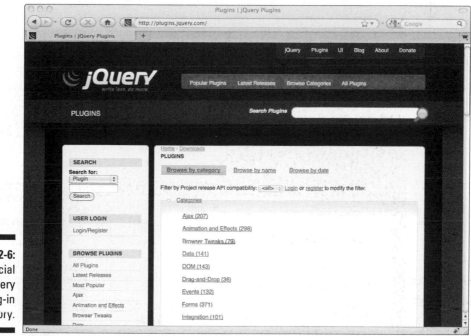

Figure 22-6:
The official
jQuery
plug-in
repository.

Smashing Magazine

`smashingmagazine.com/tag/jquery`

Smashing Magazine is an online resource for Web designers and developers. It's a great destination if you create anything for the Web, and it also has a section specific to jQuery topics (see Figure 22-7).

You can find even more articles on jQuery topics by typing *jQuery* in the search box at the upper right of the Smashing Magazine Web site. My search turned up 1,270 articles.

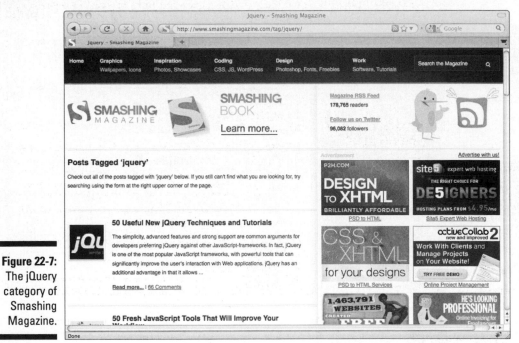

Figure 22-7:
The jQuery
category of
Smashing
Magazine.

Speckyboy Design Magazine

`speckyboy.com/category/ajax`

Much like Smashing Magazine, Speckyboy Design Magazine offers lots of jQuery information and tutorials, as you can see in Figure 22-8. The jQuery topics are found by clicking the AJAX & JavaScript link on the left side of the main menu.

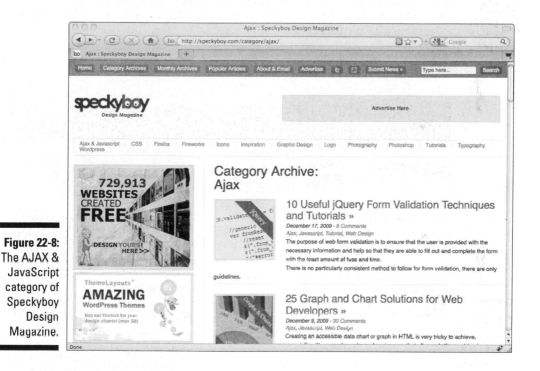

Figure 22-8: The AJAX & JavaScript category of Speckyboy Design Magazine.

Nettuts+

`net.tutsplus.com/category/tutorials/javascript-ajax/`

Nettuts+ is a Web site devoted to tutorials on Web design and development topics. They have a number of solid jQuery tutorials worth checking out. You can either use the search box in the upper right to find jQuery topics or click JavaScript & AJAX under the Categories button to the right of the main menu. Figure 22-9 shows the JavaScript & AJAX category page.

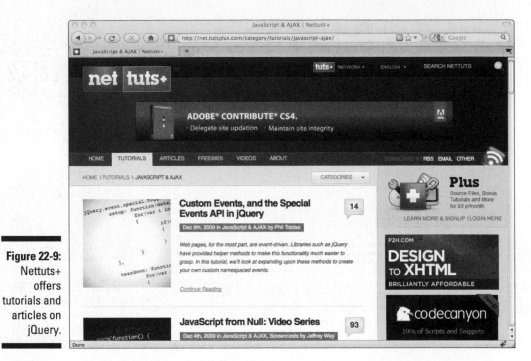

Figure 22-9: Nettuts+ offers tutorials and articles on jQuery.

You'll find lots of results when you search for *jQuery,* but not all of them focus on jQuery. Also, the site offers a paid service, so some of your search results won't be available for free.

Woorkup

woorkup.com/tag/jquery/

Woorkup is a community Web site with lots of great information for Web designers and developers. It has an entire category devoted to jQuery, as shown in Figure 22-10. To reach the jQuery category, click the jQuery link in the main menu.

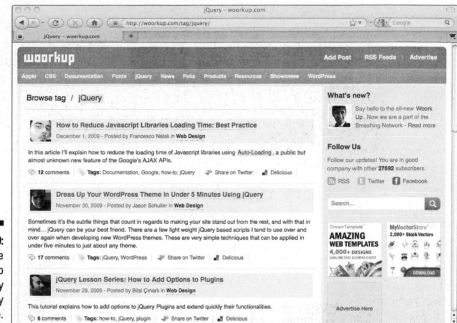

Figure 22-10:
The
Woorkup
jQuery
community
site.

Index

• *F* •

Business/Accounting & Bookkeeping

Bookkeeping For Dummies
978-0-7645-9848-7

eBay Business
All-in-One For Dummies,
2nd Edition
978-0-470-38536-4

Job Interviews
For Dummies,
3rd Edition
978-0-470-17748-8

Resumes For Dummies,
5th Edition
978-0-470-08037-5

Stock Investing
For Dummies,
3rd Edition
978-0-470-40114-9

Successful Time
Management
For Dummies
978-0-470-29034-7

Computer Hardware

BlackBerry For Dummies,
3rd Edition
978-0-470-45762-7

Computers For Seniors
For Dummies
978-0-470-24055-7

iPhone For Dummies,
2nd Edition
978-0-470-42342-4

Laptops For Dummies,
3rd Edition
978-0-470-27759-1

Macs For Dummies,
10th Edition
978-0-470-27817-8

Cooking & Entertaining

Cooking Basics
For Dummies,
3rd Edition
978-0-7645-7206-7

Wine For Dummies,
4th Edition
978-0-470-04579-4

Diet & Nutrition

Dieting For Dummies,
2nd Edition
978-0-7645-4149-0

Nutrition For Dummies,
4th Edition
978-0-471-79868-2

Weight Training
For Dummies,
3rd Edition
978-0-471-76845-6

Digital Photography

Digital Photography
For Dummies,
6th Edition
978-0-470-25074-7

Photoshop Elements 7
For Dummies
978-0-470-39700-8

Gardening

Gardening Basics
For Dummies
978-0-470-03749-2

Organic Gardening
For Dummies,
2nd Edition
978-0-470-43067-5

Green/Sustainable

Green Building
& Remodeling
For Dummies
978-0-470-17559-0

Green Cleaning
For Dummies
978-0-470-39106-8

Green IT For Dummies
978-0-470-38688-0

Health

Diabetes For Dummies,
3rd Edition
978-0-470-27086-8

Food Allergies
For Dummies
978-0-470-09584-3

Living Gluten-Free
For Dummies
978-0-471-77383-2

Hobbies/General

Chess For Dummies,
2nd Edition
978-0-7645-8404-6

Drawing For Dummies
978-0-7645-5476-6

Knitting For Dummies,
2nd Edition
978-0-470-28747-7

Organizing For Dummies
978-0-7645-5300-4

SuDoku For Dummies
978-0-470-01892-7

Home Improvement

Energy Efficient Homes
For Dummies
978-0-470-37602-7

Home Theater
For Dummies,
3rd Edition
978-0-470-41189-6

Living the Country Lifestyle
All-in-One For Dummies
978-0-470-43061-3

Solar Power Your Home
For Dummies
978-0-470-17569-9

Available wherever books are sold. For more information or to order direct: U.S. customers visit www.dummies.com or call 1-877-762-2974.
U.K. customers visit www.wileyeurope.com or call (0) 1243 843291. Canadian customers visit www.wiley.ca or call 1-800-567-4797.

Internet

Blogging For Dummies,
2nd Edition
978-0-470-23017-6

eBay For Dummies,
6th Edition
978-0-470-49741-8

Facebook For Dummies
978-0-470-26273-3

Google Blogger
For Dummies
978-0-470-40742-4

Web Marketing
For Dummies,
2nd Edition
978-0-470-37181-7

WordPress For Dummies,
2nd Edition
978-0-470-40296-2

Language & Foreign Language

French For Dummies
978-0-7645-5193-2

Italian Phrases
For Dummies
978-0-7645-7203-6

Spanish For Dummies
978-0-7645-5194-9

Spanish For Dummies,
Audio Set
978-0-470-09585-0

Macintosh

Mac OS X Snow Leopard
For Dummies
978-0-470-43543-4

Math & Science

Algebra I For Dummies,
2nd Edition
978-0-470-55964-2

Biology For Dummies
978-0-7645-5326-4

Calculus For Dummies
978-0-7645-2498-1

Chemistry For Dummies
978-0-7645-5430-8

Microsoft Office

Excel 2007 For Dummies
978-0-470-03737-9

Office 2007 All-in-One
Desk Reference
For Dummies
978-0-471-78279-7

Music

Guitar For Dummies,
2nd Edition
978-0-7645-9904-0

iPod & iTunes
For Dummies,
6th Edition
978-0-470-39062-7

Piano Exercises
For Dummies
978-0-470-38765-8

Parenting & Education

Parenting For Dummies,
2nd Edition
978-0-7645-5418-6

Type 1 Diabetes
For Dummies
978-0-470-17811-9

Pets

Cats For Dummies,
2nd Edition
978-0-7645-5275-5

Dog Training For Dummies,
2nd Edition
978-0-7645-8418-3

Puppies For Dummies,
2nd Edition
978-0-470-03717-1

Religion & Inspiration

The Bible For Dummies
978-0-7645-5296-0

Catholicism For Dummies
978-0-7645-5391-2

Women in the Bible
For Dummies
978-0-7645-8475-6

Self-Help & Relationship

Anger Management
For Dummies
978-0-470-03715-7

Overcoming Anxiety
For Dummies
978-0-7645-5447-6

Sports

Baseball For Dummies,
3rd Edition
978-0-7645-7537-2

Basketball For Dummies,
2nd Edition
978-0-7645-5248-9

Golf For Dummies,
3rd Edition
978-0-471-76871-5

Web Development

Web Design All-in-One
For Dummies
978-0-470-41796-6

Windows Vista

Windows Vista
For Dummies
978-0-471-75421-3

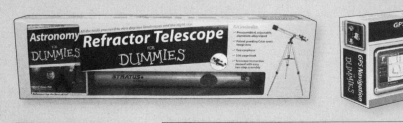
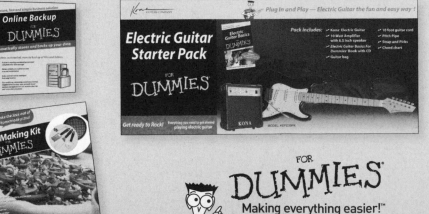